"A lively account of how the wives coped with fame, fear [and] loneliness."
—*People*
(A "Great Summer Read" selection)

"Truly a great snapshot of the times."
—*Publishers Weekly*
(starred review)

"A perfect beach read."
—*Entertainment Weekly*

"A remarkable story of perseverance and friendship in a time when women had few rights."
—Daily Beast

"A true (juicy) story... Put down that mystery and pick up some history!"
—*Redbook*

ACCLAIM FOR

THE ASTRONAUT WIVES CLUB

"The men catapulted into space in the twentieth century were interesting, sort of. The women they left back on earth were fascinating."

—*People*

"Intriguing, pleasantly gossipy, and often touching... in its light and engaging way, THE ASTRONAUT WIVES CLUB is a reflection on the gap between image and reality, and a glimpse of an unstable time when 'good wives' were reckoning the cost of that role."

—*Columbus Dispatch*

"This is one of those light, tasty summer reads you'll guzzle down like a milk shake."

—*Entertainment Weekly*

"Lily Koppel offers a grounded, irresistible and sociable social history... Koppel's book deftly delivers The Wife Stuff... [She] does an excellent job of capturing a group portrait with enough highlights, low points, sunny spots, and shadows for individual features to emerge... THE ASTRONAUT WIVES CLUB is wholly and consistently in Koppel's voice: smart, evocative, informed, and warm—an electric fireside chat with the women who put men on the moon."

—*Chicago Tribune*

"The only thing more delicious than the idea for this book is its execution. Come, all you *Mad Men* lovers, you girl-bonding-opus fans, you amateur historians who've looked under rugs for unlikely heroines: Relish this story of a bevy of women each as different from the other as their pastel shirtwaist dresses, their dutiful-wife exteriors, and their dowdy-pert hairstyles were not. THE ASTRONAUT WIVES CLUB rockets us back to the innocence of a unified mid-century America's space race triumphalism and to an unselfconscious sisterhood-is-powerful in the bud—nice things to recall, and maybe take a tiny bit of heed from, in these more sophisticated but much more complicated times."

—Sheila Weller, *New York Times* bestselling author of *Girls Like Us: Carole King, Joni Mitchell, Carly Simon—and the Journey of a Generation*

"Engaging... [Koppel] hits the mark, crafting an exceptional story that seriously examines the imperfection and humanity of America's heroic astronauts, their wives, and their families. This work will hold vast appeal for armchair historians, and those interested in feminism, women's history, and twentieth-century history."

—*Library Journal* (starred review)

"THE ASTRONAUT WIVES CLUB is spectacular, both in its intimacy and its reach. Lily Koppel pulls out delicious behind-the-scenes details of the stresses, formalities, pleasures, and travails of being the women behind the men on the moon."

—Karen Abbott, bestselling author of *American Rose* and *Sin in the Second City*

"*Mad Men* fans and history buffs alike won't want to miss a new book about... the lives of the astronauts' wives... We meet the Mercury Seven women in the first chapter of THE ASTRONAUT WIVES CLUB, and author Lily Koppel does a nice job of staying close to their stories. By the time you see the women's faces in the pictures, you'll feel like you're a member of the gang... It's hard to believe no one has already written their story, and this reader is glad Koppel finally did."

—*BookPage* (A "Nonfiction Top Pick")

"Lily Koppel writes with humor, cunning, and integrity. I found her recounting of the Mercury, Gemini, and Apollo programs riveting. Highly recommended!" —Douglas Brinkley, author of *Cronkite*

"[The wives'] story turns out to be much more than a pale reflection of the space race. It's an integral part of it. —*Times* (London)

"Insightful social history with a light touch." —*Kirkus Reviews*

"Koppel has launched her talents into another orbit by writing a book about America's space program that is not only smart, but also fun and sexy... THE ASTRONAUT WIVES CLUB is a clever and engaging book celebrating a group of women who, today, are often overlooked—if not forgotten... Pack this book along on your summer vacation and you are assured to have a good read, as well as a conversation starter, wherever your spacecraft takes you."

—Bookslut.com

"Reminiscent of the non-fiction prose of Norman Mailer."

—*National Post* (Canada)

"If you thought the only heroes in the history of NASA were its astronauts; if you thought the all-American family regularly seen in the pages of *Life* magazine was the full story of those astronauts' private lives; and if you've ever dreamed of supersonic romance, dinners at the Kennedy White House, through-the-roof beehives, a group of friends and neighbors going through this crazy time with you, and a celebrity-hero husband who is the most admired man in the nation (yet could die at any minute)... then you're ready to sign up for Lily Koppel's thrilling, magical, nostalgic, and eye-opening Atlas rocket of a read, THE ASTRONAUT WIVES CLUB."

—Craig Nelson, bestselling author of *Rocket Men* and *The Age of Radiance*

ALSO BY LILY KOPPEL

The Red Leather Diary

The Astronaut Wives Club

A True Story

Lily Koppel

GRAND CENTRAL
PUBLISHING

NEW YORK BOSTON

For the wives, who have the "right stuff"

Photo credits are located on page 303.

Grand Central Publishing
Hachette Book Group
237 Park Avenue
New York, NY 10017

www.HachetteBookGroup.com

Printed in the United States of America

RRD-C

Originally published in hardcover by Hachette Book Group.

First trade edition: May 2014

10 9 8 7 6 5 4 3 2 1

Grand Central Publishing is a division of Hachette Book Group, Inc.
The Grand Central Publishing name and logo are trademarks of Hachette Book Group, Inc.

The Library of Congress has cataloged the hardcover edition as follows:
Koppel, Lily.
The astronaut wives club: a true story / Lily Koppel.
pages cm
Summary: "Bestselling author Lily Koppel reveals for the first time the stories and secrets of America's unsung heores—the wives of our original astronauts"— Provided by publisher.
ISBN 978-1-4555-0325-4 (hardback)— ISBN 978-1-4555-2958-2 (large print hardcover) (print) — ISBN 978-1-4555-0323-0 (ebook)
1. Astronauts' spouses—Texas—Houston—Biography. 2. Women—Texas—Houston—Social life and customs—20th century. 3. Astronautics—United States—History. I. Title.
TL789.85.A1K67 2013
629.450092'655097641411—dc23

2012045976

ISBN 978-1-4555-0324-7 (pbk.)

Contents

The Astronaut Wives

The Original Seven

In April 1959 NASA's first spacemen, the Mercury Seven astronauts, were announced in Washington, D.C., and their wives were like America's first reality stars:

Rene Carpenter—wife of Scott Carpenter; JFK made it clear that platinum-blonde Rene was his favorite of the astronaut wives.

Trudy Cooper—"Gordo" Cooper's wife; Trudy was the only licensed pilot among the astronaut wives.

Annie Glenn—wife of John Glenn, the first American to orbit the Earth; Annie was what NASA wanted the wives of its seven astronauts to be.

Betty Grissom—wife of Gus Grissom, the second American to go into space on a suborbital flight; Hoosier from Mitchell, Indiana.

Jo Schirra—wife of Wally Schirra, the practical jokester among the astronaut corps; Jo was Navy royalty.

Louise Shepard—wife of Alan Shepard, the first American to go into space; the other wives called her Saint Louise because she was so serene and ladylike.

Marge Slayton—wife of Deke Slayton, Coordinator of Astronaut Activities; known as Mother Marge, she ran the Astronaut Wives Club.

The New Nine

The second group of astronauts was announced in September 1962 to man the next phase of the space program named Gemini, featuring two-man space capsules and the first American space walk. Enter nine new wives:

Janet Armstrong—wife of Neil Armstrong, the first person to walk on the Moon during Apollo 11.

Susan Borman—wife of tough-as-nails Frank Borman; a model of composure at A.W.C. meetings.

Jane Conrad—wife of Charles "Pete" Conrad, otherwise known as "Princeton Pete"; tall and model-thin Jane attended Bryn Mawr.

Marilyn Lovell—wife of Jim ("Houston, we have a problem") Lovell, the famous commander of Apollo 13 and the command module pilot of Apollo 8, the first mission to orbit the Moon, given a fifty-fifty shot.

Pat McDivitt—wife of Jim McDivitt, Ed White's partner for the first American space walk.

Marilyn See—wife of Elliot See.

Faye Stafford—wife of Tom Stafford; the Astronaut Wives Club's top pastry chef and Harriet Eisele's best friend.

Pat White—delicate-as-porcelain blonde wife of Ed White, aka the "next John Glenn," the first American to perform a space walk.

ini, and '70s suburban psychedelic for Apollo. *Life* magazine had been awarded exclusive coverage of the astronauts, and always sent its top photographers to cover them.

In the home of the lucky woman whose husband was "going up," each wife was assigned her duty. One manned the coffeepot while another dumped out heaping ashtrays, chain-smoking being the occupational hazard of the Astrowives. Solidarity was essential; who but another Astrowife could understand what the wife of the moment was enduring? Of course the harrowing worry and stress was the wife's alone. If she did ever care to share it, newsmen were stationed right outside, eager for a quote.

The ever-growing group of astronaut wives relied on each other more and more to negotiate their own roles at the forefront of history. As next-door neighbors in the space burbs, they kept each other grounded while their husbands headed to the Moon.

"We formed our own traditions as we went along," said Marge Slayton, who was essential in organizing the wives' get-togethers, "and they were good traditions."

The astronaut wives instituted official monthly coffees and teas; everyone knew their unspoken promise: "If you need us, come."

The story of the astronauts is well known, but this is the first time the wives' story has been told. We have heard and seen so much about the technological aspects of the space race, but not enough about the extraordinary day-to-day lives the wives experienced behind the scenes.

This book tells the story of the women behind the spacemen, from Project Mercury of the Kennedy Camelot years (1959 to 1963, which launched the first American into space and eventually into orbit around the Earth), to the Gemini missions (1962 to 1966, notable for two-man space travel and the first U.S. space walk), through the Apollo program (1961 to 1972), which finally landed a man on the Moon.

Ultimately, the wives' story is about female friendships and American identity. While their husbands were launched into space, they were being launched as modern American women. If not for the wives, the strong women in the background who provided essential support to their husbands, man might never have walked on the Moon.

Barbara Young—wife of John Young, who many now say reminds them of Don Draper, the fictional *Mad Men* character.

The Fourteen

The third group of astronauts was announced in October 1963 to crew the upcoming Gemini and Apollo Moon missions. This meant another gang of gals:

Joan Aldrin—actress wife of Edwin "Buzz" Aldrin, the second man to walk on the Moon after Neil Armstrong on Apollo 11.

Valerie Anders—wife of Bill Anders, the rookie astronaut on Apollo 8.

Jeannie Bassett—wife of Charlie Bassett.

Sue Bean—wife of Alan Bean ("Beano"), fourth man to walk on the Moon during Apollo 12 and a painter; best friends with the other blonde Texan, Barbara Cernan.

Barbara Cernan—wife of Gene Cernan, last man to walk on the Moon during Apollo 17; best friends with Sue Bean.

Martha Chaffee—drop-dead gorgeous wife of Roger Chaffee; resembled the model Twiggy.

Pat Collins—wife of Michael Collins; Irish Catholic girl from Boston.

Loella Cunningham—wife of Walt Cunningham.

Harriet Eisele—wife of Donn Eisele; four-foot-ten, pint-sized, big-hearted mother of four who filed for the "First 'Space Divorce.'"

Faith Freeman—wife of Ted Freeman.

Barbara Gordon—wife of Dick Gordon.

Clare Schweickart—wife of Rusty Schweickart, the "token hippie" in the Astronaut Office.

Lurton Scott—wife of Dave Scott.

Beth Williams—wife of C. C. Williams; former AquaMaid, professional water-skier at Cypress Gardens.

The Nineteen

Selected by NASA in 1966, the new boys called themselves the "Original Nineteen." Their wives included:

Joan Brand, Nancy Bull, JoAnn Carr, Dotty Duke, Mary Engle, Jan Evans, Ada Givens, Mary Haise, Mary Irwin, Kathleen Lind, Gratia Lousma, Liz Mattingly, Bernice McCandless, Louise Mitchell, Wanita Pogue, Joan Roosa, Suzanne Weitz, and Pamela Worden.

Author's Note

To be an astronaut wife meant tea with Jackie Kennedy, high-society galas, and instant celebrity. It meant smiling perfectly after a makeover by *Life* magazine, balancing an extravagantly lacquered rocket-style hairdo, and teetering in high heels at the crux of the space age.

The astronaut wives were ordinary housewives, most all of them military wives living in drab housing on Navy and Air Force bases. When their husbands, the best test pilots in the country, were chosen to man America's audacious adventure to beat the Russians in the space race, they suddenly found themselves very much in the public eye.

As her husband trained for every possible aspect of spaceflight, each woman had to prepare for the day when she would have to face the television cameras, when the world would be scrutinizing her hair, her complexion, her outfit, her figure, her poise, her parenting skills, her diction, her charm, and most of all, her patriotism. She had to appear calm and composed while her husband was strapped atop what was essentially the world's largest stick of dynamite, seconds away from being blasted off into space.

To help cope with the astronomical pressures of publicity, the wives couldn't turn to their husbands, who were too busy training, or to NASA, which was too busy figuring out how to get their husbands to the Moon. So the wives turned to each other.

Louise Shepard, wife of the first American to go into space, had learned the hard way that she needed to prevent overeager photographers from pressing a lens to her window and sneaking a shot of her living room. Drawing curtains against the press was only the first of many tips, tactics, and secrets that would be passed among the astronaut wives, for enduring what was known to the public as the launch report, but which one of the wives renamed the Death Watch.

Years later, by the time NASA put a man on the Moon, this excruciating pageant, with the wives' photogenic children, helpful neighbors, and publicity-seeking preachers, had evolved into a gathering somewhere between a celebration and a wake. In a singular Houston neighborhood known as Togethersville, this diverse group of women—over coffee and cigarettes, champagne and cocktails, tea and Tupperware, society balls and splashdown parties—shared laughter and tears, triumph and tragedy, as their husbands streaked through space.

The Astrowives learned that they needed to comfort each other during the agonizing minutes, hours, and days they had to wait at home for their husbands' safe return to Earth. They brought potluck spreads—Jell-O molds, casseroles, frosted cupcakes stuck with little American flags, lasagna, deviled eggs, pigs in blankets, strawberry angel cake, marshmallow brownies, and homemade "Moon Cake," a coconut cream pie topped with meringue swirled to look like the lunar surface. There was always champagne on hand, ready to be popped upon a successful splashdown. The wives dressed in their fashionable best: Doris Day–like finery for the Mercury missions, '60s mod for Gem-

1

Introducing the Wives

They had endured years of waking up alone, making their kids breakfast, taking them to school and picking them up, fixing dinner and kissing them good night, promising that Daddy was thinking of them all the time. There had been lonely nights when they fell asleep wondering how they were going to get by on their husbands' measly pay for another month. During tours of duty in World War II or Korea or both, their husbands had nearly become mirages. Navy deployments had taken their men away on six- to nine-month cruises to the far corners of the Earth. They'd each wait for half a year imagining their man, trying not to forget what he looked like, only to have him come home hungry and tired. They'd miss him even before he left.

Things were no easier in peacetime when he was back home on base serving as a test pilot. There were times when squadrons would lose as many as two men in a week. The wives couldn't do a thing about it but pray for their prowess over the 5 a.m. skillet, hoping they'd cooked their husbands a good breakfast of steak and eggs before they left to go fly, so they'd be alert up in the air. They went to friends' funerals, sang the Navy hymn, and wore white gloves and clutched a handkerchief to catch the tears. They'd become conditioned to living with the daily fear that their men might not be back for dinner, or ever.

For Marge Slayton, whose wide, pale Irish face and expressive eyes made you want to hug her, it was the sound of a helicopter that sent her into a tailspin of fear and nausea. Hearing the blades of a chopper whirring overhead almost always meant that the men were searching for a plane that had gone down. Long after she stopped living on remote air bases, such as Edwards in the Mojave Desert, the sound of a helicopter still struck fear in her heart.

If a husband was out testing a new experimental plane and didn't come home by five o'clock, almost all of the wives experienced the same waking nightmare, imagining the dark figure of the base chaplain ringing the doorbell, telling her she was now a widow. They had rehearsed that awful scene in their minds, over and over. Such was the life of a test pilot wife. They could not possibly have imagined all that would be in store for them as astronauts' wives.

The United States was well behind in the space race. Soon after launching *Sputnik* in 1957, the Russians launched *Sputnik II* with its passenger Laika ("Barker," also known as Little Curly), the Soviet space dog. She was a female stray found on the streets of Moscow (and those godless Soviets let her *die* in orbit). The United States had responded by trying to send up its own satellite on a Vanguard rocket from Cape Canaveral, Florida, but it disastrously exploded on the launch pad, leading the press to call it "Kaputnik." In the following months and years the United States tried to send up bigger rockets, such as the Atlas, but nearly every one of them had exploded before reaching outer space. Now the United States was determined not only to catch up but to pull ahead. It was a national priority in those fervent days of the Cold War.

America's space age was officially announced on April 9, 1959. In Washington, D.C., at the buttercup-yellow Dolley Madison House, across Lafayette Square from the White House, the seven men who'd been chosen to be the nation's first astronauts were officially presented to the world. They sat onstage at a blue felt–draped banquet table under NASA's round red-and-blue logo of a planet and stars, nicknamed the Meatball. Onstage with them was a model of the tiny Mercury capsule on top of an Atlas rocket, which would fall off once the capsule had passed through the Earth's atmosphere and entered outer space. At promptly 10 a.m., the press conference began. T. Keith Glennan took the podium. A natural-born showman who had previously worked at Paramount and Samuel Goldwyn, he was now the administrator of the National Aeronautics and Space Administration.

"Ladies and gentlemen," he announced, "today we are introducing to you and to the world these seven men who have been selected to begin training for orbital spaceflight. These men, the nation's Mercury astronauts, are here after a long and perhaps unprecedented series of evaluations which told our medical consultants and scientists of their superb adaptability to their upcoming flight. It is my pleasure to introduce to you—and I consider it a very real honor, gentlemen—Malcolm S. Carpenter, Leroy G. Cooper, John H. Glenn Jr., Virgil I. Grissom, Walter M. Schirra Jr., Alan B. Shepard Jr., and Donald K. Slayton... the nation's Mercury astronauts!"

The ballroom burst into applause. The Mercury Seven astronauts were instantly beloved, embodying the country's optimism and excitement. Space capsules and rocket launchers and men in silver suits in outer space; it was a brave new world. The stuff of science-fiction novels was now coming true. These seven young flyboy test pilots, with their strong jaws and military buzz-cuts, were the best America had to offer. Glennan explained how the seven were chosen out of 110 test pilots considered for the job. Most of all they were healthy small-town Americans. None was older than forty.

Glennan touched on how fierce the competition had been. The Mercury Seven had been exhaustively tested and checked out down to their innermost orifices at the famed Lovelace Clinic in Albuquerque, selected for its secluded location. There were all kinds of "wild theories" about zero gravity, as one NASA doctor later put it. "Some people said the astronauts' hearts would explode, or that their blood pressure would fall to nothing. Some said they would never be able to urinate, and others said they'd never be able to stop urinating." Physicians did a complete medical, psychological, and social evaluation of the astronauts. NASA looked into the backgrounds of not only the men but also their wives.

Since all of America's new astronauts were drawn from the test pilot world, they were military men who would retain their rank while on loan to the new civilian space agency. They would work together now, so rank would no longer be important. They wouldn't wear uniforms besides their silver space suits. And they wouldn't only be pilots. Each would be in charge of a particular ingredient of spaceflight, such as the capsule, communications, recovery, or navigation.

When it was question time, the reporters shot up their hands and leaped out of their seats. It turned out they were mostly interested in what the astronauts' wives had to say about their men being blasted into space. It was insanity, wasn't it? Or was it the American dream? Didn't their wives want to bring the country down to earth, say there had been some mistake? *No*, you cannot send my husband to the Moon. What kind of woman would actually let her husband be blasted into space on a rocket? The newly christened astronauts were in the process of formulating answers when John Glenn piped up.

"I don't think any of us could really go on with something like this if we didn't have pretty good backing at home, really," he said, speaking of his Annie. "My wife's attitude toward this has been the same as it has been all along through my flying. If it is what I want to do, she is behind it, and the kids are, too, a hundred percent."

When the press conference ended, reporters dashed from the room to instruct their editors to dispatch their minions to track down the Astrowives. John Glenn, who would remain very protective of his wife throughout the space race, always did his best to shield her from the press. The other wives, however, were open game. There were seven of them scattered across the country: Air Force and Navy wives, and Annie the lone Marine wife. They had spent the best years of their lives raising kids and supporting their husbands' careers and moving their families from one end of the country to the other, from one dismal base to the next. Now their husbands were astronauts, and they, too, were instant celebrities.

NASA didn't provide the wives with any instructions. No NASA public relations spokesmen contacted them with tips on how to deal with the press that day. The wives would have to handle the reporters the way they'd handled all the ups and downs of service life—with slightly knitted eyebrows, perfectly applied lipstick, and well-practiced aplomb.

The reporters hunted down the wives, showing up at their doorsteps and even chasing them at the grocery store. Out in Enon, Ohio, Betty, new astronaut Gus Grissom's wife, was having a hellish time dealing with the journalists, who were practically crawling through the curtains into her house. Gus had vastly underestimated the new situation the night before, when he'd called from Washington to warn her, "It's a good bet you'll be pounced on by the press." She'd been sick, running a temperature of 102. Her curly brown hair was a mess. So was the house.

Betty Grissom had never thought of Gus as a potential hero. They'd met back in Mitchell, Indiana, where Gus, too short to make the basketball team, had to be satisfied with being the leader of the Boy Scout honor guard. Betty played the snare drum in the pep band. "The first time I saw you I decided you were the girl I was going to marry," he'd tell her.

Betty had put Gus through engineering school at Purdue, slaving away on the 5 to 11 p.m. shift at Indiana Bell in a room full of exhausted working girls plugging in telephone connections. Her graveyard shift gave her husband some quiet to study. She had to work hard in those days because they lived off her pay. Betty didn't have any education beyond high school, but she often joked about her hard-earned "P.H.T." degree—Putting Hubby Through.

She had sweated out Gus's tour of duty in Korea, where he

flew an F-86 Sabre on one hundred combat missions. Gus was promoted, but Betty was devastated when he actually volunteered to stay in Korea to fly another twenty-five missions.

After the war, Gus was stationed at Wright-Patterson Air Force Base in Ohio. He was now a test pilot, and they were finally living under one roof, with their two little boys. Even though Gus was home, he was often off flying. Betty knew flying was Gus's life, and she supported him without question.

"If I die, have a party," Gus once told her after one of their test pilot friends crashed and burned.

"Okay," she promised. "We'll have a party."

"If something happens to me, I don't want people sitting over here, crying."

In January 1959 Gus had received the top-secret telegram. Gus wasn't much for words, but Betty usually knew before he did what was on his mind. In fact, they both figured that she was a little psychic. That night, as the Moon hung over Enon, Ohio, and the two boys were finally in bed, he read the telegram aloud. A couple of sentences long, with the usual confusing military acronyms, it "invited" Captain Virgil I. Grissom to come to Washington, wear civilian clothes, and not utter a word of this to anyone. Neither of them had any idea what it meant, so Betty blurted out the craziest thing that popped into her head. "What are they going to do, Gus, shoot you up in the nose cone of an Atlas rocket?"

She had heard Gus talk about the Atlas rocket, which was being tested in secret at Cape Canaveral in Florida. It wasn't much of a secret, seeing as reporters had watched it blow up from the nearby town of Cocoa Beach. The rocket was unstable, and kept on exploding at liftoff after liftoff. Did men in the government really reckon someone was supposed to *ride* that thing?

Gus laughed. Soon Betty began to feel like a spy girl in a James Bond thriller. Federal investigators were canvassing Enon, making inquiries into the character of the Grissoms: How patriotic was his wife? How many times a week did she make home-cooked meals? Did she drink too much? Did communists regularly appear on their doorstep?

Finally, Gus asked Betty's permission to accept the dangerous mission. She looked at him and said, "Is it something you really want to do?"

"Yes, it is."

"Then do you even need to ask me?"

On the day of the astronauts' press conference, Betty had gone to the doctor and gotten a shot of penicillin. She stopped at the grocery store on the way home to pick up a few things for her and her boys, eight-year-old Scotty and five-year-old Mark, who were still at school. A reporter-photographer team from *Life* had interviewed her neighbor and tracked Betty's trail to the store. They came right up to her as she was wheeling her shopping cart through the vegetable aisle. Being a polite midwesterner, Betty invited the duo to her home, though they would have followed her through her door whether she wanted them to or not.

As soon as she let the *Life* fellows in, other reporters and photographers started arriving. They didn't even knock, just marched right in her front door and made themselves at home. Asked all sorts of personal questions, Betty didn't view these invasions as a welcome opportunity to become famous.

Sitting off to the side in her living room, as if the men wanted to photograph her dingy furniture and not her, Betty slung one saddle-shoed foot over the other, hoisted up her bobby socks, and watched suspiciously. Her big round owl glasses almost hid how cute she was. A perpetual worrier, she noted every time one of the men used the toilet (which she scrubbed herself) or plugged heavy equipment into a socket without permission. She didn't like the reporters: she hadn't prepared for this at all.

Betty didn't mind putting up with a lot for Gus. But she expected some common decency.

On the other side of the country, on a windswept shore near her home in Virginia Beach, Louise Shepard had taken her three lovely girls to the beach to escape the reporters who would surely be ringing her bell at home. Louise walked slowly up the shoreline as her blonde-haired girls built sandcastles and waded in the surf.

"Mrs. Shepard?" The press had tracked her down. "We're from *Life* magazine, Mrs. Shepard. We'd like to take some pictures."

Louise had always played a supporting role to her husband, Alan. She was a Christian Scientist and did not like this invasion of her quiet life, but assumed her new role was beginning, and she handled the press gracefully. She smiled tentatively at the two men from *Life* and told them it would be okay if they took a few pictures. She smoothed out the girls' windblown hair and posed for the photographer.

After Louise let them instruct her to look left and look right, look up toward the sky, where her husband's *bird* might one day go, she was ready to get out of there. She looked at them kindly, smiled a smile that meant, *That's enough*, then put two slender fingers in her mouth and whistled. "Laura, time to go."

The men were flummoxed. Louise rounded up her girls. They thought the attention was fun, but they followed their mom to the car. Louise calmly steered toward home, expecting that by now, any press that had come calling would be gone.

She was wrong. When she turned onto her quiet street, lined with wooden houses with pleasant gardens hemmed in by picket fences, she could hardly believe her eyes. There must have been a dozen news trucks in her yard.

"How does it feel being the wife of an astronaut?" The men started flinging questions right away. "How long have you been married? What do your kids think?"

Louise stared into the exploding flashbulbs.

"Do you really want him to go?" asked another newsman. "Aren't you worried he'll be killed?"

That was the question that really disturbed her. Louise had been living with the fear of Alan's death ever since he started test-flying high-performance jets. The death rate for men like Alan was staggering. If Alan didn't call or come home by five o'clock sharp, Louise would start looking at the sky for the ominous black clouds near an air base that rose from a plane crashing to the ground.

Finally, she enveloped her children in her arms and ushered them through the crowd, away from all the attention. Down the street, the neighbors were watching the drama unfold in the Shepards' yard, and a mother told her son to be a dear and go see what all the hoopla was about. He ran back home and announced, "Mom! Mom! You gotta hear this! Mr. Shepard's going to the Moon!"

* * *

Rene Carpenter's husband, Scott, had called from Washington, D.C., the night before to tell her that the press was likely going to be coming this morning. Rene dressed in a classic sheath and planned to outfit her two toddler-age girls in matching red dresses piped in gold and black rickrack.

As the sun rose over the Carpenters' house on Timmy Lane in Garden Grove, California, the reporters started arriving. Soon one of them was knocking on the front door.

"Mrs. Carpenter?" the reporter asked.

"Yes?"

"We know you can't talk to us till seven a.m. But do you mind if we set up a few things in the yard?"

"Yes, *please* do."

The thirty-year-old mother of four had a welcoming smile, green eyes, platinum hair, and deep dimples. She was a winning combination of beauty and bookishness. In high school, she had wanted to be an actress and a writer. At the University of Colorado, the intellectual Tri Delta sorority girl had been writing a paper on *Paradise Lost* when she'd met Scott during her shift at the Boulder Bookstore. He showed up one afternoon after spotting her for the first time at the Boulder Theater, where she also worked, as a movie usherette. After they discovered they both loved to ski and discuss literature and philosophy, they decided to build a life together and got married. She helped support them, continuing to work at the bookstore as Scott made his way toward his degree. Before graduating, he joined the Navy.

Soon the reporters were again at the door, asking if they might come in to take some photos. She knew how to be a gracious hostess, having been a Navy wife for a decade now. As

Rene invited them in, the reporters took note of how she pronounced her name; it rhymed with *keen*. She let the reporters tour her home, filled with cherished family items like the teardrop-shaped monkeypod coffee table. Rene had picked up the raw wood for it when they were stationed in Hawaii. She had fashioned it into a base for the coffee table herself. One of the few perks of being married to an aviator was that the Navy would move your furniture for free, as you uprooted yourself from one base to the next.

Rene offered the newsmen coffee to go with the donuts some of the more enterprising of them had brought. They rearranged the furniture to make way for the lights and cameras now unblinkingly trained on her family.

Sitting on her orange couch with her gang of four, Rene posed for more photos. Nine-year-old Scotty Jr. had donned his dad's flight helmet, dark visor down, breathing into its ventilator tube hanging from the snout. He made quite a subject for the photographers.

Rene was as excited about this bold new endeavor as the newsmen. "We all want to go with him!" she told them. "Even the two dogs!"

Finally the reporters packed up and left. "It's as if I'd been acting on a dark stage all my life," Rene said later. "And suddenly someone turns on the spotlight."

Marge Slayton welcomed the press boys with her silent-film-star smile. She and Deke were stationed at Edwards Air Force Base in the Mojave, where Joshua trees rose like gnarled arthritic hands out of the lakebed runway. She had been gung ho ever since the space race began on an October night in 1957 when Russia launched *Sputnik* over the United States on the same evening *Leave It to Beaver* made its television debut. *Sputnik* means "fellow traveler" in Russian.

As the 1950s had progressed, the threat of nuclear war became more and more real. In schools, children practiced "duck and cover" drills, crouching under their desks and covering their heads with their arms. Fallout shelters abounded in towns and cities. Some families constructed their own bomb shelters in basements or backyards, stocking them with survival kits complete with bottled water, evaporated milk, and enough canned goods to last through the nuclear winter. As the Americans and Russians continued to build up their arsenals, the country lived in fear of thermonuclear war. It was a devil's bargain to keep the peace known as MAD, or mutually assured destruction.

On the night of October 4, 1957, terror in their hearts, men, women, and children ran outside to search the nighttime sky for the Russian interloper, masterminded by the shadowy Soviet chief designer. The unmanned aluminum satellite orbiting the Earth looked like a spiky silver bug. What might the Soviets do next? America had nightmares of future *Sputnik*s dropping atom bombs onto their happy homes. Nobody wanted to live under a communist Moon. Texas senator Lyndon B. Johnson feared precisely that, saying, "I'll be damned if I sleep by the light of a Red Moon... soon they will be dropping bombs on us from space like kids dropping rocks on the cars from freeway overpasses." The next morning, the front pages of newspapers across the country bore images that looked like the old Martian-infested EC Comics, predecessor to *Mad* magazine. Nikita Khrushchev bragged that the U.S.S.R. could mass-produce rockets like "sausages." Important officials called the launch of *Sputnik* "a technological Pearl Harbor."

A few nights after *Sputnik*, Marge and the other wives at Edwards Air Force Base got an idea to give their men a much-needed laugh. They dressed up like Playboy Bunnies in sexy black seamed stockings, black bathing suits, and little skirts. When their guys gathered at a lonely supper club out there in the middle of nowhere, the women came out dancing in a chorus line. They had affixed miniature *Sputnik*s on top of their caps, which whirled along with the dance. Marge's husband, Deke, whistled as the girls shook their *Sputnik*s. *Come and get me*, beckoned Marge and her *Sputnik* sweetheart revue. At one point, the gals turned around and flipped up their skirts and shook their fannies. When assembled, the secret message could be deciphered. Written in white lettering across their black bloomers were the words TAKE ME TO YOUR LEADER.

"Of course, I'm pleased my husband was selected as an astronaut. It's a great honor. Do I have any fears about the unknowns of spaceflight? Do you know of anyone who's going to be boosted out of this world who wouldn't be apprehensive?"

The reporters' questions brought Marge back to reality.

"Yes, I'm familiar with the dangers. Yes, I've lived with them for years through Deke's service as a fighter pilot and a test pilot," she said. "Yes, I stand by him. Yes, I support Deke all the way. No, I have no reservations about what he has chosen to do."

Marge told the reporters how she had met Deke in Germany after World War II, where he was a bomber pilot and she was a secretary for the civil service. They met at a volleyball game on base. Marge hit a spike and broke her wrist. She described for the newsmen how tough-looking Deke carried her to the base hospital, her very own Prince Charming. Marge couldn't help but be reminded of her Irish father, a rough-and-tumble detective for the railroads. He drank too much and was often violent. Deke was much, much kinder. They both thought there was something a bit odd about the doctor who set Marge's wrist, but just figured he was a kook. A couple of weeks later, the doctor was found in his room, painted up with iodine like an Indian and shooting holes in the ceiling with a Colt .45. Another doctor had to break Marge's wrist again and reset it, and throughout the whole awful process, Deke was with her every day, so gentle. They soon bought a velvety gray Weimaraner puppy together and named him Acey. Seeing Deke pet the pint-sized Acey simply made Marge melt.

Deke was so different from her previous husband, but Marge didn't want *anyone*—especially at NASA—to know she had been divorced. Divorce was taboo at the space agency, which believed that stable home lives were essential for success in orbit. One of the first among NASA's many unofficial rules was: if you don't have a happy marriage, you won't have a spaceflight.

Suddenly the phone rang. It was Deke calling from Washington after the press conference.

"Hi, honey."

Marge pressed the receiver of the black phone to her cheek while she surveyed her quarters. Her two-year-old son, Kent, was fighting the photographers like a diapered Don Quixote. All at once, her whole world had changed. Marge brought Kent close to her, holding him out of harm's way.

The photographers took a shine to little Kent. On one occasion, *Life* got him to ride Acey, who, now full grown, weighed ninety-eight pounds and towered over Kent. They took a photo of the astronaut's son riding the dog like a nursery pony. Unfortunately, Acey was a maniac, and every time Kent tried to pet him, the dog tried to bite him.

Trudy Cooper and her husband, Gordo, were also stationed at Edwards. Any wife would be happy to leave this place where sandstorms blew through the cracks and crevices, turning base housing into a veritable hourglass, with sands pouring down through the light fixtures onto freshly set dinner tables.

One of the first household tips the Edwards wives passed down was "Don't move a *thing.*" The sand problem was so bad that if you moved anything—a book, lamp, paperweight—it left a shadow ringed with a fine layer of dust. If you liked rearranging things, you'd be dusting until kingdom come. Another piece of advice was to watch out for the snakes; there were all kinds of poisonous ones, including Mojave greens and sidewinder rattlers.

An enigmatic woman who was always conspicuously quiet with reporters, Trudy relied on her kittenish eyes to say, *I'm happily married.* It was all that anyone seemed to be able to get out of her.

Trudy's husband, Gordo, was a tanned, cocky little fellow with a wide country boy's grin. He was the youngest of the astronauts, and the most experienced pilot in the group. He was real slow-talkin' and from Oklahoma. When chestnut-haired Trudy met Gordo at the University of Hawaii, she was already a pilot herself, dashing in Wayfarers as she purred over Oahu Island in a Piper Cub. Her heart was set on entering the Powder Puff Derby, the women's transcontinental air race founded decades earlier by Amelia Earhart and Pancho Barnes. Pancho had once run Pancho's Happy Bottom Riding Club, a bar on Edwards Air Force Base, and led a gang of hellcat aviatrixes in Pancho Barnes's Mystery Circus of the Air. Gordo was used to adventurous women. Hell, his eighty-six-year-old grandmother, still kicking in Shawnee, Oklahoma, was a rootin'-tootin' cowgirl who said she'd go with Gordo into space if she could.

The reporters pressed on. It was amazing how an adventurous gal like Trudy—the only licensed pilot among the new astronaut wives—was so damn quiet. Well, maybe she'd adopted some of the stoicism of her male counterparts. Compared to some of the chattier wives, her silences were almost rude, frankly. The truth was, Trudy didn't want anyone to find out her dirty little secret. Gordo had gotten up to more mischief than she could handle at Edwards.

Before the astronaut selection process had begun four months before in January 1959, Trudy had left Gordo after twelve years of marriage. ("Because he was screwing another man's wife out there in California," one of the astronaut wives would later reveal in a loud whisper.) She gathered her two daughters, Camala Keoki and Janita Lee (she and Gordo had named them with a Hawaiian nostalgia), and took off to San Diego, ready to start a new life for herself and her girls, sans Gordo. After years of supporting Gordo's career only to find him cheating on her, she now had the chance to pursue her own dreams.

Then one day, Gordo came banging on her door wanting her to come out and talk. With his aw-shucks demeanor, Gordo could somehow manage to look both dejected and excited. He was pretty sure he'd aced the extensive testing NASA had put him through. (Sperm counts, electrical stimulations, *five* barium enemas? Good God.) He'd been thoroughly checked out, stamped, and approved as grade-A American beefcake. He scored big on all the psychological tests at Wright-Patt, and the headshrinkers concluded that Gordo was just like any other supernormal fellow with a *healthy* male appetite.

Gordo always talked slowly, even if his wheels were spinning. It was the chance of a lifetime—he'd be shot up on an Atlas rocket into space! He was about to be an astronaut; all that was left for him to succeed was to produce a loving wife. A good marriage would ensure his appointment. After all, how could an astronaut handle the pressures of getting shot into the heavens if he couldn't even handle his wife on Earth? (Not to mention that if Trudy stuck around, she'd prob'ly reap plenty of goodies and rewards herself.)

At the very least, the flying part was enough to excite Trudy. Gordo was the best pilot Trudy had ever seen, and she was a good judge, being a damn good pilot herself. If anyone was going to outfly those Russians, it was Gordo.

Honey, Gordo's smile seemed to say, *think about the girls, think about Cam and Jan. I don't want to leave them behind when I'm a famous as hell astronaut.* Gordo had a way of making Trudy feel like she was not quite up to the challenge. He'd go around behind her back calling her a prude because she was very proper, the top button always done up on her tailored shirt. So what if she didn't like to get undressed in front of other women in the locker room of the Officers Club on base? Perhaps it was the competitive pilot in Trudy, but she couldn't bear to let such a choice assignment be forfeited. She'd go along with him. And she'd have to get over that stoic demeanor because talks were already under way to give *Life* magazine exclusive coverage of the astronauts' and their wives' "personal stories." They would do a major story on the seven astronauts together, then on their seven wives. Separate stories on each family would be published over the course of Project Mercury. The reward would be big—$500,000.

If there was anything more amazing that Gordo could have told Trudy, she didn't know what it was. Like all of America's new astronaut wives, Trudy had become adept at stretching Gordo's military pay of around $7,000 a year. The idea of half a million dollars, which was to be divvied up equally among the seven new space families (that meant over $70,000 each), was like winning the lottery. You could only laugh at that number.

Turning a blind eye to Gordo's affair, Trudy decided to go along with him on his space adventure. She let Gordo drag her back to godforsaken Edwards. Just like that, Trudy and Gordo and little ten-year-old Cam and nine-year-old Jan were back together living the American dream. She'd fooled NASA easily.

Stork-like blonde Jo Schirra sat on her couch in her quarters at the Naval Air Test Center at Patuxent River in Maryland, otherwise known as Pax River, where her husband, Wally, was a Navy test pilot.

Jo was Navy royalty. Her stepfather, four-star admiral James L. Holloway Jr., known as Lord Jim, had been appointed by President Eisenhower to be in charge of all United States naval forces in the eastern Atlantic and Mediterranean. She knew very well the proper codes of behavior, taught to her by her Navy-wife mother, Mrs. Admiral Holloway—how to dress, how to serve tea to an officer, how never to go to an official function without her white gloves, pearls on, and calling cards. And how to always say the right thing. If Jo had any questions about the customs of the service and the management of a shipshape Navy household, she could always turn to *The Navy Wife*, the bible for any service wife, written by two inimitable Navy wives, Anne Briscoe Pye and Nancy Shea. Throughout her husband's early officer's career, Jo followed "the rules" to the letter.

Before she was a Navy bride, she was a Navy brat who'd spent her teenage years in Shanghai with a rickshaw running her and her sister through the city streets on their way to the American Officers Club. When she first married Wally and they were stationed in China, where he was a naval attaché, Jo felt as if she were going home. As a young bride, she had her very own amah, the lady who drew her bath and laid out her clothes on her bed canopied in mosquito netting. The more exotic something was, the more Jo loved it. And space was very exotic.

John Glenn, Gus Grissom, Alan Shepard, Scott Carpenter, Deke Slayton, Gordon Cooper, and Wally Schirra were about to report for duty at Langley Air Force Base in Virginia, NASA's headquarters for Project Mercury. Training would start there in the late spring of 1959. As Vice President Richard Nixon declared in the so-called Kitchen Debate that summer with Khrushchev, the Russians might be ahead in rocketry, but America was ahead in the accoutrements of middle-class life. The wives were prime examples, helpmates in complete operational control of kitchens chock-full of nifty new gadgets—dishwashers, Frigidaires, electric can openers, and Westinghouse electric ranges. None of the seven astronaut wives knew exactly what lay ahead for them, but they believed they were living on the winning side of the Cold War.

2

Think Pink

Most of the wives would rather have gone out for a night on the town than be stuck inside the kitchen fighting the good fight on the domestic front, but over the course of being a test pilot's wife, none had much opportunity to be wined and dined. Their husbands might take them out to dinner now and then, but it was easier to stay at home, because they didn't have the money for both a babysitter and a night on the town. Nevertheless, the wives had become worldly through studying women's beauty and fashion magazines. They were looking forward to tasting what they'd experienced only through pictures. Some were imagining buying designer dresses rather than having to settle for copies. All of the wives felt they were now due a little payback for waiting those long, lonely months during World War II and Korea. They were ready to be treated like queens.

Their astronaut husbands now had a hotshot celebrity attorney, Leo DeOrsey, who took everyone out to dinner. At his fancy Columbia Country Club in Chevy Chase, Leo brought the men into a private room, ready to smoke cigars and talk business. Leo was handling the $500,000 *Life* deal pro bono, as a public service to America's new heroes. This included a $100,000 *Life* insurance policy, seeing as no insurance company would underwrite an astronaut. He negotiated TV and film rights for them, as well as things they "couldn't imagine."

The wives didn't exactly appreciate being left out of Leo's wheelings and dealings, but then again, they were used to it. In 1950s America, women were usually excluded from business and decision making. Their realm was limited to the domestic—housekeeping, childrearing, cooking, and cleaning. Many women, like most of the wives, dropped out of college early, favoring an "M.R.S." degree over a college baccalaureate (or in the case of Betty Grissom, her hard-earned P.H.T. degree). Even a strong woman such as Rene Carpenter said, "We were *complete* traditionalists: hats, gloves, entertaining machines, eyes glued on husbands' careers." In fact, one of the first jokes that broke the ice among the wives was admitting that they were a little perplexed by the press saying that their husbands all had genius-level IQs. Well, not quite, they opined, but only to each other.

Luckily, Leo had talked "Ike," President Eisenhower, also his client, out of making the families live in secrecy. Eisenhower had wanted all the astronaut families to live in a secluded village like the Soviet Union's Star City, so secret that the cosmonauts couldn't even tell their babushka-covered wives what they did for a living. Instead, America's astronauts would be out in the open, ready for public consumption. The new Mercury families were invited to live at Langley Air Force Base in Virginia. Langley offered typical military base living, nothing to write home about, but there was a palpable excitement in the air because of the extraordinary reason they were all there.

The Coopers and the Carpenters moved into officers' duplexes along pleasant Eagan Avenue. Having moved from military base to military base during Gordo's Air Force career, Trudy got to work on the bare, no-frills quarters, deftly unpacking the family treasures, all part of the ritual of making a new home.

Down the street, Rene's girls played dress-up in her old outfits. Gauzy creations spilled from a cardboard box—in tulle, satin, and parachute silk. There were many styles from over the years. There had been so many homes, going all the way back to their remote white clapboard house in the mountains in Colorado, its fireplace roaring with the discarded telephone poles that handsome Scott would chop into logs. His acoustic guitar had made it through this latest move unscathed. Before long, he'd be lounging in the living room, strumming away and singing.

Rene unpacked boxes of letters from over the years, pages full of memories. They were very open with each other, and now that Project Mercury was underway, they would even share journals.

"If this comes to a fatal, screaming end for me," read Scott's long letter about his new astronaut job, "I will have three main regrets: I will have lost the chance to contribute to my children's preparation for life on this planet, I will miss the pleasure of loving you when you are a grandmother, and I will never have learned to play the guitar well."

Scott was different from the other astronauts. He didn't join Gus and Deke, who were getting to be good friends, on their weekend hunting trips in the Great Dismal Swamp in Virginia. He was a bit of a pacifist and tended to drift off into his own world. He loved to look through his telescope at the stars, searching for a glimpse of what he might discover when he was sent out to space.

Another unusual fellow was John Glenn. Before he'd been selected as an astronaut, John was a project officer for the Navy in Washington, where he'd sit up in the Senate gallery with his wife, Annie, and listen to the debates, as optimistic as the Boy Ranger troop leader turned senator in *Mr. Smith Goes to Washington*. Whatever John did he gave his all to, and Annie supported him "a hundred percent."

When the space program began, Annie agreed that John should throw his whole self into it. They decided that Annie would remain in Arlington with their two kids, twelve-year-old Lyn and thirteen-year-old Dave, and John would live on base at Langley, 120 miles away. John spent weeknights at Langley Air Force Base's Bachelor Officers Quarters, his spartan room furnished with training manuals and a well-worn Bible. On base, John would jog in his sweatsuit, doing his "roadwork," as he called it. John was a cheerful, freckle-faced fellow who wasn't afraid to puff himself up and play the alpha dog. To one of the new astronaut wives, sitting outside sipping her coffee as John jogged by, he huffed, hardly out of breath, "Oxygen. Oxygen to your brain." Coffee wouldn't do her a bit of good, he told her. It was the lack of oxygen to her inner circuitry making her tired. Oxygen would make her more energetic, increase her ability to best support her astronaut. Oxygen to the brain was what she needed, he assured her.

"I'll have Annie send you our book on the Royal Canadian Air Force Exercises," said John. "It will change your life."

The book featured strange silhouette diagrams of the eleven-minute 5BX physical fitness plan, detailing toe-touches, push-ups, and scissor jumps for men, as well as the twelve-minute XBX plan for women, which Annie was on. Even in the early days, it was hard to live up to the Glenns.

Every weekend John drove home to Annie in his Prinz, a boxy British clunker that got terrific gas mileage. The other astronauts teased him mercilessly about the car. Alan, Gordo, and Gus were big racers, loved fast cars, and were planning to realize their hot-rod fantasies with their *Life* money. In the meantime, Gus and Deke continued to hunt in the wilds outside of Langley.

"Hey, where'd you get that *cat*?" asked Betty Grissom's son Scotty about the black bear his father and his new astronaut pal Deke were dragging into the garage one Sunday. They'd brought home their kill, displaying the all-American frontiersman spirit that made the press call the boys "the greatest heroes since Christopher Columbus. The men who will take us to the stars!" The wives just looked at each other with frozen eyes.

"Thank goodness we got that money for our stories from *Life*," said Betty. She believed she and Gus well deserved their extra $24,000 a year, which was to be paid out over the three years Project Mercury was scheduled to run. She'd suffered a lot of hardships supporting Gus through college and sweating out his service in Korea. Betty, ever practical, was hoping that with this new astronaut business, Gus would have a more stable job, like a salesman taking a silver briefcase into space. Maybe he could spend some more time with the family.

The Grissoms, Schirras, and Slaytons had decided to forgo the Langley duplexes for Stoneybrook, a subdivision about fifteen miles away. The families moved into tract houses practically identical except for their color. The houses were comfortable, actually rather terrific, the gals thought, compared to what they were used to. There was even a swimming pool at the community club, private for Stoneybrook residents. Betty, Jo, and

Marge, in an adorable new stars-and-stripes-skirted swimsuit, spent their off hours lounging by the pool, dipping their toes into the water, feeling a little self-conscious as the ever-present *Life* photographer snapped from the sidelines. The astronaut children liked to cannonball off the diving board and douse everyone.

Before Betty moved to Virginia for the space program, her fellow test pilot wives at Wright-Patterson Air Force Base in Ohio had given her a silver charm bracelet with coins they'd engraved with all of their names, *Ginny* and *Peggy* and *Gladys* and *Violet.* They knew Betty was a homebody, and worried that she wouldn't be socially up to par with the other astronaut wives.

"They're all going to play bridge, and you're not going to know how to play," they warned her.

"That's okay, I don't want to play bridge," said Betty. "Gus Grissom didn't get where he is today because I sat around and played bridge." She was more of a poker player anyhow.

As it turned out, the only one of the astronaut wives who played bridge was Gordo Cooper's wife, Trudy. So Betty said to herself, "Betty, you're safe on that one." She didn't care too much about getting close to Trudy, seeing as Gordo, Gus's old flying buddy from back at Wright-Patt, had once almost gotten Gus killed in a plane crash.

One evening, Trudy and Gordo came over to the Grissoms' house to toast their new enterprise with champagne. Gus kept filling Trudy's glass over and over again. Trudy, who was usually uptight, let loose a bit. She loved her champagne. She was having a really good time.

After the Coopers left, Betty turned to Gus. "Tomorrow, Gordo's going to be dead. She's going to blame him for getting her drunk, she's not going to blame you." Betty had a sixth sense about these things.

Soon the boys were being sent hither and yon for astronaut training: to the Navy's human centrifuge in Johnsville, Pennsylvania, for "eyeballs in, eyeballs out" tests where they were whirled around to see how many g-forces they could withstand; to the Morehead Planetarium in Chapel Hill, North Carolina, where they studied the stars to help them navigate the skies. With their husbands away so frequently, the wives often got together. Back in their Navy and Air Force days, they would lay their young children out on a bed in someone's house and stay up all night playing cards, drinking Pepsi-Colas, staving off the loneliness. Sometimes a kindly neighbor might watch the kids. Now that they were astronaut wives, they arranged joint babysitting or dropped their kids off at military daycare at Fort Eustis, near Langley.

They tried to meet every few weeks at the yacht club restaurant at Fort Monroe, also near Langley. One night, Marge was driving Betty and Jo when she ran out of gas. They were stranded until a man came along and offered to give Marge a lift to the closest filling station. Proving she was not technically oriented like her husband, Marge said to the girls, "If you get cold, just turn on the ignition."

Betty and Jo were still laughing when Marge finally returned with the canister of gas. "Just how exactly can we turn on the ignition, Marge, if we don't have gas?"

Marge was always the most amusing of the wives. She loved telling stories about Japan. After World War II, before moving to Germany, she'd lived in Tokyo with a roommate. Marge would walk by the bombed-out Imperial Palace every day and had a prized photo of herself sitting on a cushion in a traditional flowered silk kimono, holding a fan.

Her stories about Japan became a euphemism for her previous life as a divorcée. She cracked the other girls up with her story about when she'd first arrived in Japan and found it very strange. One evening she went with her boss, the general for whom she was working as a secretary, to a formal Japanese house. When Marge spotted a beautiful black-lacquered tray arranged with lovely little pink melon balls, she thought, "Oh, finally something I can eat." She popped one in her mouth and realized with horror that it was raw fish.

"I don't think I ever chewed so long in my life," recounted Marge. She said she just looked at her boss and her boss looked at her and it was understood: *You are going to eat that and you are going to enjoy it.*

Another time, her boss woke Marge in the early hours to type an emergency memo for General MacArthur, and looked over her shoulder as she typed while MacArthur dictated. She was barely awake, extremely nervous, and hardly dressed for work in her housecoat and slippers, but knocked it out without any mistakes!

Marge seemed to have a story for everything. When the astronaut wives were invited to be guests on *The Bob Hope Show*, she told them, with a wink-wink expression, "My roommate and Bob Hope would go *out on the town*," if they knew what she meant. Bob did not recognize Marge under all the makeup his cosmeticians had slathered on her face, but Marge didn't mind. To the wives, she was the star of the show that day.

All of the wives were getting used to dealing with their new fame—even though it would be two years before any of their husbands would be shot into space. They prepared as best they could, coaching each other and offering bits of advice like "Trust yourself. You know more than you think you do," a message gleaned from Dr. Spock, the childcare expert whose advice was taken as gospel at the time. All of them had young kids, at least two, except for Marge with little Kent. A born leader, Marge told the ladies that if a reporter came up to them and asked about a technical aspect of spaceflight they should never admit ignorance, but just look him dead in the eye, smile, and say, "I'm sorry, that's classified."

She told her friends and an eavesdropping *Life* reporter about what happened one day at the Langley Air Force Base Officers Club swimming pool when she was introduced to a young woman as "the wife of one of the astronauts."

"The girl I was meeting looked like she expected me to sprout antennae over my ears," said Marge. "'Oh, I'm so sorry for you,' she said." Marge bugged out her eyes to dramatize the story. "I honestly cannot understand that kind of reaction!"

All the wives felt as Marge did. They knew the stoic code of the test pilot wife. If any one of them lost her husband in a crashing hulk of metal, she'd have to take it quietly and bravely. That was part of the job.

One of the first challenges the wives faced was dealing with the ghostwriters from *Life*. The magazine was planning its first big cover story on them for September 1959.

The writers, when calling to schedule appointments, or dropping by for supper or to take them out to dinner, acted as though the ladies were their long-lost best friends. There were three *Life* reporters assigned full-time to the husbands and wives, including Loudon Wainwright, whose son would beget a musical dynasty. The contract stipulated that each wife would have a piece ghostwritten that would be presented as authored by her—"by Betty Grissom." Having a ghostwriter was a relief to Betty, who'd never been much of a reader or a writer. She liked jigsaw puzzles mostly, complicated ones that she slaved over. When she was nearly finished, her boys would usually run in from playing outside and fit in the final pieces, or Gus would show up, put in the last piece, and claim all of the glory.

Betty found it just plain weird to be shadowed everywhere, even when she chauffeured her kids to school or tidied up her home. "They act like I'm the most interesting thing since sliced bread," she marveled.

The seven wives hosted their ghostwriters at their homes and let them tag along as they went about their daily routines. The girls found their real selves disappearing behind *Life*'s depiction of what it meant to be not only the perfect fifties housewife, but the perfect astronaut's wife, molded like the popular Barbie doll that had first appeared on store shelves that spring. The wives felt keenly the pressure to do everything just so, now that the whole country was watching them.

The *Life* feature would be a multiple-page spread with profiles of each of the seven wives complete with a portrait, as well as group shots, one of which would grace the cover of the magazine. It was Marge's idea that they all go on a diet to firm up in light of their newfound fame. They had all read the articles about how eating avocados and taking sauna baths could help weight loss. Marge marched the gals into the Langley Air Force Base Officers Club sauna. She thought she'd won over her troops, but wrapped in a white towel, glowering at those red rocks, Betty said it was hot enough to roast a turkey! She couldn't decide if she could breathe or not in that little cedar cell. Finally Betty just had to get out of there. "That one fell apart pretty quickly," she said.

The wives concurred: they simply were not the exercising type. They decided they got quite enough of a workout just running after their little kids, and it wasn't so hard to shed a few pounds, what with someone constantly following you and noticing everything you put in your mouth.

They were, however, all consumed by a burning question: what would they wear for the *Life* pictures?

The editors told them that the cover shot would be taken from the chest up. *Life*'s instructions, coordinated with NASA, were that the women wear prim and proper tailored pastel shirtwaist dresses for one of the group shots. Their big national magazine debut, and NASA wanted them wearing plain-Jane shirtwaist dresses?

The wives discussed it endlessly over the phone, starting the astronaut wife tradition of the round-robin phone call, a party line that would stretch throughout the space race. How dare the government tell them what to wear? They were astronauts' wives now!

There was also lots of discussion about what color lipstick they should wear for the cover picture. Most of the wives didn't wear any makeup except for lipstick, so the color was very important.

All the fashion and homemaker magazines suggested that they "think pink." Pink was the color of the First Lady, Mamie Eisenhower. The wives had read all about Mamie and her "million-dollar fudge," which the thrifty housewife could make as a special treat for her husband without breaking her grocery budget. They knew about Mamie's White House routine. At 11 a.m. every day, she had her hair done in her famed Mamie bangs. She dabbled in correspondence and women's luncheons, and then she and Ike usually had dinner in front of the five o'clock news.

In the Pink Palace, as reporters acerbically called the White House, several rooms had been repainted "Mamie Pink," the First Lady's signature Pepto-Bismol hue. Pink was in vogue: pink dresses, pink pocketbooks, pink carpeting, pink Maytag washing machines, even pink poodles, which were all the rage among fashionable Parisians.

So it was agreed: Responsible Pink for the perfect Astrowife.

The Astrowife round-robin kept the women up to date on what the other wives thought about this or that, and allowed them to scheme together accordingly.

"*Hmm*," thought Betty, if one of the girls fussed over her looks too much. "She's one of *those*."

Betty wasn't gung ho for group activity, but she was grateful that the round-robin gave her a chance to hear what the other wives were up to. Not that the Grissoms gave a damn about keeping up with the Joneses.

One day, Marge invited some of the wives over to her house in Stoneybrook to try out a facial mask (a favorite was the Edna Wallace Hopper white clay mask), but Betty had already decided she wasn't going to spend an extra dime to go to the beauty parlor. Not that Gus complained about what she spent. Gus was not cheap about certain things. He was the only astronaut to splurge on air-conditioning in their car, the latest luxury for automobiles. When the *Life* money had rolled in, the only thing Gus said to Betty was, "There are two things that I request. Do not do anything different with your hair. And no frilly bedrooms."

"I don't think you are going to have to worry about either one of those," Betty assured him.

She felt pleased with the all-yellow ensemble she had pulled together for the photographs—a marigold scoop neck for the cover, and for the group shot with the Mercury capsule, a sunny yellow shirtwaist dress, cinched at her slim waist with a belt. She had taken some care to find yellow sunglasses and perfectly matching yellow button earrings at a local department store, and considered herself the best dressed of the wives. Like Trudy, she would wear her NASA dress buttoned up to the top. Gus was more of a leg man anyhow. Whenever he'd tell her, "Your legs are good-looking," Betty would shine inside.

"Betty's a Hoosier," someone explained on the party line, "and she's kind of stubborn and she's not as socialized as the rest of us."

Nevertheless, when the big day of the shoot rolled around, Marge and Jo didn't mind Betty chauffeuring them in her air-conditioned car. She pulled into Jo's driveway bright and early. It was true what the other wives said about Jo. She was the perfect Navy wife with her white gloves and pearls. Today she was wearing seventy-dollar white high heels.

Marge was late, making Betty and Jo wait in the car while she put on her finishing touches, probably going to work with her tweezers on her "beauty mark." Jo thought Marge, a fellow Navy wife, should be abiding by their code, the first rule of which was to always be on time. It was important to have a good memory for things like what O-hundred hour your husband's ship was to sail. And as they waited, it got closer and closer to the hour scheduled with the photographer.

"Shoot," said Betty. That was one of her favorite expressions. She honked her horn.

Jo could hardly keep from rolling her eyes at Betty's unladylike turn of phrase; "very Air Force," she thought.

Marge finally came out of the house, waving her hands about madly. She made some excuse about having to feed Acey. As soon as Marge offered her a cigarette, Jo forgave her.

Marge and Jo were the smokers of the group. Betty was not too happy to have these chain-smoking chimneys in her car. She hated smoke. Back in Mitchell, Indiana, she'd had to endure Sunday drives with her dad, who smoked big cigars and insisted that all the windows be kept closed. It always made Betty sick. Finally she convinced her mother to let her stay home. She'd even been willing to forgo a delicious three-scoop cone from the place that made its own ice cream in order not to have to ride around in a cloud of smoke.

Now she was an astronaut wife and had to get along with her cohorts, so she set her jaw and pressed the pedal to the metal.

At Langley, Ralph Morse, the *Life* photographer, looked through the viewfinder of his camera. The women were all noticeably nervous, so Ralph kept on moving around and talking in his New York accent while he set up hot lights. It was better this way because if he stopped for a moment, the women might pass out cold. *Life* had big plans for the wives and he needed the pictures to be perfect.

For the cover shot, Ralph arranged the wives like numerals around a clock face. Their formation mimicked the placement of their husbands, whose cover story, "The Astronauts—Ready to Make History," would come out the week before the wives'. The wives smiled and blinked into the bright popping flashbulbs. There was plenty to chat about while Ralph set up the next shot, like how the boys had all decided to quit smoking now that they were astronauts and starting their training. Jo's pack-a-day husband, Wally, claimed to have kicked the habit so as not to have a nicotine fit in orbit. He would still light up cigarettes, but wouldn't inhale. Jo was almost ready to throw him out of the house, he was so irritable.

The crowning shot was taken on a grassy Langley field under a perfect blue sky. Ralph set the ladies up in a pleasing arrangement, positioning them on the metal apron of the red model of the Mercury capsule their husbands would ride into space. This very capsule had recently been dropped into the Atlantic and survived! Instead of some egghead from Langley Research Lab giving the women a little lesson about where the parachute was folded away in the capsule, the wives got something along the lines of: "You in the pink, sit next to the gal in the yellow, yeah, yellow, don't move, you're in the middle next to Snow White—"

The wives looked like scoops of ice cream around an upside-down cone. Just as NASA and *Life* had ordered, they were all in their pressed pastel shirtwaists, white and pale blue and—*roses*? Rene had astonished the wives by wearing red heels and a bold dress, blooming with red cabbage roses. Actually, Rene's dress matched the space capsule perfectly! How could the *Life* editors not be amused? Rene really made the shot zing. The wives each placed a manicured hand on the capsule, like models selling a Maytag. Perfect!

* * *

It was torture waiting weeks for the magazine to come out, but finally the day came, September 21, 1959. The cover bore the headline "Astronauts' Wives': Their Inner Thoughts, Worries." There they were, seven well-coiffed "typical" American housewives with smiling red lips. The wives had been airbrushed to perfection: there were no pimples, no puffy eyes, no crow's-feet or fine lines around the lips. But what *about* those lips? They had all worn pink lipstick, but here they were in *red*?

The wives were completely shocked, worrying about how America would judge them. They would *never* wear such a bold-colored lipstick. They were mothers, not vixens done up in Racy Red. What had happened to Responsible Pink?

In the towering Time-Life Building in New York City, the editors had decided against Mamie Pink because it was fast going out of style. This was the space age after all, and the flare of a bright Patriotic Red on the Astrowives' lips better promised America the Moon and the stars. Soon, bouffant hairdos whipped up to the heavens appeared on runways, on sidewalks, and in typing pools, along with frosted "Moon Drops" lipstick, launched by Revlon as "the lipstick to wear to the moon."

The wives pored over their fifteen-page "Seven Brave Women Behind the Astronauts" spread. Through touching up and editorial tinkering, *Life* had transformed seven very different, complicated women into perfect cookie-cutter American housewives. There was not a whiff of domestic turbulence.

In her *Life* profile, Trudy came out strong for her Gordo, proving herself his biggest supporter with total faith in his piloting skills and his grace under pressure. Deke's wife, Marge, certainly didn't mention her ex-husband, a lesser Air Force pilot who had turned out to be a pathological liar. It was because of him that she'd left the United States for Japan and then Germany, where she met Deke. She knew *Life* wouldn't want that piece of history anyway. A perfect Astrowife being a divorcée?

Instead, Marge's ghostwriter had put in how sick Marge was of the Hollywood version of a military pilot wife, crying into her dirty dishwater over the loss of her man. Marge had seen more than a few girls turn into widows at Edwards, and promised herself that if she lost Deke in space, she'd take her lumps without sugar.

"You learn to take the things your husband does in stride," Trudy told her ghostwriter, but she didn't care to elaborate on that statement.

It had taken some overtime for the New York editors to turn Betty Grissom into the quintessential fifties housewife. Sucked dry of all her character and verve, Betty could now be admired by readers across the country and held aloft as a role model. Whatever eccentricities the wives displayed, *Life* was complicit with NASA in erasing quirks such as thirty-year-old Betty referring to herself, because of all she'd been through, as "ole Betty."

As far as being a red, white, and blue all-American, no one could beat Annie Glenn, which led to a complaint that none of the wives could explicitly state on the round-robin: why hadn't *they* gotten the lead? The answer was right there on the page. Annie's dark hair perfectly framed her face, which, just like her balding redheaded spaceman's, was sprinkled with freckles. The seemingly perfect Annie had known John all her life, having met him when they were just toddlers in their hometown of New Concord, Ohio. Annie's dentist father, Doc Castor, stuck her in a playpen with Johnny during their local teetotalers' monthly dinner club potluck.

Color photos featured Annie in a cherry print headscarf driving the boat as Johnny water-skied across the glistening blue Chesapeake Bay inlet, a more middle-class version of Senator John F. Kennedy's family at Hyannis Port. Annie was just what NASA wanted the wives of its seven astronauts to be—a squeaky-clean American housewife standing proudly beside her husband with her spatula ready to whip up something tasty for her hero who was beating those godless Russians in the space race. Annie fit the part perfectly; she even played the organ for Sunday evening home sing-alongs, which featured Broadway hits and Presbyterian hymns. Like Miss America contestants, she had her "talent." Annie was the Ultimate Astrowife.

Annie spoke of faith in God and country. When John was picked for the program, she said she went to see her family minister to make sure the higher power approved of man's exploration of its realm. "There's no religious reason why mankind, and John in particular, should not explore space," Reverend Erwin assured her.

"What if that thing is up there going around and around," she confessed to America, "and they aren't able to bring him back? What would I do?"

In the Glenns, people across the nation saw America's values and ideals—faith, bravery, family—personified. And in Annie's confession, their own hopes and fears about this crazy, bold, amazing step America was going to take were reflected back at them.

If the other wives didn't want to watch John Glenn become the first man to go into space, they had their work cut out for them.

3

The Cookies

Across the land, housewives opened their glossy *Life* magazines and saw seven glorious women they could look up to and emulate. If only *they* could whip up an apple pie or a perfect batch of chocolate chip cookies like Annie Glenn, maybe their husbands would be more productive, better fit their gray flannel suits, and get ahead in business.

Nobody wanted to be left in the backwash of the space age, so the pressure to have an exemplary family life, from Walla Walla, Washington, to Presque Isle, Maine, was greater than ever. No matter what a wife had to sweep under her carpet, keeping a peaceful marriage was not just an imperative of American womanhood, but in this day when everything could be wiped out at the push of a button, a matter of national security. The seven Astrowives would show them the way.

Soon, the astronauts were off to the Convair plant in California. Here was where they were building the Atlas rocket that would fulfill Project Mercury's goal of putting a man into orbit around the Earth before the Russians did. As usual at these Astro-junkets, the red carpet was rolled out and the boys were put up in the first-class Kona Kai Resort, a tropical oasis of lush gardens with torchlights and white-sand beaches on the shores of the Pacific at the tip of Shelter Island off San Diego.

Alan Shepard got a room with twin beds, which didn't exactly fit his plans for the evening, so he asked to switch rooms with Scott Carpenter, who'd been assigned a full-sized bed. Scott handed over his key and Alan headed off to his new room. Why did Alan need the extra mattress space? As the story went, Alan had gone across the border and picked up a *chiquita* in a bar in Tijuana, the den of sin for many a lonely sailor stationed in San Diego.

In the middle of the night, John Glenn was woken up by a phone call from John "Shorty" Powers, the NASA press officer known as the "voice of the astronauts and Mercury Control," who had been a cheerleader in high school. Shorty had gotten a call from a paper that was ready to run a story, complete with incriminating photos.

John was livid. He convinced the reporter and the photographer and the editor, who he got out of bed, not to run the story. It was a matter of national security. The next morning, John asked for a "séance," which was what the seven astronauts called their closed-door meetings. This one would be forever known as the Kona Kai Séance. As John saw it, any astronaut who couldn't keep his "pants zipped" threatened to ruin everything and squash America's opportunity to beat the Russians, not only in space but also on the grounds of moral superiority. They all had a responsibility to the country to be the wholesome heroes they were sold as. John went head-to-head with Alan over the issue.

They didn't come to any agreement, but the overriding feeling was that any extracurricular monkey business was each man's own private affair, so long as he kept it out of sight. All the same, Alan didn't exactly try to hide his philandering. He was seen at swinging parties and golf tournaments with multiple women hanging off his arms and was spotted cruising the Strip in Cocoa Beach in his white Corvette, customized by Chevrolet with a "space age" interior and racing tires. Thank God *their* husbands weren't like Alan, the wives thought.

"How do you think Louise puts up with him?" they asked. But of course they didn't want to pry too much or say anything that could even remotely affect the competition that was foremost on everybody's mind—which of the astronauts would be the Chosen One to go up first?

The astronauts were spending most of their days down in Cocoa Beach, the "Jewel of the Space Coast," working overtime at nearby Cape Canaveral, the military base that housed the astronaut headquarters, including their "procedures trainer," a spacecraft simulator. The Cape was where the actual launch would take place in the spring of 1961. The big day was fast approaching when, after a massive and intensive effort by NASA, the titanium Mercury capsule would be nearly complete. One of their husbands would ride this "can" into space for the first suborbital flight—just a fifteen-minute shot up and down, but long enough to assure his place in history as the first man in space.

Soon the wives were going down to Florida for a glimpse of what their husbands were doing. Driven from the airport in convertibles, they held on to their hats and squinted through cat-eyed sunglasses at this fabulous space frontier town of coconut palms and white stucco motel architecture, with blinking neon signs advertising nightclub acts. Along the stretch of Highway A1A known as the Strip, Cocoa Beach was exploding with rat-shack motels, popping up overnight with names like Starlite, Polaris, Sea Missile, and Astrocraft. The Satellite Motel spun its famous Earth-orbiting signpost. A rocket took off in neon from the Starlite Motel. The famous Mouse Trap steakhouse crowned a Miss Orbit every year. The Vanguard was a lousy-looking joint, but it had topless waitresses.

The Holiday Inn was the classiest of the new accommodations along the Strip. It looked like a giant live-in cocktail, garnished with a huge green neon star on top. This was where the wives would be put up for this and all subsequent visits to Cocoa Beach. The tanned, smooth-talking manager, Henri Landwirth, pronounced with a dramatic French accent, met them at the door and welcomed them chez *Henri*, offering his master-of-ceremonies services for the wives' weekend.

As the husbands escorted them in, the women were alarmed to see a crowd of astronaut groupies waiting in the lobby. Stewardesses with flexible flying schedules, hotel clerks, and diner waitresses seemed to magically appear wherever an astronaut was to be found. Two of these Cape Cookies, as the boys called them, dropped to their knees as the group entered, prostrating themselves before the astronauts. The wives were taken aback at the sheer number of these pretty, tanned young things with their scantily clad bodies, obviously willing to do anything a spaceman desired. Dear God!

"I mean, these Hollywood types—they need this and they want this," said Jo, looking around at the rest as if to say, *But our guys don't, right?*

The boys didn't mind the attention one bit. The MO, as it had always been for a Navy wife worrying about her husband (who might be cozying up to an exotic Asian dancer in a dark tiki bar on the other side of the globe), was to play a cool hand.

Pretty soon the wives learned the lay of the land at Cocoa Beach. It was chock-full of promoters and public relations men, each trying to get in a word about his product and solicit an astronaut's endorsement. The party followed the astronauts wherever they went. When the astronauts had first rolled into town, everyone went to the Cape Colony Inn because that's where the astronauts were. After they packed up and moved the party permanently to the Holiday Inn, everyone followed them there. The hotel bar would be empty, then an astronaut would walk in; within minutes the bar would be full. The bartenders tipped off reporters, who would literally chase the astronaut children down hallways. The kids thought it was funny. The rabid press didn't get to them the way it got to their mothers, who didn't like their husbands being walking advertisements for the bald smooth-talking types who offered a variety of perks and bargains while picking up the cookie crumbs left in their wake.

For the time being, the boys ignored the cookies, instead reminding their wives what a terrific rate the Holiday Inn was giving them. Their rooms cost only a dollar a night, not to mention free all-you-can-eat dinner buffets, which featured shrimp cocktails shaped like rockets. And there was an even better perk: down here in Florida, each astronaut was given a dollar-a-year Corvette.

Al, Gus, and Gordo befriended Jim Rathmann, who'd won the Indy 500 that year. Jim owned the local Cadillac-Chevrolet dealership in nearby Melbourne, and, under the auspices of doing his patriotic duty, he arranged an out-of-this-world deal with the president of General Motors. An astronaut could "executive drive" a Corvette for a year, then trade it in for a new one the next year. All he had to do was plunk down another dollar. Meanwhile, the wives were doomed to drive station wagons; family rooms on wheels were deemed the perfect vehicle for these all-American mothers. Trudy, who was not only a pilot but liked to race cars, yearned to get behind the wheel of something with a little more horsepower. But the ad men of America told her that a station wagon, with plenty of room for kids and groceries, was more suitable.

As for Betty, she thought Gus was in a little over his head, always talking about his "friends" at Rathmann's house. It was a fast crowd, and they all raced cars. Betty didn't like it a bit. Finally she had a chance to see the place for herself. After dinner in the formal dining room, Betty, who usually didn't like to cause a fuss, pointed out to Gus, "It's *you* they're after, not me."

The astronauts weren't exactly tall, NASA's requirement being that they all had to be less than five foot eleven—small enough to squeeze into the cramped quarters of a spacecraft. But they were enormously competitive. Anything, no matter how insignificant, might become a test of their manhood. At a mere five foot five, little Gus wanted to prove to the others that he was the most macho of them all. The boys liked to play handball, but they turned this simple street game into an epic battle. Gus was the champion, except for the one time when he supposedly let Alan beat him so he wouldn't feel bad. To make sure that never happened again, Gus strutted around the Cape squeezing a spring-loaded handgrip to strengthen his hand and wrist muscles so that he could smack the ball even harder, faster. Gus had to win, all of the time. Dominating his peers, even at handball, just might make the hairbreadth of difference when it came to winning the prize of being first into space.

Ultimately, NASA would decide who was the One, but the question would also be posed to the astronauts themselves: "If you can't make the first flight yourself, which man do you think should make it?" Each would vote for the man he thought would be the best among them to go first. No one was allowed to vote for himself, obviously, since each felt very strongly that he should be chosen.

So they had to prove themselves to their peers, all of the time. If the boys were going waterskiing at the Cape, whoever was in charge of getting the speedboat had to make sure he got the fastest one on the dock. Pansy tourists might like to slalom, but astronauts preferred barefoot skiing, which required far more horsepower. NASA worried that their national treasures might break an ankle going fifty miles an hour on the choppy water, but the astronauts just went faster. Even at a friendly astronaut barbecue, the boys would jockey for position to be the one manning the grill. The wives would roll their eyes while each secretly hoped *her* husband got the apron and tongs.

When the wives were together, they tried to avoid talking about their husbands' competition because it was so ferocious. Betty didn't think Alan liked Gus one bit, and in fact thought Gus was a shade ahead of Alan (and driving Alan nuts because he couldn't catch her Gus). The competition reached pathological proportions one day at the Cape when Gus spontaneously started shimmying up one of the guy wires that held up the rocket on the launch pad.

"Get down!" the engineers ordered, but Gus wasn't about to let some pencil neck tell him what to do. Strong as a bear, he climbed higher and higher. This sent the rest of the boys into a tizzy. Alan hopped on the wire and climbed after him, ready to beat Gus to the top.

"Get down!" the engineers called again, but the guys were too pumped on adrenaline to even hear them.

Wally Schirra's gambit to beat out the rest of the boys was through practical jokes. If the astronauts were on the golf course together and Alan was about to tee off, Wally might goose him with a putter. If Wally "gotcha," as he called his pranks, that meant he had triumphed over you, at least in his own mind. To his wife, Jo, Wally didn't care to sugarcoat his competitive nature with jokes. They competed at everything—swimming, diving, waterskiing. One time, when they went out on the tennis court, Wally served as hard as he would to an astronaut, as if his wife were somehow competing with him to be first in space.

But Jo was no shrinking violet. Instead of thwacking back the ball to Wally, she would give it a light tap so it would just go *boop* over the net. Wally didn't know how to handle it. Jo "got him." When Jo won a match she didn't brag to the other wives, lest they mention it to their husbands. Wally would go ballistic if his comrades knew he had lost in anything to his wife.

After having spent a couple of nights in Cookie Land, the wives could joke about the absurdity of the scene, and each went to sleep glad *her* astronaut was diligently sticking to his training schedule during his many months down at the Cape. But was her man *really* staying in like John Glenn with his Bible? Or, God forbid, panting around until the wee hours like Alan, chasing tail like a hound dog, taking advantage of the Strip's easy drive-up-to-the-door motel access (so you didn't have to sneak cookies in through the lobby).

The possibilities for extracurricular activities made Marge Slayton, for one, see double. God knows what her Deke was nailing down in Cocoa Beach. What was so top-secret that the Cape, the actual rocket launch site, was declared "off-limits to wives"? Who knew what went on at the top-secret Cape with the astronauts' secretaries and nurses? Marge was no dummy. She'd been a secretary on an air base in Germany. That's how she'd met Deke!

Marge decided enough was enough, and she finally gave Deke an ultimatum. "Tell them I'm coming to wash your damn Ban-Lon shirts. That I'm looking for a job. That I'm your girlfriend. That ought to do it!"

Deke drove out to the Cape and shot the breeze with the guards at the gate while Marge hid on the backseat floor underneath a couple of blankets. Recounting her adventure to the wives afterward, she said, "I was having a nicotine fit, and I just about jumped up and asked those guards for a cigarette."

She didn't want to get Deke in trouble for breaking the rules, or to do anything to jeopardize his chance to be the first man in space. After she popped up her head, she realized there wasn't much to see at the Cape, only scrub grass and a couple of lonely launch pads, where she hoped Deke would make history. Suddenly, she looked over and saw Christopher Columbus Kraft Jr., the appropriately named flight director, who would have no small part in making the big decision of who would go up first. He stared right at her. Marge could have just died.

On another occasion, the wives were treated to a sporting boat trip down the coast to ooh and ahh over technological marvels created for their husbands' journeys, like the green dye marker that would show the rescue crews of frogmen where their husbands' "can" had landed. Its brilliant color was now spreading across the waves. After this fun fact was pointed out to them, perfectly bred Jo, emboldened by the company of the wives, asked, "Is that how we'll know where to throw the wreath?" She made them all laugh through their fears.

The grand finale was getting to watch the test firing of the Atlas rocket, which would first be manned by Enos the chimpanzee, then by their husbands for the orbital flights. It was an ominous, gray, overcast day. Everyone on the beach craned their necks to see the magnificent bird rise in the distance from its launch pad on the Cape on a red-hot thrust of flame.

The girls looked on in amazement. Then *kaboom!* The rocket exploded like a bomb.

"Oh, thank God the monkey wasn't in that one," cracked one of them.

The wives knew NASA was looking not only at how their husbands flew, but how they lived at home. Alan Shepard offered an easy scapegoat, comedian Will Dana's joke being if he had slept with as many women as he was rumored to, "his dick would have fallen off." Besides, why would Alan want to squash the rumors? His reputation for astronomical virility might even help him outshine the competition! Wasn't riding a rocket the biggest test of manhood around?

Still, the wives felt terrible for Louise. They called her Saint Louise, not because the Christian Scientist was churchy like organ-playing Annie, but because she was so serene and ladylike. She smiled so genuinely; often she seemed to glow from within.

Finally, in their own version of their husbands' Kona Kai Séance, the wives broached the subject during a get-together at

Jo's house. They asked Louise if she knew what her husband was doing. It was so obvious. How could she turn a blind eye to Alan's constant fooling around?

Louise had to catch her breath before she composed her answer—"Because I'm the one he really loves."

The wives thought it was just awful. Louise was in total denial, lost in her own world and glued to her great consolation and time-passer, needlepoint. She would sit for hours sewing light yellow into the depths of brown, giving shape to florals, flame stitches, even abstract designs. She never stuck the wrong color in the wrong square, and rarely seemed to miss a hole. Neither did Alan.

At home during the week in Virginia Beach while Alan was off at the Cape training, Louise managed a household of girls, looking after her two daughters, Laura and Julie, and a niece, Alice, who had lived with the Shepards ever since Louise's sister had died from mysterious causes. Louise had already gone through long periods of separation from Alan as a Navy wife. As the other wives noticed, Louise had an unusual elegance and reserve about her. She had been raised at Longwood Gardens, the spectacular Du Pont estate in Kennett Square, Pennsylvania, where her father was the chief groundskeeper and engineer.

Longwood Gardens was America's Versailles, more than a thousand acres comprising formal Italian and French gardens, English rose gardens, woodlands, meadows, and a glass-canopied conservatory lush with orchids and exotic flowers. Inspired by the grand Italianate marble fountains of Europe, Mr. Du Pont had created similar wonders on his estate. Louise's father was a favorite of his and he sent her parents all over Europe to study these great fountains, so her father could design and construct water marvels for the Du Pont estate.

The most splendiferous feature Louise's father designed was a massive pipe organ connected to an extensive system of fountains and colored lights. As a girl, Louise had often helped her father create brilliant bursts of colored water with the push of a button or the press of a pedal. The ever-changing colors of the water jets provided a magnificent backdrop for the ballets staged at the Du Ponts'.

Old man Du Pont didn't have any children, so the couple was especially attentive to Louise and her older sister, Adele, who were affectionately known as VIP kids around the estate. When they were little girls, they used to play hide-and-go-seek in the underground passage that connected the groundskeeper's cottage to the main house. They enjoyed tea parties in the trellised garden with their dolls and teddy bears, and when they were older they were invited to the formal tea dances, garden parties, and lavish balls the Du Ponts hosted. Louise was like Audrey Hepburn, starring in *Sabrina* as the chauffeur's daughter living on a wealthy estate. The Du Ponts even returned from one of their many tours of the Continent with new dresses for the sisters.

When Louise was a teenager, her parents sent her to Principia in St. Louis, a private Christian Science boarding school. People dismissed Christian Science as that religion that didn't allow you to go to a doctor, which was true, but in the East, Christian Science had high social cachet. At Principia, Louise was known as "Frosty" because of her icy reserve. They also called her "Miss Westinghouse," after the refrigerator. It was at Principia, at a Christmas dance, that she met Alan, who was there visiting his sister Polly. He, too, had grown up going to a Christian Science church (although his faith didn't particularly carry into adulthood). Louise's schoolmates thought he was an arrogant jerk and didn't want her to marry him, but marry him she did, and she was not sorry about it.

Keeping up her calm and elegant demeanor, her "Frosty" façade, proved to be a perennially challenging part of being Alan Shepard's wife. Louise took her role as a Navy wife seriously. She was loving but strict with her girls, and she used secret codes to keep them in line. If they didn't put their napkins in their laps, Louise would look over and very quietly say, "White Sails." If, after taking a serving of fruit cocktail, the girls had neglected to return their spoons to the doily on their place setting, Louise would say, "Star-Spangled Banner." That meant, "Spoons out of the bowl, girls, spoons by your plates. Mind your manners!" It was a monumental challenge for Louise to maintain her composure when she and her daughters were invited to an opulent invitation-only luncheon in the wardroom of Alan's ship, which was docked in port. Louise's girls observed the linen tablecloths and silver service and asked, "Mommy, how come Daddy is so rich and we are so poor?" There were no secret codes to answer that question, which struck at the heart of Navy life. The men were heroes and the families were broke.

Louise's religion had helped her survive Alan's days as a Navy test pilot. Her bible, Mary Baker Eddy's *Science and Health*, stressing the power of positive thinking, was always near and dear. Mrs. Eddy counseled not to dwell on dark thoughts, which was perfect for a test pilot's wife. Still, Louise insisted that if Alan was going to be even a little late coming home, he had to call her at exactly five o'clock to warn her. Otherwise she'd be squinting at the sky, looking for those awful black clouds that meant someone's husband had crashed to the ground in a burning hulk.

On the day that Alan was announced as one of the Mercury Seven astronauts, one of the newspaper photographers had snapped a photo of Louise posing rather awkwardly in front of her mailbox. When the papers came out the next day, the address on her mailbox, 580 Brandon Road, could clearly be read. Louise received a boatload of mail, letters written by housewives across the country with cheery messages like *Good Luck!* and *God Bless You, Dear*, some clipped to a check written out for a generous sum. It seemed most of the women in the country believed Louise would end up a widow now that Alan was officially an astronaut.

On January 20, 1961, while the wintry light shone on the crowd huddled before the Capitol steps for John F. Kennedy's inauguration, the handsome new president, beaming with hope, spoke of a "New Frontier" that, as it came to pass, would include going to the Moon by the end of the decade. "Ask not what your country can do for you," Kennedy said, "ask what you can do for your country."

The day before, the astronauts had been called into NASA head Bob Gilruth's office for a meeting. "I have something important to tell you," Gilruth said. NASA had made its decision. "This is the most difficult choice I've ever had to make. It is essential this decision be known to only a small group of people. We'll make it known to the public at the appropriate time. Alan Shepard will make the first suborbital Redstone flight."

They were all stunned, especially John Glenn, who had been sure he was going to be chosen to be the first man in space. Instead, he was slated to be the backup pilot not only to Alan, but also to Gus, who would make the second suborbital flight. John would have to go up third. It was a difficult pill for him to swallow. Where was the glory in that? The *third* man in space?

Perhaps it had something to do with the Kona Kai Séance, which had turned a few of the boys against John. Not long after that caper, the astronauts had to rate each other for their "peer vote." John called it "a popularity contest." In the weeks after the decision, he fought NASA until he was finally told to be a good sport.

Alan managed to control his jubilation by forcing his expression to stay neutral and staring at the floor. Freckle-faced John was steaming, but he reached out and gave Alan a congratulatory handshake; all the other guys followed suit. Then they left the room. Standing there alone, Alan realized there would be no celebratory drinks tonight; still, he was elated. So he raced down the highway to his home in Virginia Beach. Alan strode into the house, looking into the living room where Louise liked to sit on the carpet and play solitaire. "Louise! Louise, you home?"

She came into the room. "You got it! You got the first ride!" She could tell by his smile. He hugged her, squeezing her so hard she nearly squealed.

"Lady, you can't tell anyone, but you have your arms around the man who'll be the first in space!"

"Who let a Russian in here?" was Louise's naughty reply.

The only catch, Alan explained, was that though he was definitely going to be *first,* NASA wanted to withhold the news until the day of the launch. This would protect Louise and the girls. Otherwise, the press would be all over them like on that first day.

NASA told the press that the choice would be among the three men—Alan Shepard, John Glenn, and Gus Grissom. *Life* promptly nicknamed them the Gold Team. (The editors acted like it had always been clear that these three were the most impressive of the seven.)

Louise couldn't tell her two youngest girls, her daughter Julie and her niece, Alice, both of whom were chatty little girls and would surely tell their secret. Louise did tell her oldest daughter, Laura, who was thirteen and, like her mother before her, attending Principia boarding school. For Laura it was torture keeping the secret, as it must have been for Louise. "It's going to be John Glenn," Laura's friends at school taunted. Laura, who was blonde and as competitive as her dad, had to bite her tongue because she had been sworn to secrecy.

The launch was scheduled to take place in the spring. All of the wives were counting on "Miss Frosty" to show them how a proper wife acted when her husband was shot up into space. Louise knew the worst could happen on Alan's shot, but she didn't give in to her fears. She sat calmly and worked her needlepoint. In *Life*'s first feature on the wives, under the headline "Just Go Right Ahead, by Louise Shepard," Louise told readers, "I suppose I have the same faith in technology that most Americans have: this continuous steady feeling that the wheels of the car will turn and the brakes will work when I come to the next stop light. But I am a Christian Scientist and have a strong spiritual faith. If the brakes don't work, I know that something else will."

In the accompanying photo, she was wearing Bermuda shorts

and a sleeveless white oxford blouse. She was dealing out a game of four-way solitaire to her girls, who wore outfits identical to their mother's. Her serene smile hid a tremendous will to keep everything looking perfect at their home.

Louise's "Who let a Russian in here?" comment to Alan turned out to be not so witty as when she'd made it. In April 1961, when Alan's launch was originally scheduled, NASA delayed the flight, suddenly wanting to make two additional tests of the Redstone rocket, including one with Ham the chimp. In the meantime, Alan was beaten to the chase by Russian cosmonaut Yuri Gagarin, who made history by actually *orbiting* Earth.

A reporter woke up Shorty Powers early one morning at the Cape to get NASA's reaction. A groggy Shorty yelled into the phone, "We're all asleep down here!" The morning's headline followed: "Soviets Put Man in Space. Spokesman Says U.S. Asleep." Alan was disgusted. "We had 'em," he said. "We had 'em by the shorthairs and we gave it away."

Alan was already in his capsule on the day of his flight when the big announcement was made that he was the One. Then the weather fouled up and the launch had to be postponed. Now that the surprise was blown, Louise worried that on the day of his rescheduled launch, May 5, she would be completely overrun by the press. She called the local police, but the chief's only suggestion was "Why don't you book yourself into a motel under a new name, lady?"

Louise decided she simply couldn't run away. She would speak to the press, but not until Alan was safely back on Earth. Still, there was one reporter and one photographer in her home with her. The *Life* contract stipulated that they would have intimate access to the astronauts' wives during their husbands' flights. So Louise had to smile and remain calm as *Life* looked on.

The night before the launch, Louise tiptoed out on her front porch and taped a message to the door: THERE WILL BE NO REPORTERS IN THE HOUSE. I WILL HAVE A STATEMENT FOR THE PRESS AFTER THE FLIGHT. All night long she heard reporters creeping across her porch reading the note. In the special astronaut quarters in Hangar S at the Cape, Alan awoke at 1:10 in the morning and sat down for his special "low residue" launch breakfast, which had been specifically designed by the NASA doctors to ensure no bowel movements in space. Amazingly, it included bacon-wrapped filet mignon, scrambled eggs, OJ, and coffee, sans milk.

In the morning it was little Alice who woke up first. It happened to be her tenth birthday, but Louise had decided to postpone the party and dolls and tea sets until the following day. After all, Louise's two little girls still had no idea Alan was going into space. Alice crept downstairs and drew back a corner of the pink homemade curtains. Lo and behold, a carnival had landed in her front yard, only it was a frightening kind of carnival because there were policemen with shiny badges and guns and German shepherds sniffing in Mommy's pretty flowerbeds around the house. Alice worried the police had come to take Louise away, and she ran upstairs, where Julie was asleep in their shared bedroom. "Julie, Julie, wake up! Mommy must have done something really bad!"

Together they went into Louise's room to tell her the terrible news. Louise was getting dressed. She said very calmly, "Now, girls, your father is going up in a Redstone rocket into space today." Then she led Julie and Alice downstairs, where Louise's parents, who had come to keep her company for the launch, were already making breakfast. Grandparents, mother, and daughters sat at the dining room table and held hands in a group prayer. The *Life* photographer had his perfect family portrait.

After breakfast, they all got ready to watch Alan blast off on the black-and-white TV. In only fifteen minutes, he would fly in a parabola 116 miles above the Earth into "outer space" and back. Louise sat in a chair holding a little all-weather transistor radio. She was concentrating deeply, repeating over and over in her mind, "Alan will be in the right place at the right time. *Everything will be A-OK.*"

Her belief in the trinity of America, NASA, and the Shepards, all operating under a heavenly umbrella, was unshakable.

As planned, Alan fell safely back to Earth fifteen minutes after he'd blasted off, dropping in his capsule into the Atlantic. After NASA called Louise to tell her that Alan was safely aboard the USS *Champlain*, a Navy jet flew over her house making an *S* in its contrail. Louise stepped out of her house, pink sweater draped around her slight shoulders, and met the press, kicking off another new Astrowife ritual—the post-flight press conference on the lawn. Though still not thrilled that their own husbands hadn't been picked to go up first, the other wives did have to admit Louise made a wonderful First Lady of Space.

4

Jackie

Pinch me, please. Louise was on cloud nine during the ceremony in the Rose Garden of the White House. "Ladies and gentlemen," said President Kennedy, "I want to express on behalf of us all the great pleasure we have in welcoming Commander Shepard and Mrs. Shepard here today." Alan winked at Louise. While Kennedy continued talking, Louise watched Jackie standing by his side, like something conjured up in a dream. When the NASA Distinguished Service Medal slipped out of the president's hand and clattered onto the felt-covered stage, Jack picked it up and handed it to Alan, but Jackie had a better suggestion for her husband, telling him, "Jack, *pin* it on him."

Jacqueline, who pronounced her name *Jackleen*, in the French style, was a breath of fresh air after Mamie. What could be more perfect than the Kennedy White House with its resident queen? Jackie was not model thin, but her dress, one of many specially designed for her by the best designers in the world, made her look svelte and glamorous. She was dressed in an elegant midnight blue sheath, her only jewelry a thick gold chain around her neck and a small gold bracelet around her left wrist. She was perfectly regal. Louise thought she and Jackie had a lot in common; both having been raised in aristocratic surroundings on the East

Coast, Louise at Longwood Gardens and Jackie summering at Hammersmith Farm in Newport, Rhode Island. Even though Louise was only the groundskeeper's daughter, she always held herself as if she were a Du Pont.

After the ceremony, Jack led Alan and his fellow astronauts off to the Oval Office to talk about the program, specifically his grand plans for NASA to go to the Moon. Kennedy's recent failed Bay of Pigs invasion of Cuba had been an absolute disaster and international embarrassment for the president, and he was hoping to neutralize it with his ambitious space program.

"We're not about to put you guys on a rocket and send you to the Moon," said Kennedy from his rocking chair. "We're just thinking about it."

Meanwhile, Jackie held court with the women in the formal Green Room. Louise was wearing a beige suit and a white hat with a big starched bow. She was fixated on Jackie, memorizing her every move and mannerism. Jackie, who was *hatless*, apologized that all the White House kitchen had to offer were crackers because the Kennedys had just gotten back from Hyannis Port. After a bit of small talk, Jackie tucked her arm into Louise's and led her off for a private tour of the White House.

After Louise returned to Virginia and back into the fold at Langley, the wives were desperate to hear her report. "What's Jackie like? You two hit it off, didn't you? She's lovely, isn't she?" They were hoping for some good gossip; they wanted to know what Jackie was *really* like. Louise acted sisterly, but she was perfectly politic. "She has big feet, just like me," she said, hinting that Jackie was "bigger-boned" in person. Soon all the wives knew that the First Lady's dress size was the same as her shoe size, which was a ten.

What was nice about Louise was even though her every movement and observation was controlled, she really made an effort to be just one of the girls. Louise would come at the drop of a hat to Langley to visit with the girls or meet them at the yacht club at Fort Monroe. She understood her new role as the First Lady of Space, especially when, a calculated twenty days after Alan's flight, President Kennedy announced to a joint session of Congress his goal of putting a man on the Moon by the end of the decade. In this speech Kennedy appealed to Americans' dreams for the future: "I believe that this nation should commit itself to achieving the goal, before this decade is out, of landing a man on the Moon and returning him safely to the Earth... in a very real sense, it will not be one man going to the Moon; if we make this judgment affirmatively, it will be an entire nation. For all of us must work to put him there."

He also asked Congress for some Moon money, to the tune of an estimated $40 billion, but no matter: "A great nation was one that undertook great adventures."

Since becoming an astronaut wife, Betty had developed expensive tastes. It was impossible to find really nice outfits at the dinky department stores near Langley. Gus knew his wife put up with a lot from him, and she never asked questions if he wasn't around much on the weekends. As a trade-off, he didn't complain about what she spent. Betty appreciated that.

"You know," Gus had told her, "we really have never had any money, but you always know what our limit is. You know what we can do and what we cannot do. I expect you to have clothes when you need them. I do not want you to have to go out and buy something at the last minute."

Five-foot Betty had once wanted to take to the skies as a stewardess, but Pan-Am required its hostesses to be at least five-two. She was so short that everything she wore needed tailoring. Nothing off the rack ever fit; the sleeves and pant legs were always too long. Since Gus would be next to go up into space, he wanted his wife to look her best. So he gave Betty some mad money to go out and buy new outfits, something to make her look as good as Louise had when she stood next to the Queen of Camelot, Jackie.

The other wives still thought of Betty as an unsophisticated Hoosier and didn't know that Betty (whose full name was Betty Lavonne) saw herself quite differently. Betty cared a lot about fashion and thought she was the best dresser of the group. "The wildest, too," she bragged (in the near future she would be the first Astrowife to buy fur hot pants).

Not many in the group sought out her friendship, but Louise Shepard was always sweet to her. She always complimented her on her adorable new accessories, a watch or a pair of screw-back earrings, color-coordinated to one of her spiffy outfits: "If there is anything out new like that," Louise would say, gently touching a new wristwatch, "you've got it, Betz." Louise was the only person who ever called Betty Grissom *Betz*—like she was Bette Davis or *someone*.

"I need some clothes! I'm not doing too well down here," Betty complained at one of the wives' get-togethers. Hearing her cry for help, Annie Glenn invited her to come to Arlington for the weekend, and they would go shopping in Washington.

On the train, Betty wondered if she'd in fact invited herself up and Annie had just been too polite to turn her down. She'd never been to the Glenns' home, and she didn't know Annie as well as the other wives. Annie had been a little aloof since the beginning of the program, especially since John had chosen for her and their two kids, Lyn and Dave, to remain in their house in Arlington rather than move near Langley as the other families had. Annie didn't talk much at wives' gatherings either, just smiled, as if she were above it all. The other wives initially mistook Annie as standoffish until they finally realized the source of her extreme shyness.

The *Life* ghostwriter, Loudon Wainwright, in vigilant keeping with the magazine's no-flaws policy, had glossed over what was embarrassingly obvious in person. Annie had a terrible stutter. She'd had it since childhood, as had her father, Doc Castor. The only time Annie could get through an entire sentence unstuttering was when she sang hymns behind the organ. John boasted, "Annie could make an organ talk." In public, Annie usually just smiled and nodded.

When Annie met her at the station, Betty nervously prattled on about whatever was on her mind, while Annie silently listened. Annie was very sensitive to others speaking, for she knew that when she herself needed to speak, her interlocutor would have to wait out her stutter and be patient while she formed her words. She didn't want anyone finishing her sentences for her. Betty had to bite her tongue to hold herself back.

As the two women roamed the big Washington department stores like Garfinckel's and Woodward & Lothrop, running their fingers along fabrics and testing the resilience of stockings, Betty realized how difficult this simple activity was for Annie. Salesgirls would struggle to keep a straight face while she stuttered out her requests. Some even laughed. While it probably hurt her feelings more than she'd ever admit, Annie didn't seem too fazed by it. The Marine wife, the only one among the Astrowives' ranks, had developed an effective system; if she wanted anything, she'd write the salesgirl a note or bring something from home that she needed.

Betty had never been on such a shopping spree. She tried on all sorts of stylish ensembles, the whole works: heels, gloves, hats, skirts, and dresses with full "New Look" swing skirts worn with lots of fluffy, floaty petticoats—which were usually reserved for teenagers, but Betty wanted to let out her wild side. If it fit and she looked good in it, especially if it was in patriotic colors, she bought it, laying down the cash. Sunny yellow was her favorite, but the public seemed to prefer the astronaut wives in red, white, and blue.

After hugging Annie good-bye, Betty boarded the train with shopping bags full of pretty new clothes, including a light blue dress with a matching jacket-vest she had chosen to wear for the launch. As the train whipped along, she thought about her visit with Annie and concluded they'd really hit it off. Betty envied Annie's house in Arlington, far from the rest of the wives. Betty and Annie might have been an unlikely pair, but somehow they fit. They shared the same worries and concerns. Betty, who spoke in a Hoosier twang, often worried about whether she was saying the right thing. "Is that the right words?" she'd ask her ghostwriter.

Gus Grissom just wasn't the sort of man who could play Perfect Mr. Family for *Life*. That was all too apparent when Gus told the magazine in their feature about the Gold Team, "Betty and I run our lives as we please. We don't care anything about fads or frills or the P.T.A. We don't give a damn about the Joneses."

It was enough to make NASA cringe, especially from one of their elite Gold Team. They expected each astronaut not only to keep up with the Joneses, but to *surpass* the Joneses, with at least two and a half perfect strapping milk-fed children with plenty of badges from the Boy and Girl Scouts. Gus took a lot of flak for that quote, but Betty knew what he meant. She had tried going to a few P.T.A. meetings at the various bases where they had lived, but whenever she went, all the parents ever seemed to be voting on was whether or not to allow chocolate milk in the school cafeteria. Betty finally gave up. She sometimes wondered if her lack of social skills would affect Gus's astronaut career, but he reassured her, "You didn't sign up for this. I did."

She worried his personality never really came across in interviews, but Gus had a few tricks up his sleeve. "I can't act like they do," he'd complain, knowing he'd never be as polished as John Glenn, or as calculating as Alan Shepard. "I just have to do my work and mind my own business and that's it." Though he wasn't good at kissing up to NASA, or playing the perfect family man, he kept his mind on his own business and excelled at his work.

After several delays because of rain and threatening weather, Gus's shot finally took place on July 21, 1961. The wives gathered at Betty's home in Stoneybrook. Louise had ridden her mission out solo, and after the onslaught of reporters she suffered, the wives realized it was too great a burden to endure alone. Hungry for some insight into the astronaut wife, her children, anything, the press had even surrounded a hapless diaper salesman. Did Louise feed her astronaut Wheaties every morning? After the press asked the man all sorts of trivial questions, they realized he was not even going to the Shepards'! Louise didn't have a baby, and certainly no need for diapers. He was going to the neighbors'.

Betty was not intending to let the press run all over her. Gus had convinced the Newport News police to patrol his patch of green and protect it from being ruined as the Shepards' yard had been. Everything was very tense that morning, beginning when CBS's famous newscaster—Nancy Dickerson—accosted Betty when she was putting the Buick in the garage. Betty told the news lady not very politely to scram, and then shut the rolling door in her face. The other wives gave each other significant looks.

Betty and her two boys talked to Gus on the phone as he lay flat on his back in the capsule before he blasted off. Betty hadn't seen him for two weeks, but they'd talked almost daily. After receiving their many wishes for a good flight, Gus finally jokingly told his family that if they stopped yakking, he might catch a couple of winks before his flight.

There were several holds on the countdown to liftoff, and at T minus fifteen minutes, Betty went into the kitchen to soft-boil some eggs, dropping them carefully into the water. But then Marge called her back out because the countdown had resumed. At T minus five minutes, Betty suddenly remembered her eggs and dashed into the kitchen, only to realize that they were not soft-boiled, but hard. She felt like one of those hard-boiled eggs, encased in a fragile shell. Perched on the sofa in her sparsely furnished home, she watched the countdown. The last two seconds before liftoff were almost unbearable for her.

After she watched the rocket blast off Gus's *Liberty Bell 7* capsule, she stayed glued to the TV for the fifteen minutes until the news reported his successful splashdown into the Atlantic. While all of the other girls, chatting away, went into the kitchen to get something to eat, Betty alone watched the coverage of Gus's rescue. She was the only one who heard that something had gone wrong. Gus was okay, but his hatch door had blown prematurely and his capsule had flooded and sunk.

Betty was sick to her stomach with worry that Gus had done something wrong. She didn't understand a lot of the technical details of his mission, but she knew enough to know that the capsule was definitely not supposed to sink. Was it Gus's fault?

The question plagued her as she emerged to face the dozen or so reporters on her lawn. Wearing her new blue dress and white Minnie Mouse heels, flanked by a son on each side, Betty said she was happy that Gus's flight was a success, but she said with genuine regret, "But I am *so* sorry the capsule was lost."

A reporter told her NASA had reported that her husband had been tidying up his spacecraft when the hatch blew. "Is he tidy at home?"

"He does not pick up things around the house very well," Betty replied. She was smiling and animated with the reporters, though she felt on pins and needles. This interview was even more stressful than watching the flight on television, and she told the reporters as much.

Asked if she had prayed during her husband's flight, she replied, "Certainly."

Asked if she would like Gus to be the astronaut to make the big leap in Project Mercury, the first orbital flight, she replied, "I think I would because he would. I hope he calls when he reaches Grand Bahama Island. Now I can rest for a few days and get back to normal."

Betty spent the rest of the day watching television and answering the phone. Finally Gus called. Betty wanted to sound casual, so she said, "I heard you got a little wet?" "Yeah," said Gus, who was not much of a talker, especially today. The line crackled with static, but they chatted for another tense minute. Finally Betty couldn't help it any longer and blurted out a stabbing little question: "You didn't do anything wrong, did you?" "No," said Gus. "That hatch just blew." She could hear in his voice that he was wounded, but she knew he would admit it if he had done something wrong. He did not lie. He told her the Holiday Inn had lost a stack of his shirts and slacks, so when she came down to meet him in Florida, could she bring along some clean clothes?

The next day, some of the wives flew down with Betty for the post-flight press conference at Patrick Air Force Base, located just south of Cape Canaveral. Someone snapped Betty's picture standing next to Gus's other true love, his Corvette, which was waiting for him on the runway. With her skinny little legs crossed at the ankle, she clutched her new raffia purse and held her boys' hands. She was wearing a carnation corsage with a red, white, and blue patriotic ribbon pinned to her lapel and a gold pin designed especially for the Mercury wives in the shape of a seven inside the circle of ☿, the astronomical symbol for Mercury. She felt good, dolled up in one of her snazzy new outfits. She waved excitedly when she saw Gus emerge from the NASA Gulfstream. Taken to a little waiting area, where Gus was being fussed over, she stole one peck on the cheek before Gus was ushered back to a receiving line to greet the brass.

During the ceremony, under a tent set up on the steaming tarmac at Patrick, Betty felt her anger rising. She didn't know whether it was because the reporters wanted to blame Gus for his hatch blowing, or because NASA seemed to be only halfheartedly defending her husband, their least media-savvy astronaut, but she could see through their pomp.

Afterward, NASA honored the Grissoms by giving them a VIP beach house at Patrick for the weekend. There, Betty opened the refrigerator to find it stocked with bacon, eggs, and milk. Did she have to play perfect housewife today of all days? "What do these people think I am going to do?" she asked Gus. "I am not going to cook!"

"Well, you won't have to cook much," said Gus with a sheepish half grimace. "I'll be going back to work at eight tomorrow. It's a regular workday."

The worst was yet to come when Gus broke it to her that there would be no White House visit. He tried to shrug it off, saying that the president was probably busy. He had a lot on his plate. He was still dealing with the fallout from the Bay of Pigs fiasco. Betty was not buying it. She knew it was because of that lost, very expensive space capsule. Not getting a ceremony in the Rose Garden was terrible for Gus's reputation. All it would have taken was a smile from the president, a flash of that Kennedy wit with a line about getting wet, and all would've been forgiven in the eyes of America. But silence was damning. Betty had wanted so much to have her own moment alone with Jackie, and she felt humiliated having to tell the other wives that she and Gus were not to be given the special honors Louise and Alan had. She was heartbroken.

Soon she was fuming. That stocked fridge really pushed her over the edge. She looked around this rat-shack that was supposedly for Very Important Persons and pointed out to Gus that there wasn't even a TV for the kids, and the beach was across the highway. "I'd have been ready to commit suicide if I'd have stayed in that place all day waiting for him to come back home," Betty later reflected. She could call one of the girls from over at the Holiday Inn, where the rest of the astronauts and their wives were staying and probably having a ball, and say, "Somebody come get me!" But how would that look? She was supposed to be Mrs. Queen Astronaut for the weekend.

"I'm not staying here," she told Gus. "You call the Holiday and see if we can get a room." Gus got right on the phone and got Betty and the boys a room.

A couple of hours later, Betty was sitting by the side of the pool, still seething. "Hey," Gus called to Betty. He had just finished revolving-door interviews with the press. "Get dressed. You're coming with me." Betty didn't smile, but she got dressed. Someone volunteered to watch the kids at the pool, and Gus ushered her into his Corvette.

He drove her out toward the Cape. They got to the checkpoint, and Gus didn't even crack a smile at the guard. He said, "You know who I am and we're going through." The guard didn't argue. Gus took Betty up to see the giant Titan rocket, which was being prepared for the two-man Gemini flights that would follow Project Mercury. Betty got to go up the gantry elevator and touch the Titan's smooth metallic body.

Gus also screened for her the raw footage of his rescue mission, and it was terrible. Betty felt worse than ever, hearing Gus narrate the drama of flailing around in the choppy water in his silver space suit, about to drown. "Hell, I'm waving and they're waving back, and I'm saying, 'I want you to pick me up!'" he narrated for Betty. The helicopter over him had been blowing the water hard, and his head went under the waves a few times. He worried that the sharks would get him.

Betty knew Gus had carried a couple of dime rolls in the leg pocket of his space suit, which he and Betty had planned for him to hand out as souvenirs to their family and friends back in Mitchell, Indiana, and the boys' classmates. Gus had regretted the added weight with each swell from the helicopter. Betty knew he was a swimmer, but not a very strong one.

Finally a second helicopter had come to Gus's rescue and let down a harness. Gus hadn't even managed to get in it frontward, just let himself be lifted up and away. In the helicopter he had enough strength left to grab a Mae West life vest, so called because it made the wearer look big-chested.

Back at the Holiday Inn, the nightmare replayed through Betty's mind at the pool as she stared into the water. Betty realized her husband had actually thought he was going to die out there. She herself had never learned to swim.

5

Primly Stable

The United States was still behind Russia in the space race. It had been a year now since cosmonaut Yuri Gagarin had orbited the Earth. "I didn't see God," the Russian told the world upon his landing. When he posed for pictures in a veritable love embrace with the bearded revolutionary Fidel Castro in his army fatigues, Gagarin's bright smile was said to have accelerated the Cold War.

After two manned suborbital flights, both deemed a success despite Gus's blown hatch, NASA was confident that it was time to send a man to orbit the Earth. It would take more thrusting power than the Redstone rockets that had sent up Alan and Gus. They would have to use the dreaded Atlas rocket, the one that had blown up before the wives' eyes as they watched the test firing at Cocoa Beach. John Glenn was ready to saddle the beast and ride it to the stars.

America couldn't have hoped for a better choice. His sunny, freckled face was sure to eclipse the smiles of those communists. As for seeing God in space? NASA was confident that with John Glenn that would not be a problem. The man taught Sunday school in his spare time, a rare counterpoint to the hard-living, hard-playing astronaut life. He saw the grace of God in everything, especially in Annie. Annie was simply lovely—dark-haired with her wide, toothy Girl Scout grin. (One couldn't help but picture her in the sage green uniform, badge sash, and matching socks.)

Scott Carpenter, John's backup for his upcoming *Friendship 7* mission, was less tightly wound than John, and took it upon himself to help his friend let loose a little. They enjoyed eating out at a Polynesian-themed restaurant in Cocoa Beach. They cruised the Strip in Scott's Shelby Cobra with its sexy metalflake blue paint job. John was also putting his church choir tenor to good use, sweetly singing while Scott strummed his guitar.

Meanwhile, the wives got busy on Annie, offering to help in whatever way they could. The post-flight press conference on the lawn, by now a necessary ritual, was something all of the wives dreaded. None more than Annie. She could get through short, practiced phrases such as "Fine," "Thank you," "Please do," but she couldn't improvise without stumbling over her words. Annie really couldn't even get through a complete sentence except when she was singing, and she could hardly sing to the press. She was incredibly independent and self-sufficient in most aspects of her life, but she often had to rely on others when called upon to speak. She dubbed her daughter Lyn her "telephone surrogate." Lyn had been making her mother's doctor and beauty parlor appointments since she was a little girl.

To keep spirits high and light, all the wives had their ways of dealing with the press. A favorite was the comic skit Rene came up with: a one-woman show that she called "Primly Stable," starring the perfect astronaut wife Primly Stable, married to her astronaut, Squarely, with their little Dickie and Mary and dog Smiley. The Stables were suspiciously like the Glenns—

who had two perfect children, Dave and Lyn, and a dog named Chipper.

Rene usually played all the parts, changing her voice accordingly. Holding her fist up to her lips as a microphone, she launched into her routine playing reporter Nancy the Newscaster, who bore a wicked resemblance to Nancy Dickerson (the one who had accosted Betty).

"We're here outside the trim, modest suburban home of Squarely Stable, the famous astronaut who has just completed his historic mission, and we have with us his attractive wife, Primly Stable," began Rene, playing Nancy to the hilt. "Primly Stable, you must be happy, proud, and thankful at this moment."

"Yes, Nancy, that's true," Rene's ever-so-proper Primly said tentatively (or sometimes another wife would play this role). "I'm happy and proud and thankful at this moment."

"Tell us, Primly Stable—may I call you Primly?"

"Certainly, Nancy."

"Tell us, Primly, tell us what you felt during the blastoff, at the very moment when your husband's rocket began to rise from the Earth and take him on his historic journey."

"To tell you the truth, Nancy, I missed that part of it. I'd sort of dozed off, because I got up so early this morning and I'd been rushing around a lot taping the shades shut, so the TV people wouldn't come in the windows."

"Well, would you say you had a lump in your throat as big as a tennis ball?"

"That's about the size of it, Nancy; I had a lump in my throat as big as a tennis ball."

Nancy was about out of time, but she suddenly lit up with

an idea. "And finally, Primly, I know that the most important prayer of your life has already been answered: Squarely has returned safely from outer space. But if you could have one other wish at this moment and have it come true, what would that one wish be?"

"Well, Nancy, I'd wish for an Electrolux vacuum cleaner with all of the attachments."

Annie liked a good laugh as well as the others, but nothing could calm her anxiety about her husband being the first American to orbit Earth, not to mention having to face the press. Annie had become so worried during the month leading up to *Friendship 7*'s blastoff that she lost twelve pounds. The wives urged her to eat, but Annie just looked at them. "Just you wait until *your* launch."

On January 27, 1962, live on the Glenns' lawn, news reporters narrated the scene into network television cameras, affecting great concern for the poor wife while regretting that they were barred from entering the Glenns' redbrick home. And, as Annie had learned from Louise Shepard, her curtains were drawn so no reporter could get a sneak peek through the windows.

Along with her kids and some close family friends, Loudon Wainwright from *Life* magazine was with her to watch the launch. Annie's brown eyes remained glued to the unfolding drama playing on her three television sets. One was tuned to ABC, another to NBC, the third to CBS. As newscasters outside speculated about what the courageous wife could possibly be going through, Annie sat nervously in her living room. Save for a tension headache that had kept her up for several nights, she seemed perfectly composed.

All of a sudden, it was announced on the TV that John's launch had been scrubbed due to bad weather and would be rescheduled for a later date. The phone rang. Vice President Lyndon B. Johnson was blocks away in a limousine and wanted to come and comfort poor Annie in her disappointment. Oh, and he would be bringing with him the three major network news crews.

Annie wasn't feeling too well, but she didn't need to be comforted. Delays were the norm rather than the exception for launches. She needed only for the press to clear off her lawn that John always took such pains to tend. Right now, she didn't want anything to do with the swaggering Texan who would fawn over her for his own political gain. Besides, the *Life* contract forbade the wives from giving anything to the general press except for a news conference and a few measly photos. The deal was that Annie only had to come out for the post-flight press conference, and that was once John had landed!

The thought of suddenly having her home and life opened up to the general press—and her stutter revealed on *national television*? Well, it was enough to send any wife into a dither and give her a migraine. On top of that, Johnson wanted Loudon Wainwright to leave so that the networks would have a free hand. This didn't sit well with Annie. She trusted Loudon and felt as comfortable with him as she'd ever feel with any reporter. He protected her. "You sit right there," she told him. "You're not leaving this house!"

Annie and John truly understood the power of the press and the importance of good relations with the politicians. Being the good Boy Scout and Girl Scout came naturally to the Glenns; it was who they were. But this was too much for Annie. She simply would not admit Johnson and his crews into her home.

NASA couldn't believe it. As the head of the new Space Council, LBJ was spearheading Kennedy's Moon effort. He was also the prime mover behind NASA's big plans to relocate from Langley Air Force Base to Houston, Texas, his home state. It was important that NASA keep him happy. Why wasn't Annie playing ball? This was their perfect Astrowife, their patron saint? Couldn't she just let the man come in and say hello? Didn't she want to win the goddamn space race?

NASA pressed Annie. *Just let him come sit with you.* Come on, Annie, do it for America! Do it for Johnny!

Within a few minutes NASA was buzzing in John's ear about how they needed the support of Washington if they wanted to get to the Moon. James Webb, NASA's administrator, threatened to switch the flight order. If John couldn't get his little lady to play ball and let the vice president come in and sit with her, maybe he wouldn't get to be the first American to orbit the Earth.

From a phone near the launch pad, John, biosensor wires still dangling from his chest to monitor his heart in orbit, called Annie and said, "Look, if you don't want the vice president or the TV networks or anybody else to come into the house, then that's it as far as I'm concerned, they are not coming in—and I will back you up all the way, one hundred percent."

The six other astronauts backed up John, and John Glenn was still going to be the first American to orbit the Earth. When Johnson was told no, he hit the roof, but there was absolutely nothing he could do about it.

* * *

There were delays and delays on the road to John's flight, which was finally rescheduled for the following month. Just before his launch on February 20, 1962, he called Annie. Suited up in his silver space suit, lying in the tiny cockpit of his *Friendship 7* capsule, perilously perched atop a steam-hissing ninety-four-foot Atlas rocket packed with 367,000 pounds of explosive liquid oxygen, he told her, "I'm going down to the corner store to buy some chewing gum."

"Don't take too long," replied Annie, as she always did. They'd been having this same exchange ever since John was a fighter pilot, and after all the missions they'd lived through together, it had become a comforting ritual for them.

Living with danger had never been easy for Annie, but it was nothing new. That's why John called her "the Rock." She had endured John's years as a fighter pilot during World War II, left to simmer on the back burner while her husband flew fifty-nine death-defying missions in the South Pacific against the Japanese. And then there was John's service in Korea, where he attracted so many enemy MiG-15s that his squadron called him "Magnet Ass." The nickname made Annie cringe; nevertheless, John looked handsome in the photo of him in his brown leather bomber jacket and white silk pilot's scarf patterned with red hearts. And he did manage to shoot down three of the buggers from his plane with LYN ANNIE DAVE painted on the fuselage. In Korea, Johnny and his plane had survived over 250 enemy "flak holes." His F9F Panther jet interceptor looked like it was made of Swiss cheese. The Glenns' wood-paneled walls were so cluttered with pictures and certificates celebrating John's fighter pilot career, he called it a *danged* museum.

Squeezed into a flying tin can the size of a bathtub, John was to spin around the globe three times at 17,544 mph and return home in a brilliant ball of fire screaming through the atmosphere. The slightest wrong tilt of his spacecraft would fry him in an instant.

Annie waited the excruciating five hours while John orbited the Earth three times and saw four beautiful sunsets and sunrises. And he did indeed see in them the handiwork of God. Space sunsets came and went in a flash. He radioed excitedly, "The sunset was beautiful. I still have a brilliant blue band clear across the horizon. The sky is absolutely black, completely black. I can see the stars up above." He tried to pick out familiar constellations he'd known since he was a boy.

He experienced weightlessness, which Alan and Gus had only tasted a few moments of, and it felt like the most natural thing in the world to him: "I think I have finally found the element in which I belong." He radioed to the ground when he spotted some fascinating glowing "fireflies," which conjured up theories of minuscule extraterrestrial life at Mission Control.

But there was a problem, one so threatening that ground control kept the full extent of it from the astronaut. The metal shield protecting his capsule from burning up in the atmosphere upon reentry was registering a warning signal. If the heat shield came loose, John would be incinerated.

At one point during his reentry before landing, there was nothing but silence from his capsule; all signals to the Earth were lost.

Finally, a giant fireball dropped through the sky, rainbow

contrails streaming behind it. John's peppermint-striped parachute was the most wonderful sight he, and Annie, had ever seen. His capsule was hoisted safely aboard the aircraft carrier *Randolph* before he got out, to make dang sure it didn't sink like Gus's. As soon as he had the opportunity, he switched his handheld air-conditioning device from his left hand to his right. He'd worked out this signal with Annie, in the expectation that the television cameras would record it. The space-age briefcase changing hands was his way to tell her, "I love you."

A few days later in New York City, Annie sat high on the back of a convertible riding along downtown Manhattan's Canyon of Heroes next to her husband, America's new hero. It was the biggest ticker-tape parade since Charles Lindbergh's. This was Annie's sort of publicity. She didn't have to say a word. In a Jackie-inspired crimson suit and matching pillbox hat, she waved to the crowds and smiled away. In all the cities they traveled to—New York, Chicago, and Washington—they were welcomed with a blizzard of ticker tape and confetti. The other astronauts and their wives were waving from their own cars, all part of the parades because John had insisted, "They don't go, I don't go."

6

Squaresville

Like Betty Crocker and Mickey Mouse, John Glenn was now a household name. NASA was astounded at how great a hero he had become. His *Friendship 7* mission was America's greatest victory in the space race so far, packing more of a punch than Alan Shepard's first spaceflight. Deke Slayton was scheduled to orbit the Earth next, but suddenly, perhaps realizing just how valuable their astronauts were, NASA decided it couldn't take the chance. The space agency had chosen Deke to be an astronaut despite his heart murmur, but the possibility of it acting up, no matter how small, was a risk that NASA no longer wanted to take.

Deke was outraged. Dr. Bill Douglas, the NASA flight surgeon, had said he was A-OK to go up, and Deke was more than ready to go. But it just wasn't going to happen. To make matters worse, the Air Force followed NASA's lead and grounded him from flying planes. Marge was heartbroken that her Deke, all muscle and maleness, who drove his Corvette flat out at 120 mph, had been grounded.

One morning, sitting alone at home with the news, she just had to do something. The rotary phone on the kitchen wall beckoned. *Oh, what the hell.*

She picked it up and asked the operator to place a call to Pres-

The Mercury wives entertaining, Virginia, 1959. From lower left: Rene Carpenter, Annie Glenn, Jo Schirra, Betty Grissom, Marge Slayton, and Trudy Cooper with tray.

Rene and kids on the day the Mercury astronauts were announced, Garden Grove, California, 1959.

Clockwise from top left: Jo Schirra, Louise Shepard, Marge Slayton, Betty Grissom, Trudy Cooper, Annie Glenn; middle, Rene Carpenter.

Annie Glenn towing John across the Chesapeake Bay inlet near Langley, Virginia, September 1959.

Jo Schirra and Marge Slayton with kids at Stoneybrook pool, September 1959.

Marge, Rene, Jo, and Betty watch Alan Shepard's Redstone rocket blast off, Cocoa Beach, May 1961.

Betty Grissom at her Virginia home after Gus's hatch blew, July 1961.

Rene and Scott Carpenter do the Twist at the Armory dance for the astronauts, 1962.

Rene betrays the nail-biting strain during Scott's *Aurora 7* flight, May 1962.

Barbara Young chain-smokes and watches her husband's Gemini 3 mission, March 1965.

Jim Lovell kisses his wife, Marilyn, at Cocoa Beach, December 1968.

ident Kennedy. *Yeah right, lady.* The girl balked until Marge informed her she was an astronaut wife and it was a matter of national security. Finally connected to the White House, Marge was put on the line with a presidential aide.

"I'm sorry, but I would like to talk to the president."

The aide was very understanding. He said he knew the president would very much like to speak to Marge, too, but unfortunately he was in a meeting.

Marge had to tell her story to someone, so she explained to the aide how NASA had selected "these extra special men who were specimens of health and strength and all good things," and now they were breaking their promise, saying, "Oooops! We made a mistake!" As far as Marge was concerned, she was ready to shoot Deke up into orbit herself. She told the aide as much, and also that she didn't think President Kennedy could possibly be aware of this injustice.

That night the other astronaut wives gathered at Marge's house to comfort her. "I guess he was glad," said Marge about Deke's reaction to the phone call. "In fact, I wish I could have called God." Marge and her sob sisters cleaned out the liquor supply and Marge composed a press comment for the next morning. But no one ever called for a statement. Well, at least no one called Marge.

She and Jo Schirra sat at Marge's kitchen counter the next morning, smoking and crying. The two women had become extremely close over the past three years, and considered each other best friends. Although Jo's Wally had been Deke's backup and the natural replacement, Wally hadn't been given the flight. Scott Carpenter had. It was just so unfair. Marge and Jo had no idea why such decisions were made, handed down from on high by NASA. Why wasn't Wally kept on as next in line? Marge and Jo smoked more cigarettes and held ice cubes in dishrags to their puffy eyes. Seeing each other in such a sad state made the eye faucets turn on again. They were in the mood to cry for just as long as they wanted. This upset was rough on all of them, but they tried not to let feelings of unfairness and jealousy come between them. "Tough days for us gals, but we didn't let it louse up our relationship," said Marge. "The men had their job to do and we had our friendship to protect."

On *Aurora 7*, set to take off on May 24, 1962, Scott would be repeating John's flight, orbiting Earth three times, in addition to carrying out some new experiments. The Carpenters had decided that their kids should go to Cocoa Beach to see Scott's launch, so Rene called Shorty Powers and informed him of her plan ("the rebel," joked one of the wives). Rene would be the first wife to view her husband's launch.

Shorty didn't like a wife dictating her own plan for the mission, especially after Annie went rogue with the LBJ press opportunity. NASA expected the wives to do as they were told.

Rene asked Shorty to keep her plans under wraps; she didn't want a circus, the press hounding her.

"Oh, yeah, Rene. We'll take care of you," said Shorty. Then he proceeded to inform all the networks. Rene didn't let Shorty in on any more secrets.

When she got down to Cocoa Beach, she wore big sunglasses and tied a scarf around her head because she'd been warned that the news had stakeout cars along the Strip.

It seemed excessive, but coverage of an Astrowife was hot property and could be sold around the world.

Rene was determined to write her own *Life* cover profile about the tense hours she spent during Scott's launch and flight. It had become the tradition that each wife got a cover profile to coincide with her man going into space, and Rene could better describe what was going through her mind during Scott's flight than any ghostwriter.

She had been displeased with the prelaunch cover profile on Scott. Loudon Wainwright had written a more "authentic" take on an astronaut than he ever had previously.

Painting a portrait of Scott's young years in Colorado, Loudon had written how Scott had "filched a pair of tiger-eye taillights" as a kid when growing up in Boulder. Scott was known among the astronauts to go out on the beach alone and strum his guitar under the Moon, and it was this sensitive nature that Loudon touched upon in his article. Loudon wrote, "He is also concerned, in the words of Robert Frost, with his own 'inner weather.'" Inner weather? "I think I'd like to go to a beautiful unspoiled island and get back to basics," Scott said in *Life*. "There I'd just take root and grow like another tree." A *tree*? To readers of the time, this sort of earthy navel-gazing was dangerously close to the terrain of the dreaded beatnik, the current scourge of upstanding America. *Life* had recently done a glossy portrait of what they deemed the classic beatnik lifestyle, the stereotypical cool cat and his chick decked out in black turtlenecks, lounging around in *Life*'s mock-up set of "The Well-Equipped Pad," a cold-water flat complete with a single bare bulb and a set of bongo drums. In the pages of the wives' first *Life* cover three years earlier, the magazine had pitted Squaresville against Beatsville, and there was no question which side NASA wanted their astronauts on.

* * *

Rene had her own flight plan for the day. Up early, she and the kids all talked to Scott one last time on the phone as Ralph Morse from *Life* snapped away. Then they got dressed and went out to the beach to watch the launch.

Scott's *Aurora 7* capsule careened into the sky. Scott had named the capsule himself. *Aurora* happened to be the goddess of the dawn, but the real reason he picked the name was because he'd grown up on Aurora Street in Boulder.

Ralph shot Rene on the beach, against the morning sun. Was that sunburst he captured in the twin mirrors of Rene's wraparound aviator sunglasses the reflection of Scott's rocket riding a tail of fire? What a shot!

Inside, the live television updates used a cartoon drawing of a man in a space helmet to represent Scott as if he were a comic book hero. As ground control saw it, Scott seemed to be having the time of his life up there, snapping photos with his Hasselblad camera and performing the experiments the scientists had set up for him. He was the first astronaut after John to sample space food. He squeezed some radioactive food into his mouth from a toothpaste-like tube. The NASA doctors would later track this Spam glowworm as it snaked its way through his system. Scott made the fascinating discovery that his friend John's glimmering "fireflies" weren't forms of extraterrestrial life at all, but in fact were urine particles, frozen after being ejected from the spacecraft via a condom-like device attached to a tube. Fascinating!

While Scott appeared to be playing tourist up there with his Hasselblad, using his rocket boosters to position his spacecraft just so, he didn't seem overly concerned with the repeated warnings from the ground that he was using up a dangerous amount of fuel. When it was time for him to realign and burn back into Earth's atmosphere, he barely had enough fuel left to hit the proper trajectory to come home. There was silence for what seemed an eternity. "I'm afraid...we may have...lost an astronaut," reported CBS's Walter Cronkite. After a nail-biting hour, Cronkite, a.k.a. the Voice of Doom, updated his report. A member of the Puerto Rican Air National Guard had spotted Scott in his life raft, hands behind his head, snacking on leftover space food.

"Well, it started out like Buck Rogers and wound up like Robinson Crusoe," said Uncle Walter.

Wearing a navy blue skirt and white middy blouse, and holding a red scarf, Rene stood before the newsmen on a stage set up for her post-flight press conference at Patrick Air Force Base. "I was dry-eyed the whole day," she said. "I'm not a brooding person."

The newsmen wanted to know if she had said any prayers, referring to a statement Scott had already made that he wasn't going to pray before his flight because it was presumptuous to pray for oneself. "I feel the same way as Scott," said Rene, and offered the reporters something more substantial than the wives' usual Primly Stable routine.

"I have to say, that clip you get of the woman in front of the house is such an innocuous, brief thing. Every woman has her own identity. She's not just the apple-pie thing waiting back home and she's probably had to take a tranquilizer pill to step out in front. I want to say that the effort involved in one of these missions is that, at the end, we often feel emotionally drained.

We tend to fall back on the comfortable phrases and words, like 'happy, proud, and thrilled,' and we feel so much more."

Though Scott hadn't lost his capsule, he had wasted so much fuel that he overshot his landing by 250 miles. Flight director Chris Kraft vowed Scott would never fly again. When Kraft saw a photo of Scott in the morning paper floating casually in his raft, it made him furious all over again.

As for the president, Kennedy had Air Force One fly the Carpenters out to Colorado, where there were various celebrations including a parade in Denver and a hometown one in Boulder. Then there was the White House visit, and afterward, since she had not been there, Jackie personally invited Rene and her daughters back to join her for afternoon tea.

Oh, Jackie. Her hair was perfect, her skin powdered, her eyes feline. So statuesque in her lavender silk dress. Her amethyst brooch glittered.

Jackie's private sitting room was furnished with French antiques, and the walls displayed eighteenth-century French drawings, and seascapes by the nineteenth-century French artist Eugène Boudin. The White House had recently been given some paintings by the French post-Impressionist Odilon Redon. *Mon dieu!* Everything here was so *French.* Jackie had a cabal of designers at her beck and call, most prominently Oleg Cassini. For political reasons, Jackie had chosen the French-born American fashion designer to design her state wardrobe.

Before her tea with Rene, Jackie changed into a different dress, one almost identical to the one Rene wore, which Rene's seamstress had made, inspired by a magazine photo of Jackie.

Everything was perfectly choreographed by Jackie, as if it were effortless, down to the simple tray of iced tea that the waiter brought out for their tête-à-tête in the garden. The tourists pressed their faces against the gates, hoping for a glimpse of Camelot. Although the First Lady couldn't *see* all of those tourists clamoring for a peek into her world—they were blocked by the hedges and expanse of lawn—she was certainly aware of them. Jackie probably felt a little trapped. Perhaps she was lonely for female companionship.

After being an astronaut wife for three years, and being covered by *Life*, Rene, like Jackie, knew just what it was like to have reporters and photographers wanting to capture almost every moment of her life. Jackie reminded Rene about *Life*'s coverage of the astronauts' first White House visit after Alan Shepard's flight.

"You couldn't have missed that rear-end shot of me and my bow legs, walking with Mrs. Shepard," remarked Jackie.

The revelation that even the First Lady was insecure about her looks made one like her even more.

Jackie asked Rene to stay for dinner, and the two mothers and their children ate a perfect candlelit meal. To cap off the evening, they went downstairs to pay a surprise visit to the Oval Office. President Kennedy was working late. Jackie fixed his tie, and soon the First Couple escorted their guests to a waiting limousine, and hugged Rene and her daughters good night.

7

Space City, U.S.A.

The seven space families arrived to the newly named Space City, U.S.A. on the Fourth of July weekend, 1962. Houston was throwing them a big welcoming parade, to be followed by a Texas barbecue extravaganza. NASA was moving to Texas, with its huge Manned Spacecraft Center being built twenty-five miles south of Houston on one thousand acres of land (a former Girl Scout camp) donated by Rice University, thanks to Lyndon Johnson's cronies at Humble Oil.

The Astro-families strode out of the Houston airport while paparazzi eagerly snapped away. Each of the wives slid into the backseat of a personalized convertible, the name of her astronaut on a red, white, and blue banner on the side. The ladies had to protect their hair from the breeze as the motorcade cruised toward downtown Houston.

All seven wives had by this time become expert at riding in convertible motorcades. The only decision to be made on the round-robin phone calls before the parade was "to hat or not to hat." Jackie had begun being seen formally without a hat, so the wives felt they were no longer obliged to wear them either. Trudy still wanted to wear one, but her friends tried to convince her otherwise. The bold move was sure to make an impression on their latest admirers, the jewel-laden hostesses of Houston high society.

As the motorcade cruised through downtown, thousands of onlookers sweated it out on the sidewalks. The families were waving and smiling like mad, as they did at every other parade they had been in. But this one was different. The crowd just stared. Where was the clapping, the cheering, the shouts of welcome they were expecting? It was unnerving. The wives began to wonder if they had made a big mistake in coming to the Lone Star State.

The convertibles soon headed to the Houston Coliseum. The astronauts, wives, and children were led up onto a stage at one end of the enormous arena, which had become a giant Texas barbecue. Rodeo-style whoops and yahoos greeted the wives and their spacemen, all of whom were wearing white Stetsons to signal that they now considered themselves Texans. The sheriff was so excited, he wanted to make them all deputies. The astronaut families were introduced one by one and then the politicians and businessmen made speeches. The crowd was finally coming to life! Perhaps it had been just too hot outside for people to get excited and cheer.

Someone on the Welcome Wagon wrangled a little private dining space for Houston's new prize cattle and folding chairs for the astronaut families to sit on. As the wives stared curiously at their hunks of brisket, a string of VIPs were ushered into the corral to say howdy.

"Hi, there, little lady! Just damned glad to see you!" said one man. "We've heard a lot of good things about you gals, a lot of good things."

The cowboy tycoons with Texas-sized bellies rolling over

their Lone Star–buckled belts were eager to share what they had to offer: everything from the newest appliances to the latest furnishings. Lawrence Marcus, scion of the Dallas-based department store Neiman-Marcus, would later offer to outfit the wives—and hoped they'd be able to squeeze in the time to model for one of the upcoming charitable ladies' teas.

The families were offered free box seats to baseball games of the Colt .45s (soon to be renamed the Astros) and best of all, dream homes. The astronauts had never lived in dream homes, and dream homes were what they deserved after all the drab bases and Quonset huts they'd occupied over the years. Texas real-estate developer Frank Sharp had promised each astronaut family a free home, furnished and decorated, in his newly developed community of Sharpstown in Houston. What could be better than filling them with astronauts? Heck, they could even call it . . . Astronaut Row!

Unfortunately, the astronauts didn't want to live in Sharpstown, which they heard was near a ghetto. Besides, it wasn't exactly convenient, a ways away from NASA's soon-to-be-built mammoth Manned Spacecraft Center.

Could they simply take and then sell these free houses? Leo the lawyer gave the A-OK. If the spacemen weren't obligated to do anything but pose for a few photo ops of modern Astro-living, free dream homes were just another perk, like dollar-a-year Corvettes, dollar-a-night hotels, and free hunting trips at the homes of millionaire gamesmen. Said gamesmen always provided free taxidermy, too, meaning the wives would have to live with all sorts of wildlife staring at them from their dream house walls.

But the idea of a free home didn't sit too well with the press.

Who did these astronauts think they were? Superman? Soon the public was up in arms and NASA went ballistic. To make NASA happy, the astronauts turned down Astronaut Row, but by then the floodgates had opened. Tired of being barred from Astro-homes, tired of *Life*'s preferential treatment, the press took the opportunity to put a spotlight on the *Life* contract. Should it be terminated?

John Glenn was not about to let the good life provided by *Life* escape without a fight. No *Life* contract meant Annie might be subjected to the bloodhounds of the regular press, who weren't likely to be as gentlemanly as Loudon Wainwright and who'd have a field day with her stutter. A lot was at stake. LBJ, chairman of the Space Council, let it be known that he didn't particularly care if the *Life* contract was terminated. Now that he was "bigger than Jesus," as Gus put it, John worked his insider position with the Kennedys.

The Glenns were invited for a sail on the Kennedy yacht, the *Honey Fitz.* On board, John got right down to business. Losing the *Life* contract was inconceivable for the families. It would mean losing not only their protection from the press, but also their life insurance.

Jack asked for John's opinion on the *Life* contract. After all, a soldier did not expect any special compensation for risking his life for his country. Right?

True, but what if the worldwide press scrutinized every move of that soldier's wife, kids, dog? Annie was already practically living under a cake dome.

For all of the astronauts, no more *Life* would mean having to try to live on their military salaries. But the Glenns' fame made them American icons, and as a result, they wielded considerable political clout. Annie had even let LBJ into the house, finally, for John's fortieth birthday party (in this case, the Glenns decided to let the vice president into *their* orbit). She'd invited some of the other astronaut couples to Arlington, too.

"What on earth are you going to *serve*?" someone asked Annie.

"My ham loaf."

"*Ham* loaf?"

"Why not?" Annie smiled calmly. "Everybody likes it. I bet you Lady Bird asks for the recipe, too."

Sure enough, as Lyndon Johnson gave his hostess a good-night kiss, Lady Bird asked for her ham loaf recipe—two eggs, milk, cracker crumbs, tapioca, fresh ground and smoked ham and ground beef, minced onion optional, put in the oven with brown sugar sauce for two hours at 350°F, basting frequently with a heap of love. Yields eight portions. Annie was like Betty Crocker, the nurturing housewife who left all America feeling warm inside.

Ultimately, John Kennedy agreed that the *Life* contract should continue. Their slice of the $500,000 pie secure, the Glenns finally built their real dream home. The site of the new Manned Spacecraft Center was in Clear Lake City, located on the shores of its eponymous recreational lake. The Glenns preferred the quainter Taylor Lake nearby, and snapped up a lot at the head of the little canal that fed into it. They staked their flag in the brand-new subdivision of Timber Cove.

The banks had offered deeply discounted home loans at 4 percent for astronauts, and with homebuilders promising to build at cost, the Astrowives could splurge on BlueStar kitchens with electric ranges and blenders built right into the countertops. The Glenns' had sliding glass doors and a patio, which would be perfect for weekend family barbecues.

The Carpenters built next door to the Glenns, and two blocks away the Grissoms and Schirras built their own suburban fortresses. Betty Grissom would no longer have to draw the curtains on the day of a launch, because her house had no front windows. There was even a hole in the backyard fence so that she could slip, unseen by the press, over to Jo's. Both houses featured turquoise kidney-shaped swimming pools. Finally, Betty thought, Gus would get to swim in peace, far from the eyes of the inevitable space tourists.

The Coopers built a house across Taylor Lake in the subdivision of El Lago Estates. The Slaytons would move into the aptly named Friendswood, a historic Quaker community, also nearby. The Shepards were the only family who opted to live in Houston proper, downtown in the tony neighborhood of River Oaks.

During the summer of 1962, while their houses were being built, the astronaut families were housed in the cabanas at the Lakewood Yacht Club. Since their new houses wouldn't be ready until the fall, the Lakewood Yacht Club had graciously offered the use of its cabanas, on the beautifully landscaped banks of Clear Lake. There the couples and their kids lived in style, enjoying full access to the clubhouse. All the club expected in return was a Valentine's Day photo op of America's favorite sweethearts squeezed together into a rose-red heart.

Houston was abuzz with the arrival of the astronauts and their wives. The *Houston Chronicle* heralded the space ladies as members of "Houston's most exclusive women's club," even more elite than the Junior League or the River Oaks Garden Club, which invited Jo Schirra to be a special guest at the sneak preview of their annual Azalea Trail.

Back at Langley, the formal event of the year had been the Air Force Ball, but down here the social calendar offered frequent fêtes, supported by Houston's deep reservoirs of oil money. The doyennes of high society vied to have astronaut wives at their parties, and Jo was much in demand and getting plenty of coverage now that her Wally was to be the next man to go up into space. His nine-hour *Sigma 7* flight was scheduled to take off on October 3, 1962.

Though she had begun as one of the shier of the wives, Jo was finally coming into her own down here in Texas. She radiated such a healthy glow that Wally called her Sunray. She'd taken to pulling her hair back into a sporty headband, far different from her conservative "before" look in her first *Life* profile. Now the *Chronicle* featured sophisticated, blue-eyed blonde "Josephine," a regular on the Houston social circuit.

On one occasion, Jo and Wally were flown via private plane to the Coffield Ranch, an oil-bought haven for rich sportsmen who had a taste for hunting quail. Touching down on the palm-lined runway, the token Astrowife fit seamlessly into this socialite preserve. In a feature in the fashion pages of the *Chronicle* that followed, Jo looked fabulous in a cashmere sweater, checked wool pants, camel coat, cat-eye glasses, and her signature headband.

Now the Astrowife was about to host the most exclusive party in town—her launch party. Jo wouldn't have to draw the curtains because her house, like the Grissoms' next door, had been custom-built with no front windows. Joining the other wives,

Betty arrived through the rabbit hole, just like the two cats, Miss Priss and Gus. Jo had named the latter for her grouchy astronaut neighbor, who hated cats.

Outside, a pack of neighborhood dogs played on the lawn among the teeming reporters. There were more newsmen than ever, rejuvenated by the Texas-style fanfare of the space program moving to Houston. Jo fixed her carrot-topped twelve-year-old Marty some gelatin salad to snack on, hoping to distract him from the chaos outside. To no avail—the little rascal wouldn't quit playing peekaboo over the fence with the photographers.

"This tower is a real *sayonara*!" Wally said as he took off. After a few corny jokes, Jo's thirty-nine-year-old husband got down to dutiful space flying. He called it "chimp mode." No taking snapshots like a space tourist. No wasting fuel.

After Wally's successful splashdown in the Pacific, Jo stepped outside for her post-flight press conference. "It was a perfect landing, especially," she said, underscoring how her husband hadn't overshot his mark (like one astronaut whom she did not mention). Wally had landed within five miles of the recovery ship.

"Are you going to feed Wally steak and cake when he gets home?" asked the hungry press.

Jo just stared at the newsmen in bewilderment. She didn't even bake. All Wally wanted when he got to Earth was a smoke.

Nevertheless, "Astronaut's Wife Will Bake a Cake" ran the headline in the *Houston Chronicle*, the accompanying article detailing how upon her astronaut's return to his new dream home, Jo was planning to serve him an extra-special meal. The press was determined to keep her in the kitchen.

Dropped off on the *Kearsarge* carrier in the Pacific, Wally was flown to Hawaii, where he was met by dancing hula girls. He didn't arrive back in Houston till one o'clock in the morning. The mayor and the governor were on hand to welcome him back to Texas. Six police cars escorted the Schirras on the drive to Timber Cove. Jo's mother, Mrs. Admiral Holloway, was there to greet her hero son-in-law in proper form.

Finally Wally got a first look at his new California-style ranch house. He'd been training at the Cape all summer and had left Jo to deal with the movers. ("He planned that very well!" she told her friends.) Jo had furnished the house with a modern Oriental flair. Wally, who had served in World War II aboard the USS *Alaska* in Japan, and had met Jo at the train station carrying a samurai sword upon his arrival back in the States, felt immediately at home.

"My view of the Moon was so much better than what you can see from Earth," he explained to his mother-in-law. He happily reported to Marty, his pride and joy, "The Moon is *not* made out of green cheese."

It had been a long, long day, and now it was almost morning and Wally was in his pajamas, finally ready for bed. Jo asked him, "Wally, will you please take out the garbage?" He was fully down to Earth at last.

Only a week and a half later, Earth would seem almost as dangerous a place as outer space. For fourteen days the world teetered on the edge of nuclear war. Though the Russians were still ahead in the space race, America was winning the arms race. Nikita Khrushchev made a bold move to even the score: he began building a missile installation in Cuba, from which his medium-range missiles could easily target the United States.

When Kennedy learned of the site on October 15, he knew he had to stop him. He set up a naval blockade around Cuba. As Russian ships grew closer and closer to Cuba, the world held its breath. Finally Khrushchev blinked. He agreed to remove his missiles from Cuba. In exchange, the United States agreed never to invade Cuba. The world breathed a sigh of relief.

Kennedy was more determined than ever to win the space race. "We choose to go to the Moon!" Kennedy had told a sweltering crowd at Rice University in Houston in September 1962. "We choose to go to the Moon in this decade and do the other things—not because they are easy but because they are hard."

A new group of astronauts was announced to redouble his efforts. Along with the Mercury Seven, the New Nine astronauts would be manning the next phase of the space program. Named Gemini, it would feature two-man space capsules, the first American space walk, and rendezvous, a critical maneuver where two craft joined in orbit. All of this was preliminary to the Apollo program that would take America all the way to the Moon.

The New Nine were Neil Armstrong, Frank Borman, Charles "Pete" Conrad, Jim Lovell, Jim McDivitt, Elliot See, Tom Stafford, Ed White, and John Young. The test pilot world was a small one, so the Mercury wives knew some of the New Nine who would soon be moving to Clear Lake. Pete Conrad and Jim Lovell had been in the same flight training class as Wally Schirra at Pax River in Maryland, so Jo was already friendly with Jane Conrad and Marilyn Lovell. She had sent each of them an elegant cream-colored welcome card, and even offered to show them around the neighborhood and help find a builder, too, although the girls probably *wouldn't* get the great at-cost deal the Mercury families had been given.

As it turned out, they did, which gave the Mercury wives some reason for concern. At a get-together, the seven ladies discussed what they should and should *not* do for the incoming "Gemini wives" about to invade their turf.

As always, Betty was conspicuously missing from the group. She wanted to make sure she finished all her chores before she went anywhere, even next door to Jo's house. She even did the sweaty chores that Jo reserved for Wally when he came home on weekends from the Cape. Betty proudly mowed her own lawn, and expertly fished out hard-to-reach leaves and floating dead bugs from her pool. She wanted Gus to have maximum relaxation time with her and the boys when he got home, to feel like the king of his castle.

"Well, I don't intend to let them run all over me," said Betty when she finally arrived.

Would the goodies be spread too thin with the addition of these new wives? The *Life* deal wasn't due to end until the following year, when Gordo would make the final Mercury flight. A new contract was to be negotiated for the Gemini program. The new deal, rumored to be for a million dollars, would have to be divided into sixteen slices this time—the Mercury Seven plus the New Nine.

The Mercury wives looked to Jo. Wasn't Jane Conrad married to New Nine astronaut "Princeton Pete"? Didn't she already have enough goodies?

Well, the wives simply couldn't manage without all the perks their new Texas lifestyle demanded.

Out in the garage, Wally's blue Corvette convertible (he'd

later get a cherry red Maserati, which just happened to have been previously owned by blonde sex kitten Brigitte Bardot), was getting lonely. Jo had her eye on a sleek, sexy car to keep it company, a car she expected to purchase at a deep discount.

Jo had long ago chucked the archaic ways of *The Navy Wife*. Jo and Wally loved taking their new sailboat out on breezy Sunday mornings, so much that they eventually stopped going to church. Heaven would have to wait, because Jo simply couldn't get enough of the Texas sunshine. Soon she had acquired her new Toronado and was following adventuresome Trudy's lead, driving well above the speed limit. Jo and Wally would even race their cars down the highway, Jo's muscle car against Wally's sexy Corvette. Who was going to ticket an astronaut, or his wife, in Houston? They even had CB nicknames for each other: Skyray and Sunray.

The Glenns were throwing a welcoming party for the New Nine in their Timber Cove home. The new silver-suited cold warriors had been training at the Cape for a few months while their own dream homes were being built, courtesy of their share of the *Life* money. The rookies left it up to their wives to settle things on the home front—specifically, to begin building their new homes. New Nine astronaut wife Jane Conrad was still trying to sell their old home in Rancho Santa Fe, near the Miramar Naval Air Station in San Diego, where her real-estate broker put an ad in the local newspaper: "House for Sale. Owner Going to the Moon."

On the day Pete had been announced as one of America's new astronauts, Jane had answered a ring at the door and found a peppery little reporter named Regis Philbin asking for her reaction to the news. The press was already calling her husband the "tattooed Ivy League astronaut," making a big deal about the contrast of his bad-boy attitude with his preppy look. "Princeton Pete" dressed in typical Princeton attire—dirty white bucks, button-down Brooks Brothers shirt, khaki pants. Towering over Regis, Jane said this was just another day in the life of being Pete Conrad's wife. Totally surreal.

All of the wives of the new astronauts were eager to join the exclusive Astronaut Wives Club. Conrad Hilton had personally invited the ladies to be his guests for a long weekend at the Shamrock Hilton in Houston so they could attend the Glenns' party. The girls at the front desk were effusive in their welcome. Jane could certainly get used to this!

In her room, a heavy glass ashtray held a book of matches inscribed JANE & JIM. Jane grinned at the mix-up—Jim was Jim Lovell, the husband of her dear friend Marilyn from Pax River. The two attractive brunettes—Jane being tall and model thin and Marilyn a more sultry Liz Taylor type—were always being confused with each other.

At the Shamrock, Jane freshened up and went down to the lobby to find Marilyn, who'd experienced the same matchbook mismatch—her box said MARILYN & PETE. Then the two went to the hotel beauty parlor. They wanted to look their best when they met the Mercury wives at Annie Glenn's tonight.

The gals had no idea what was in store for them personally as astronaut wives, but they were convinced it would be fabulous. They'd seen the first generation on TV and in magazines. And to think, they'd now be in the same league with Jo, their old friend from test pilot school. Still, they were nervous about being accepted.

When their husbands, Pete and Jim, had gone down to the Cape to witness their old test pilot school classmate Wally's launch, they'd gotten an eye-opening initiation into astronaut life. Trolling the Holiday Inn, Jim and Pete happened to enter a room where Bob Hope was talking with some of the Mercury wives.

The group turned and looked at the boys like, *Just who the hell do you think you are?* Clearly the Mercury Wives were territorial. Bryn Mawr–educated Jane didn't need her Seven Sisters breeding to read between the lines of that cream-colored congratulatory card from Jo. Jo was a living doll, of course, but she was *terribly* busy with Wally's shot. All the grueling post-flight events: ticker-tape parades; the obligatory visit to Wally's hometown of Hackensack; the White House visit with Jackie. Jane would obviously understand.

Jane and Marilyn gabbed away as the hairdressers worked on them, piling their hair higher and higher into the beehive do that was all the rage with the stylish Houston ladies. "Gorgeous," pronounced the hairdresser when she was finished.

Balancing their new sky-high hairdos, they went to meet their husbands at NASA's temporary offices in downtown Houston. A secretary went to collect the boys.

As Jim strode toward Marilyn, he looked over his shoulder, to make sure no one was around. "Marilyn, what the hell did you do to your hair?" he whispered.

After all these years, Jim still carried in his billfold a photo of Marilyn at seventeen, wearing Bermuda shorts and a tight sweater, with her dark curly hair tousled. And that's how he liked her.

Pete was used to Jane's fashion daring, so he just laughed.

He found it hilarious that his buddy Jim got all riled up over such trivial matters. Jim was an utterly competent pilot, but Pete nicknamed him "Shaky."

Finally Jim asked, "What is that?" as he nodded at the girls' heads.

Jane and Marilyn answered in unison, "It's a beehive."

That night the couples drove out to Timber Cove, where old-fashioned gas lamps flickered along the gently curving roads. Ranch houses lined the streets with names like Whispering Oaks Drive and Pine Shadows Drive. Finally they arrived at the Glenns', on the right of Sleepy Hollow Court. The house looked sweet with its low-hanging shingled roof. The most pleasant aroma greeted them when they entered. Something savory was baking in the oven.

Everything in the house was perfect—the cozy rugs, the fireplace. Annie was a wonderful hostess, going out of her way to make her guests feel at home. Jane and Marilyn hadn't known about Annie's stutter. They'd read all about her in *Life*, but she didn't speak to the public very often. Annie just smiled and checked the ladies off her list. There were so many new wives to meet—Pat White, who looked like a porcelain doll; Faye Stafford, a big-haired Oklahoma girl; Susan Borman, with her blonde bob perfectly flipped up. There was also Pat McDivitt, Marilyn See, and Barbara Young.

Jane and Marilyn immediately ran to Jo. She looked fabulous. Perhaps it was the afterglow of her White House visit.

As the wives chatted away, the men of Mercury made it pretty clear to the new astronauts that they were not too thrilled about having to cut the *Life* pie into another nine slivers. And they would *not* be sharing "Big Daddy," a.k.a. Leo the Lawyer, the expert who had gotten them all their perks. In case there was any question of rank, some of the New Nine wives were calling Annie and Jo "ma'am," and their husbands were referring to the Mercury astronauts as "sir."

New Nine astronaut Jim Lovell had proudly picked out a lot in El Lago Estates, the development across Taylor Lake from Timber Cove—where most of the Mercury Seven lived, just "a holler" away from each other. The newer development of El Lago was where many of the other New Nine families were building their charming dream homes, because the lots were more plentiful and less expensive. But when Jim took his wife, Marilyn, to see the lot, she wasn't too crazy about it. She told Jim that she'd prefer to be on the water in Timber Cove. That's where Annie Glenn lived, and besides, that's where their best friends, Jane and Pete Conrad, were building. Marilyn, needless to say, got her way.

Marilyn had met Jim in the cafeteria at Juneau High School in Milwaukee, where she was washing dishes and Jim was serving hot lunch. They had gotten together after Jim's date for the prom dumped him at the last minute because he wasn't nominated for prom king. (Marilyn wondered how that girl felt now.) Marilyn had always wanted a life of glamorous adventure, ever since she had packed her trunk and left her home in Milwaukee to move to the East Coast, where Jim was attending the Naval Academy in Annapolis. Jim was very handsome and ever so bright. He seemed to know a little something about everything. And now he was an astronaut!

And she'd get to live on Lazywood Lane in Timber Cove, which was very, very glamorous because all of the men in the neighborhood were going into space, and then to the Moon. There was, however, one catch.

"You have to build the house," Jim told her. "I'm going to be too busy training."

Jim went off to the Cape and left Marilyn with the blueprints. The same builder was also constructing Jane's house around the corner on Whispering Oaks Drive, and he frequently confused the two brunettes. He'd walk with his drill into Marilyn's and start putting something up that Jane had ordered, and Marilyn would have to correct it. The builder was not the only one in the neighborhood who had trouble keeping Marilyn and Jane straight. So did the butcher, and even the gynecologist. Once, with Jane on his examining table, peering into her nether regions, he said, "You remind me so much of Mrs. Lovell."

"Inside or out?" quipped Jane, fast on the uptake.

Despite the little annoyances along the way, both women loved their new homes. Marilyn had the builder copy the design for her family room from a magazine, and the result was exactly as she'd imagined it. Connected by a bar to the brick kitchen, with big exposed ceiling beams and a brick fireplace, the family room was Marilyn's pride and joy. The walls featured paintings by a Navy wife friend of Marilyn's of the Spanish Steps in Rome and a Utrillo-style Parisian cityscape, but the pièce de résistance was an oil portrait of Jim. Though critics would be critics (not a very good painting, noted one reporter), Marilyn adored it. To her, this beautiful family room was the apotheosis of the American dream.

Life in Timber Cove seemed blessedly *normal*, and after years of following Jim from Navy base to Navy base, normal was how Marilyn wanted to live. Only one thing wasn't. When the house was finally completed, it somehow seemed a little—off. The builder had miscalculated and built some extra steps and levels. From the family room, steps led up to the front door, and down to the bedrooms, all on slightly different planes. They christened it "Lovells' Levels." Marilyn kept on staring at the brick fireplace in her family room, and it finally hit her that, like the house, it was also cockeyed. She later learned that the man she had hired was a one-eyed bricklayer.

Jane often came over, and so did another New Nine wife who was also named Marilyn—Marilyn See. Susan Borman, Pat White, or Faye Stafford would drive over from El Lago to drop in to Lovells' Levels for coffee or a cigarette. Marilyn was always grateful for the company.

She couldn't believe how lucky she was, to be able to have the girls in her kitchen where she could gaze over the bar into that wonderful family room. At night, after reading her three small children their bedtime stories and tucking them in, she'd slink into bed and open up her own book. She'd read, then try to fall asleep, but she'd just start thinking, thinking, thinking. Her house was so cozy, and beautifully decorated to boot—she was very talented in that regard, and she had a great eye for art. In the weeks to come, Marilyn realized there was something more than the levels of her house that was off-kilter. One thing, essential for her happy home, seemed always to be missing—Jim.

Across America, women were falling asleep with Betty Friedan's *The Feminine Mystique* on the bedside table, which detailed a world of suburban malaise and the underlying causes of the dreaded "Housewife's Headache" that aspirin ads in *Life* offered a remedy for. "The problem with no name" seemed to require more than a pill to cure. The book offered some tantalizing ideas about what life beyond cooking, cleaning, and housekeeping could be. But the clarion call of the beginnings of "women's liberation" was not heard on the shores of Taylor Lake, a place that seemed so very, very far away.

As one by one the new wives got settled into Timber Cove and El Lago, they began to feel rather unmoored, or just the opposite, trapped inside a giant "goldfish bowl," as Marilyn put it. Each of the new Astrowives tried to live up to the gold standard of what the public expected of them.

NASA had a protocol officer conduct a New Nine wife orientation, where he prattled on about how astronauts needed a good breakfast before flying off to work—eggs, bacon, hell, why not steak or fried chicken? Feed him well. Praise his efforts. Create a place of refuge. Adjusting to normal conditions after a week in the pure oxygen bubble of a space-training capsule could knock a husband out, so he shouldn't be expected to do menial chores around the home. And for God's sake, keep the astronaut away from stress. He should never have to worry about the plumbing, or the dental bills, and he should never be nagged about his lack of initiative in the bedroom.

New Nine wife Susan Borman knew the drill. She'd heard it all before in her military days back at Edwards Air Force Base when the commanding officer's wife would scare the daylights out of her young minions by declaring that a woman's mastery of the 5 a.m. breakfast was a matter of life and death for her man in the air. Susan did exactly as ordered. She lived to support Frank, and, like any good Air Force wife, fully subscribed to the protocol of visiting her commanding officer's wife once a week.

Gung ho as all get out, she intended to take her Frank to the stars, because everyone knew that the tighter the marriage, the better the flight position. Just look at the Glenns. That was the sort of family NASA wanted, and that's exactly what NASA was going to get from the Bormans.

One of the first things Susan did when she moved into her new home on Bayou Drive in El Lago was to open up her closet and organize her clothes like soldiers in formation. She had outfits for every occasion. But then she discovered that there was no official wives' organization here in NASA-land! Where was she going to wear all of these outfits? At every Air Force base she'd ever been, there had been an Officers Wives Club.

No wonder the rest of the ladies in El Lago were feeling a little out to sea. There was no organization! No structure, no discipline! A self-described do-gooder, the former Susan Bugbee decided to do something about it.

Unlike most of the Mercury wives, who found Susan a little too *enthusiastic*, Marge appreciated her energy. Marge was already thinking she should probably get something going for the wives, especially because of Deke's new position. Disqualified from flying because of his heart murmur, Deke had been given the job of Coordinator of Astronaut Activities. Well, that made Marge the unofficial Coordinator of Astronaut Wife Activities. Except that if there was one word the ladies of Mercury abhorred, it was "organized." They'd finally escaped the dingy quarters of base life and the required Officers Wives Club gatherings, and they had no intention of repeating those awful days in their glamorous new lives.

But Marge met Susan halfway and organized a luncheon to welcome the New Nine at Louise Shepard's swank Houston apartment in an elegant new high-rise called the Mayfair.

Like in the old Langley days, the Mercury wives carpooled to

Louise's. They all wanted the meeting with these "younger ones" to go smoothly, but they were worried.

Betty's husband, Gus, had already butted heads with some of the rookies who were strutting around the Cape as if they owned the place. That kind of attitude might work with the NASA higher-ups, but not with old Gus. He made this clear to the new guys by telling them, "Don't feel so smart. You're just an astronaut trainee" and "You're not an astronaut until you *fly.*" Gus wasn't about to let these newbies roll in and act like top guns. Neither was Betty.

Greeted by the doorman, the wives took the elevator to the tenth floor. As soon as the door opened, Picasso, Louise's bearded collie, began running around sniffing the ladies' ankles. Betty volunteered for the job of writing out the nametags for the new wives in her careful cursive. Soon the foyer was full of fresh faces. As Betty handed Susan Borman her nametag, which read "Sue," she faced a glacial blue stare.

"My name is *Susan*," said the blonde, "not Sue."

Betty looked her square in the eye. She reached for the nametag and slowly ripped it up. "Okay, *Sue*."

She thought she probably should have just kept her mouth shut, but she could already sense the attitude of the new cohort.

On the ride over, the Gemini wives had also discussed what to expect. They had all sorts of what-if and how-to questions they were eager to ask the Mercury women. Now, feeling the tension in the room, they were afraid of saying something stupid or naïve.

Susan Borman plowed ahead with her agenda. If only she could get the rest of the wives as organized as they had been in their military days. Back at Edwards, Susan *never* missed an official tea or Officers Wives Club meeting. She shone on these occasions. "This is fun," she said. "Let's start doing this on an organized basis... How about a newsletter?"

Betty locked eyes with Jo, Jo looked at Marge, and all their eyes rolled.

Susan tried again. "What advice do you have for us?"

The room fell silent. Then Marge volunteered to take that one. "Just plan to cry a lot!"

The Mercury wives decided that was enough coffee talk for now. The tense meeting broke up and the gals folded themselves back into the car for the ride home.

"Well," blurted Betty, thinking of all those beehive hairdos, "they're a showy bunch!"

"And how did you like that newsletter bit?" asked Marge.

They got the giggles and couldn't stop laughing. Despite their differences, today they had found out that they were a very cohesive group. Well, they assured each other, these babes in the woods—in space—would be just fine. After all, *they'd* somehow been able to figure it out.

8

The Galaxy Ball

Every weekend the New Nine astronauts and their wives were guests at Houston society parties. While the men were training and competing for assignments on the first Gemini flights, the women competed for invitations to the most desirable social events.

Everyone wanted to be invited to the fabulous parties thrown by Joanne Herring (played by Julia Roberts in *Charlie Wilson's War*) at her mansion in River Oaks, the city's most affluent neighborhood. A fixture on the Houston society circuit, Joanne was throwing a major party for the opening of the Broadway musical *Camelot* that was coming to Houston. Joanne was notorious for her decadent parties: for her second husband, oil baron Robert Herring, she'd hosted a wild toga party that featured copious amounts of Chianti, "Nubian slaves," and even a "Christian girl" being "burned" at the stake. Joanne was a good friend of Texas congressman Charlie Wilson, who often attended her parties. She was also quite knowledgeable about Middle East politics and later served as honorary consul to Pakistan and Morocco. She often invited Third World dictators like Egypt's Hosni Mubarak and the Philippines' Marcoses to her parties. At one of these affairs, surrounded by heart surgeons and oilmen, Marilyn Lovell met "sheiks and what have you."

One of the bizarre "perks" the New Nine wives received were $1,000 gift certificates to Neiman-Marcus from an anonymous priest, who had anticipated that the ladies would be going to plenty of these sorts of affairs, and would not always be able to afford the right clothes. So, the new Astrowives bought dresses for the launches and press conferences and social events they'd be expected to attend.

Later, before she was to go on a NASA world tour, Jane Conrad recruited her mother to go shopping and spend the gift certificate with her at Neiman's in downtown Houston. Mrs. DuBose had come from a wealthy Philadelphia "Mainline" Social Register family. "Mimi" had once been chauffeured in Rolls-Royces and taken on transatlantic ocean liner voyages. Her mother took her to Europe for a month to forget a cowboy she had fallen in love with on a dude ranch. On the Continent, Mimi met Gary Cooper, who had his eye on her, to no avail. She was going to give up all the trappings of her privileged youth for love. Jane thought it was the most romantic story she had ever heard, her mother leaving a life that featured movie stars and elegant ocean cruises for a rugged life of adventure with a cowboy.

Neiman's featured all the latest fashions—Yves Saint Laurent's "young natural" daytime attire, which tomboy Jane looked great in. For the nighttime, the look was ultrafeminine—long gowns featuring bare shoulders, bare backs, and plunging necklines outlined in fur, feathers, sequins, or beading.

While Jane was trying on all sorts of confections—with their price tags further reduced by darling Lawrence Marcus, who adored the astronaut wives—Jane's mother wandered over to the shoe department to sit down for a rest. Who should happen by but Henry Fonda (Jane's mother was a magnet for Hollywood stars). The dear woman was all "twizzled" and although it would have been nice to tell the famous actor about her daughter's husband, the astronaut who would probably be going to the Moon, she would *never* brag about that. Her mother was aware that one of the first rules Jane had learned about being an astronaut wife was: do not advertise. None of the wives ever volunteered that information unless specifically asked about their new Astrowife "status."

Jane was the only wife invited to join Houston's prestigious Junior League, largely because of her pedigree. She had grown up on a ranch in Uvalde, Texas, outside San Antonio, which was overseen by her rancher father and paid for by her mother. Jane loved ranch life—she even had her own horse to ride—but after high school, she chose to go East for college.

At Bryn Mawr, Jane had her formal "coming out" as a debutante. She first saw Pete at a deb dance at the Gulph Mills Golf Club in Conshohocken, Pennsylvania. She noticed the funny-looking fellow with a blond crew cut, and wasn't even sure why she was so attracted to him. At five foot eight, she was almost two inches taller than Pete. He had bright blue eyes and a big gap between his two front teeth that she found irresistible. It wasn't until several months later, at a Princeton party, that she finally met him. Spotting him across a crowded, smoke-filled room, she dragged her date over and made him introduce them.

It was only then that Jane noticed the anchor and rattlesnake head tattooed on his left forearm. He explained to her that he'd had it inked during World War II when he was fifteen. Although he was from the same ritzy part of Philadelphia as her mother, he'd wanted to look like a sailor, though he was too young to see combat in World War II or Korea. He was currently attending Princeton on a Navy ROTC scholarship, since his father had lost most of his money in the stock market crash and drank away the rest. When Jane took Pete home to the ranch, he got along so well with her daddy that she often wondered if that's why Pete proposed to her.

Nancy Robbins, a prominent Houston socialite, who collected Madame Alexander dolls (and now a token Astrowife), sponsored Jane for the Junior League.

Since none of the other astronaut wives had been invited to join, Jane made light of it by saying, "I had *no* intention of joining the Junior League, but these friends of mine worked to get me in, so I couldn't refuse. I guess it's an honor, and I've always liked volunteer work..."

She laughed, but secretly she did consider it an honor. To join the Junior League, Jane had to take a course three days a week for six weeks, to learn about the city and the various charitable programs the league was involved in. Once she became a member, she worked one day a week as a waitress at the Junior League tearoom in downtown Houston. It was a social commitment and all profits went to charity. She hoped she'd be able to work as a league volunteer in one of the hospitals as soon as all four of her young boys were in school. For now, she had caught the eye of Joanne Herring, host of a daytime talk show on Houston's KHOU-TV. After interviewing Jane about what it was like to be married to an astronaut, woman to woman, Joanne took quite a shine to her and invited her to a fancy River Oaks Country Club luncheon, where she introduced Jane to one of her literary darlings, Truman Capote.

Jane happened to be wearing one of her new suede hats, and was all ready to answer any questions he might have about the space program. The pale-faced Capote looked her over, from her new heels to her odd-looking hat that fit her head like, well, a *helmet*, and asked drolly, in his high nasal twang, "Are you trying to be an astronaut like your husband?" Suddenly Jane didn't feel so stylish. It felt like a slap in the face!

Since that joint session of the wives at Louise's apartment, the New Nine and the Mercury women had continued meeting for coffee, but in separate camps. It was springtime 1963, time to melt the frosty relations between the two groups of women. Enough was enough; it was time for a détente.

At the invitation of the Austin Rotary Club, the wives were flown by the Air Force to Austin, and were met at Bergstrom Air Force Base by the city council and the University of Texas Silver Spurs, an honor group of college boys wearing chaps and cowboy hats, boots, and spurs. Colonel Homer Garrison, president of the Austin Rotary Club, was there on behalf of the city.

"I've never seen a Texas Ranger in uniform," said one of the wives, so he hurried right home to change into his.

Unfortunately, his wife had informed him that it was too blasted hot here in Austin in the high-eighties spring temperature for his winter uniform (and his summer uniform was *dirty*), so the colonel assigned two muscle-bound Rangers, fully uniformed in broad-brimmed hats, knee-high boots, and silver star badges, to escort the ladies throughout their visit.

The wives were driven to the governor's mansion for coffee with the First Lady of Texas, Nellie Connally, who gave them a tour of her Greek Revival–style mansion. The wives counted twenty-five rooms and seven bathrooms! *This* was a dream home! *How many kids do y'all have?* Nellie wanted to know, so the wives commenced a "countdown of brats."

They crossed the street to the pink granite Texas State Capitol. One senator told the ladies he was so happy to see them, because "I've never *met* women who make love to men from outer space!"

Everyone was letting loose a little now that Project Mercury was coming to a close. On May 15, 1963, Trudy's Gordo was to fly the last of the Mercury missions. The Mercury wives drove over to El Lago, and Louise roared up in her new Plymouth Sport Fury convertible. They were all wearing matching headscarves and bearing gifts. Marge brought Trudy the dozen long-stemmed roses Deke had just given her for their anniversary. Betty had swiped two bottles of "Gus's good champagne." The wives didn't think he would mind.

All of the New Nine had been invited to this last launch party of Project Mercury. They were out in the living room watching the TV while the Mercury Seven set up camp in Trudy's bedroom.

Huddled together like schoolgirls, the wives listened to a high-frequency radio Wally Schirra had lent them. He'd explained this nifty gadget, saying that when Gordo was flying over Houston, they'd be able to pick up the chatter between Mission Control at the Cape and Trudy's slow-talkin' Okie. They'd hear him twenty-two times in all, once for each time that he passed overhead while he whizzed around the Earth. Trudy hoped Gordo might send her a personal message, but all the wives could hear when Gordo soared overhead was static. During his fourth orbit, Trudy was just able to make out three of his words: "Roger, *Faith Seven*," the name of his ship. She was making preparations to jet off to Hawaii with her daughters for a reunion with Gordo after he splashed down into the Pacific.

"Gordon is a good pilot," Trudy thought. She always knew he'd do a bang-up job. Who knows, being a damn good pilot herself, maybe she'd be the first female astronaut. But the prospect did not look promising.

The summer before, John Glenn had testified before the House Space Committee against sending a woman into space. Sitting in the back of the room, Annie had nodded in complete agreement with her man. What woman could imagine going to the bathroom, let alone having her *period*, in that *can*?

But only a month after Gordo's twenty-two orbits around the Earth, Russian cosmonaut Valentina Tereshkova waxed his tail by orbiting Earth forty-eight times, doubling Gordo's achievement. And comrade Valentina was *pregnant* at the time.

Still, Gordo had closed out Project Mercury in style, taking it easy the whole time, even catching a nap in the capsule on top of his giant Atlas rocket before liftoff.

Following the flight, Mercury director Walt Williams announced that the project had achieved its goals. "The program is closed," he said. "When we started it, our object was to prove man's capability in space. I think the record shows that man is capable in space. Man has a place in space."

Jackie had invited all the Mercury families for cocktails on May 21 at the White House to commemorate the project's successful conclusion. After the gathering, over the course of a White House dinner, the president gave the recap to journalist Benjamin Bradlee, who later wrote, "He said two or three times that evening that he finds Rene Carpenter the most attractive of the wives."

The wives had made what, unbeknownst to them at the time, would be their final official visit with the Queen of Camelot. Smiling, laughing, a little tipsy, they posed for a group photo, not realizing they would never again be as close as they had been during Mercury. Though the Mercury astronauts had originally been slated to fly some of the upcoming Gemini and Apollo missions, almost half of them had already been removed from active flying status. NASA still would not overlook Deke Slayton's heart murmur. Soon Alan Shepard was diagnosed with Ménière's disease, an inner-ear disorder that causes vertigo. In keeping with the teachings of Mary Baker Eddy, Louise saw his affliction as Alan's *dis-ease* with himself. Until he reached a healthy balance in his own life, she believed, and perhaps gave up his dalliances with other women, he'd be stuck on Earth, just like Deke.

Scott Carpenter was still working for NASA and took part in the training, but it was clear he wasn't going to get another flight assignment. Scott was on the outs. He might be John Glenn's next-door neighbor, but they were worlds apart. The artisan Mexican door that opened up to Scott's home said as much.

In Timber Cove, Scott got busy in the backyard digging a hole wide enough to accommodate a trampoline. He was adamant: he wanted his trampoline ground level. It would make it not only pleasing to the eye, but also very safe.

His gymnastics coach from his Navy preflight training was a trampoline pioneer, and had taught Scott all about doing flips. Scott loved teaching the neighborhood kids in turn. He'd even made some headway with NASA, convincing the agency to use trampolines in its training, sort of like simulating zero gravity. But NASA still reminded Scott at every turn that it could do without him.

At a lecture at MIT, Scott met underwater explorer Jacques Cousteau and was totally inspired by the Frenchman's passion for the magical life under the sea. Scott asked Cousteau if he could please come aboard his research vessel and join *Calypso*'s red-capped aquatic team. There were just a few problems, as the Frenchman saw it—for one, he had a limited budget to pay Scott a salary, and the astronaut unfortunately didn't speak French. Scott was also not an experienced diver.

In the autumn of 1963, NASA gave Scott leave to train for Sealab, the Navy's man-in-the-sea project, where he would become an "aquanaut," living in an experimental underwater habitat. He committed himself to being an underwater guinea pig, allowing scientists to study his physical and psychological changes while living for long, isolated periods below the sea. It was sort of like being in space, only far away from the NASA bureaucracy.

As a debutante and now a Junior Leaguer, Jane Conrad had plenty of experience with formal balls. Her fellow New Nine wives had finally gotten used to black-tie events, but the upcoming Galaxy Ball in Fort Worth was to be the grandest of the grand. Unfortunately, the wives didn't have the money for the sort of gowns they felt they needed—couture, not off-the-rack dresses. Jane took it upon herself to find a consignment shop in downtown Houston, and rallied her troops into station wagons to go dress hunting. The Second Hand Rose turned out to be a major find, filled with designer clothes—Givenchy, Balenciaga,

Chanel. All the wives found something that fit perfectly; Jane only prayed that they wouldn't bump into the society ladies who had originally worn their dresses. Jane found a green satin frock by none other than Oleg Cassini, Jackie's designer.

On the big night, the astronauts and their wives were given free rooms at the Six Flags Hotel in Fort Worth. They were driven to the ball in limousines with a full police escort. In the sumptuous ballroom strung with tiny white lights, shimmering into infinity in the gilt mirrors, each couple was introduced as if they were royalty.

They drank and danced the night away, leaving the ballroom well after midnight. But when they wandered outside, tipsy and dreamy, their limos and police escorts were nowhere to be seen.

A Volkswagen bus pulled up before the couples, shivering in their finery.

"Y'all looking for a ride?" the driver called out.

All nine couples crammed into the minibus.

"We've turned into a bunch of pumpkins," said Pete, looking at Jane.

On September 20, 1963, John F. Kennedy addressed the United Nations and proposed the unthinkable—a joint U.S.-U.S.S.R. mission to go to the Moon. JFK and Khrushchev had managed to figure out how to avoid blowing up the world during the Cuban Missile Crisis. Why not forge ahead and explore the new world together?

"Those were anxious days for mankind," said Kennedy before the UN. "Today the clouds have lifted so that new rays of hope can break through."

A new spirit of optimism rose over Clear Lake. The Mercury and Gemini astronauts welcomed the idea of a joint mission with the cosmonauts. The thought of working hand in hand with the Russians made it a little easier for the wives to accept that NASA had just chosen a brand-new group of astronauts, "the Fourteen," to help crew the upcoming Gemini and Apollo missions. This meant *another* gang of gals would be moving in, ready to take their share of the Astro-goodies. Oh dear.

A few months later, the infinite possibilities, from the sublime to the ridiculous, fueled the excited chatter at an Astrowives luncheon in the home of Del Berry, the wife of Dr. Berry, the "astronauts' doctor." When the telephone rang, Del, who was Trudy's best friend, answered. She gasped in shock and began urgently pointing to the television. One of the wives ran over to turn it on. Hands flew to mouths and cries filled the room. They couldn't believe it. The president had been shot.

All of the Mercury wives had met Jack and Jackie. The First Couple hadn't yet blessed the New Nine, but they'd met Governor Connally and his wife, Nellie, who were riding in the convertible with the Kennedys in the motorcade in Dallas. The wives were frightened and horrified—Kennedy had just been in Houston the night before, following a visit with the astronauts at the Cape! As the shock sank in, they couldn't avoid thinking about their own situation. Would the country still be committed to going to the Moon now that the president was dead? That gamble had been Kennedy's big idea.

Later that day, many of the Mercury and Gemini families gathered at the boat slip in Timber Cove, rolling their barbecue grills from their backyards down the streets to the landing. Somehow it just didn't seem right staying at home. The Glenns would soon be off to Washington; they were the only astronaut couple that had been invited to the funeral.

Continuing full steam ahead on Kennedy's dream of going to the Moon by the end of the decade, President Johnson renamed Cape Canaveral as Cape Kennedy a week later. A month and a half after Kennedy's death, John Glenn resigned from NASA to run as a Democrat for the U.S. Senate in his home state of Ohio. Robert Kennedy had suggested he do so two years before, and JFK had felt that Glenn was too valuable an American to risk his hide riding on a rocket again. Running for office now seemed like the right thing to do. America needed leadership more than ever. John knew it would be hard on Annie, who wouldn't be able to hide from the spotlight. Part of him felt guilty about constantly putting her in the firing line, but Annie always said she'd be up for whatever he was, a hundred percent.

Unfortunately, John slipped in the bathroom of his rented apartment in Columbus on a new throw rug Annie had laid down to soften the place. He hit his head on the bathtub and was laid up for weeks, leaving Rene to become the voice of his campaign. Rene had volunteered to help out on the stump, driving home John's message that politics didn't have to be a dirty enterprise, but could be as exciting and inspirational as sending a man into orbit.

In every town and city on the campaign trail, Annie would say to the crowds, "Hello, I'm Annie Glenn." Then there would be a pause as she struggled to form her sentence. "You know I stutter," she'd continue. "So here's Rene."

The daily avalanche of mail was stacked in piles at the Glenns' in Timber Cove, where Annie would type replies.

"I thought it was wonderful for her to campaign for you while you were recovering," one woman wrote to the Glenns about Rene.

To this letter, John replied: "Rene's doing such a good job that she could probably run for office herself."

Ultimately, the injury forced John to withdraw from the Senate race. His neighbor was soon to join him in infirmity. During Sealab training in Bermuda, Scott hopped onto his motorbike and crashed into a coral wall, smashing his left arm and foot, crushing his big toe. It was no use. Scott was just not going to be able to make it for the underwater mission, although there was hope for Sealab II.

9

Togethersville

"Togethersville" was the ironic name journalists gave to the space burb of Clear Lake City, the "City of the Future," with its subdivisions of Timber Cove, El Lago Estates, and the newest community, Nassau Bay. As if adhering to the social hierarchies of the astronauts, this was where most of the new group of fourteen astronauts chose to build their dream homes. Cocky young Gene Cernan had a bird's-eye view of the developments from the cockpit of his sleek T-38 Talon jet fighter, nicknamed the "White Rocket." The space agency had chosen the plane, which boasted a cruising speed of 600 mph, to be its official astronaut trainer. All the astronauts were given one to fly to and from the Cape. Though, if you asked Gene, or "Geno" as the boys called him, he'd tell you the rest of the astronauts couldn't handle it quite the way he did.

From up high, Togethersville looked like Disneyland, complete with its own space-age fortress—the Manned Spacecraft Center on NASA Road 1, a complex of white, mostly windowless buildings in a quad housing gigantic, state-of-the-art computers. The astronauts loved to water-ski on Clear Lake, but none of them could compete with newly arrived Fourteen wife Beth Williams, who had been one of the beloved AquaMaids, the professional water-skiers who stood on top of one another's shoulders in pyramid formation at the Cypress Gardens theme park in Florida.

When Gene was flying below in Timber Cove, at the end of the cul-de-sac on Sleepy Hollow Court, he could make out the Glenn-Carpenter compound with Scott's big trampoline in the backyard. The neighborhood kids swung onto it from a tree rope. They were much better at it than Gene's colleague Walt Cunningham, who had volunteered for the NASA trampoline instruction program and promptly broken his neck. Luckily, he not only lived, but was soon back in the astronaut training rotation.

The community pool in Timber Cove was obviously designed to be admired from the sky. It was supposed to look like a Mercury capsule. Over at the Keys Club in El Lago, where most of the New Nine families lived, there was a synchronized swim team for the kids called the Aquanauts. They performed in aviator-style swim caps. Their best routine was a swim-dance to "Puff, the Magic Dragon." Another of the Aquanauts' big hits was set to "Goldfinger," the theme song from the latest James Bond movie. Gordo's teenage daughters, Cam and Jan, were the stars of that routine, covering themselves in gold paint they'd bought at the hardware store. Trudy was horrified when she saw her painted-up girls, perhaps taking too seriously the warning in the movie that gold paint suffocates the skin and could cause death if the full body were painted.

Over there was Nassau Bay. Some of the stuffier types in Togethersville thought it the gaudiest of the space burbs. It had the biggest houses, but from where Gene was flying, square in the catbird seat, they looked A-OK.

He could decipher quite clearly the Bean-Bassett-Aldrin compound on the corner of Point Lookout Drive. Hell, you probably couldn't miss that one if you were in orbit. The backyards were daisy-chained, and the three families were very friendly. A prizewinning local architect had designed the Bassetts' house, a sandy-colored castle. The Beans built a pink brick chateau-style house. Sue Bean decorated it with imitation Louis XIV furniture, describing her taste as "almost French." The Aldrins' house was a two-story English Tudor. Joan Aldrin decorated Buzz's study in mahogany and midnight blue, with plush carpeting and heavy curtains, so that Buzz could have a home refuge in something resembling space.

The Chaffees' was coming into sight. Roger and his wife, Martha, had attended Purdue University with Gene. Purdue, with its advanced-technology aviation program, came to be known as "the cradle of the astronauts." In all, twenty-two of the astronauts were Purdue graduates. The Mercury astronauts had been picked for their physical stamina, but as the program progressed and technology became more important, the astronauts' IQs and educations became more and more important, with many of them holding advanced degrees in engineering. Gene and Roger had both been in fraternities. Not long after Martha had been named homecoming queen and "Eternal Sweetheart" by a rival frat, Roger nabbed her. Lucky dog. That girl was drop-dead gorgeous, but no more so than his own wife, Barbara.

Gene had first noticed her at LAX, when he was a Navy pilot on leave. She was a big-haired, green-eyed Texas blonde, and beautifully filled out her snug navy blue Continental Airlines stewardess uniform ("We really move our tail for you" was the airline's slogan). Continental's signature red beret and white gloves captured his attention. Gene eavesdropped when she gave her last name at check-in—Atchley. She was flying out for a girls' weekend in Vegas. Pulling out his little black book, Gene wrote down the vitals along with the note *Continental.* He didn't even try to talk to her, but on his flight home to Chicago he got the girl's first name from the stewardess. After telling his immigrant father that he'd seen the woman he wanted to marry, Geno used so-called "devious means" to ring the girl up and insist that she knew him. She didn't believe him, but she made a date with him anyway. Lucky guy.

Gene took his T-38 down to buzz the roof of his low, cream-colored ranch house on Barbuda Lane, making the whole place vibrate. It was his way of saying to his wife, "Barbara, I'm home." After zooming overhead, he landed at Ellington Air Force Base and parked along the line of astronauts' T-38s. Here, NASA prepared its boys for weightless spaceflight in KC-135 airplanes, dubbed "Vomit Comets." They would take off and fly in parabolas that included thirty seconds of zero G. Floating in orange and blue NASA flight suits and black combat boots, the men squeezed meal bags of condensed beef with gravy and shrimp with cocktail sauce into their mouths. They tried not to throw up from "space sickness." They brought home their food as homework. Once, a six-year-old named Sandy asked his father, "Are you eating space food, Daddy? When are you going to start floating around?" An astronaut son playing house with his kid sister was overheard by a *Life* reporter as saying, "I'm going to work, I'll be back in a week."

Geno was back from his week at the Cape, where the rookie astronauts were training for the Gemini flights. It was a pain in the ass of a thousand-mile commute to go home as often as he did, but it wasn't like he was some schmo in a Ford clanking down the Gulf Freeway. He was burning it out in his sleek T-38. And was ready to enjoy the pleasures of home. His fully stocked walk-in bar would be open for business and the hi-fi would play rock and roll all weekend long, baby.

Gene had been mowing his lawn in his sweaty T-shirt one weekend when one of the annoying Astro-tourist buses pulled over. The driver called from the window, "Hey, buddy? Any astronauts live around here?" As if he'd find Gene in a silver space suit walking his blonde cocker spaniel, Venus.

"I think a couple of 'em live over yonder somewhere," said Gene, pointing down the street.

Come Monday morning, Gene would return to the Cape, leaving his wife, Barbara, to deal with the critters in Togethersville. There were skunks, possums, armadillos, and cottonmouth snakes. The wives regularly found copperheads sunbathing on the hot hoods of their station wagons. Not to mention all the gawking sightseers from the space tour buses who climbed over fences to steal a glimpse of a real spaceman.

It hadn't taken Barbara long to realize how famous her husband was because he was an astronaut. On one of their many trips to Las Vegas, they'd met singer Wayne Newton. He was so taken with Gene and Barbara that he gave their daughter Teresa Dawn an Arabian colt.

Barbara's best friend was Sue Bean. Both were blonde Texans, although Barbara was more outgoing than demure Sue. There were no sidewalks in Nassau Bay, so Barbara and Sue often walked together down the middle of the street, pushing their daughters in strollers before them. They always shared their concerns. "Everyone wants to touch him," Sue mused.

"They don't just want their autographs when they get off the plane either," said Barbara.

Well, what could they do about that now? Not a thing.

Sue didn't want her man's head turned by all the women now available to him. She had met her Alan when they'd both been on the gymnastics team at the University of Texas. Soon they were doing backflips for each other. Sue always called him Alan, but everyone in the astronaut corps called him Al, or "Beano."

The man was a perfectionist, with an engineer's exacting eye for detail. He was very particular about Sue's wardrobe, favoring her in pastels. He had such a precise hand that before one of Joanne Herring's parties, Sue's friends lined up to have Alan put on their fake eyelashes for them. He could align and glue the black wisps ever so precisely. Once he even dyed and styled Sue's blonde hair, pinning it around her head like a crown of spilling curls.

On his worktable was a half-finished mosaic of the astronaut insignia for the counter of their bar. Alan would work on it late into the night when he was home for the weekend, cutting glass and porcelain pieces in lunar white, mauve, taupe. Sue thought what he was making was beautiful, but sometimes she wished he'd leave the damn thing alone so they could just enjoy their bar.

Sue wasn't sure what to think when Alan also began painting. He wore an old flight suit when he did so and kept his brushes clean and meticulously organized. They didn't even look as if they'd been used. His latest painting was of a clown, holding a red umbrella, balancing on a high wire. It was signed Al Bean, underlined.

One night, fun-loving Gene and good-time Barbara invited

them to accompany them to a party, but Alan just shook his head and muttered about his workload. Since he'd been working all week and dined out every night, when he was home on the weekends all he wanted was a good home-cooked meal. On the other hand, Sue had been cooped up at home all week and longed to go out, or at least spend some much-needed family time together. But Beano didn't want to be distracted from his art, which he tackled as he did any other engineering problem—obsessively.

The Mercury and New Nine astronauts had already undergone desert survival training in far-flung locations like the active volcano of Mount Kilauea in Hawaii and a secret location in the Nevada desert. There, in the 150-degree surface temperature heat, the Fourteen underwent a demanding course in how to "live like an Arab." In billowing white robes made from parachutes, they sat for their graduation photo in gold aviator sunglasses and dirty long underwear, looking like deranged Bedouin.

Next they went to Panama for jungle survival training. The Fourteen parachuted in pairs from helicopters over the jungle, carrying only the survival gear they'd have available in a Gemini capsule. They were to live off the land for a week. It was a once-in-a-lifetime opportunity to live in nature—and eat fireside meals of iguana kabob served on a machete tip by natives in loincloths. NASA insisted that since a spacecraft might land anywhere on the Earth, an astronaut had to be prepared for every climate and terrain. To the wives it seemed a little ridiculous—were their husbands really going to overshoot splashdown by a few thousand miles and land in the jungle? And if they did, wouldn't the natives serve *them* on kabobs? Why was NASA always finding ever more ways to keep their men away from home?

Sick of being grounded while their astronauts headed off to yet another exotic locale, Sue Bean, Joan Aldrin, and Jeannie Bassett, all part of that daisy-chained compound in Nassau Bay, had gotten to talking. It was high time they did something about these absentee husbands. The three gals decided to greet their savage beasts in Mexico City upon their return from the jungle. It was at least halfway to Panama, and was sure to be a lot more civilized and enjoyable than the Panamanian jungle.

Sharing a hotel room in Mexico City, the ladies picked a restaurant out of the travel book that turned out to be just as advertised: warm and festive, with chilies and colorful strings of lights dangling from the ceiling. They passed by a long table of women having a grand old time.

Joan spoke a little high school Spanish, and soon enough the three ladies were sitting with the locals, drinking margaritas, sampling the spicy salsas, and having a blast.

All of a sudden Joan got up and said, "We're going, get your things." She had a tendency to be dramatic, and was insistent they leave posthaste. Soon the three ladies were back on the street, a little tipsy.

"Why in the world did we leave?" asked Sue.

"Didn't you see that woman put her hand on my leg? Inching ever *upward*?" asked Joan.

The gals made it back to their hotel and woke up to find their guys strutting into the room, reeking of maleness. That was more like it.

The couples spent a few days sightseeing. The wives enjoyed

being regular wives, doing tourist things with their husbands, rather than serving as arm candy for macho spacemen in aviator glasses, playing "his charming wife." It was a too-short vacation, but it was so nice to be with their men on holiday for a change.

Buzz had smuggled a monkey onto the NASA Gulfstream that had brought them from the jungle to Mexico City. It was a miniature marmoset secured in a cage for the flight home.

Buzz named his monkey "PoPo" and left the little ragamuffin to look after Joan when he flew back to the Cape. Joan fell in love with the little guy. She fed him with a spoon and tucked him into a basket on a shelf in the kitchen. It nearly killed her when PoPo was diagnosed with terminal encephalitis. Buzz had to have a NASA doctor at the Manned Spacecraft Center give him a sniff of something to hasten him to that great jungle in the sky.

Joan was heartbroken. She swore she'd never have another monkey.

Grinning jack-o'-lanterns lined the brick entryways of all the new homes in Nassau Bay. The best part about this Halloween 1964, the first in Togethersville for the Fourteen Astro-families, was that it fell on a Saturday. That meant Daddy would be coming home for the weekend after training all week at the Cape. Putting on plastic masks and eye-patches and face paint, the slew of neighborhood Astrokids got ready to ring the bells of the Cernans' and Chaffees' and Beans' and Bassetts', hoping Cinderella would greet them at the door of her castle with armfuls of Jujubes.

With her dog "Red Dammit!" generally being a nuisance, hence his name, Faith Freeman helped her ten-year-old Faithie get into her costume. The sharp-looking Connecticut blonde was finicky about details (especially her jewelry; Faith hated to jangle). She was so busy putting on the final touches, she almost forgot that tomorrow was the first day of the month, and that she'd repeat the good luck charm she'd started last month.

Ted would be fast asleep at her side, and she'd wake him up good by screaming, at the top of her lungs, "Rabbit!" Faith had heard that yelling "Rabbit!" as soon as you woke up on the first day of the month offered a bubble of protection to last all month. Like many of the wives, Faith wasn't above using superstitious rituals to keep her man safe in the sky.

"Rabbit!" had served her well so far. She figured she'd try it again.

Truth be told, Faith was looking forward to sending her Faithie off trick-or-treating with the neighborhood kids so that when Ted got home she could settle back with him, drinks in hand, to greet the ghosts and goblins.

The doorbell rang, and Faith padded over to find a reporter from the *Houston Chronicle* at her door. He was here to find out some information.

"There's... been an accident."

Accident?

A Canada snow goose had smashed through the Plexiglas bubble canopy of Ted Freeman's T-38, sending shards of glass like gigantic plastic teeth through the intake system and causing the engine to flame out. Ted, a birdwatcher who loved geese, had punched out, but he was too close to the ground. His parachute only partially opened before he smashed down by his plane's wreckage near Ellington Air Force Base.

Faith completely lost it. Little Faithie, who hadn't left yet to go trick-or-treating, was there to hear the terrible news. Soon the neighborhood wives found out what had happened and came over to be with Faith and Faithie.

The round-robin was on fire. How could NASA have let this happen? The military had an exact protocol for how news of a death should be officially delivered. First and foremost, a man on the inside, a base chaplain or a high-ranking official, should be the one to bring the bad news to the family. But in Togethersville, it seemed nobody was in charge. The first death got the community up in arms and NASA got busy coming up with a protocol in case the worst should happen again.

On the morning of Ted Freeman's funeral, Betty Grissom kept an eye on Gus as she dressed in his least favorite color. She added the finishing touches to her black outfit: gloves, a modest gold watch.

Gus hated black. He was still sitting on the bed, slumped over his knees, head in hands. He wasn't budging or even looking in his closet. Betty knew what his intentions were—he refused to go to funerals, insisting he would only ever go to one, and that would be his own. He felt funerals were bad luck.

"I'm going back to work, I'm going to go back to work," Gus kept on repeating, hardly looking at Betty.

Finally he started putting on his formal Air Force uniform decorated with honor patches.

Betty feared it was only a matter of time before Gus crashed in his own T-38. The damn thing was too fast and dangerous, especially after Gus had been working for hours on end. He'd hop in that sporty little death trap to check on the progress of his Gemini space capsule being built at a NASA contractor in St. Louis, then zip back to the Cape. Betty didn't care to think too much about it; she had two boys to raise, and a house to clean and a yard to mow, but she strongly believed Gus was living in too many damn time zones, and she told him so.

The first Gemini mission, which Gus was scheduled to command, was only a few months away, and Betty had finally managed to convince her husband to squeeze in a little relaxation time at their ski chalet in Crested Butte, Colorado—Crusted Butt, her boys called it. They'd bought it with the Coopers, only Betty wasn't a skier like Trudy, who could fly down the mountain, so she kept the bar open and the fire burning while working on Playboy Bunny jigsaw puzzles, which proved to be the perfect decoration for the chalet bar.

Over in Nassau Bay, Sue Bean crossed her backyard and went over to Joan Aldrin's for their ritual afternoon tea. Joan's mother had been of British parentage, so teatime was always a genteel treat. The poor woman was dead now from a freak accident, having crashed in a private plane into the side of a mountain. It made it a little weird that Joan had married Buzz, a pilot, a year later.

A coppery blonde Jersey girl, Joan had always intended to become an actress. She'd received a master's degree in theater arts from Columbia University and would let you know she'd had a walk-on role on the TV show *Playhouse 90*, not to mention a couple of lines on the live mystery series *Climax!* She'd always been attracted to struggling actors and suffering artists, and there were plenty of those floating around New York in the fifties.

Then her mother had introduced her to a handsome, blond twenty-two-year-old Air Force lieutenant. His name was Edwin "Buzz" Aldrin (who when he was very young was called Buzzer by his little sister—she couldn't pronounce *brother*, and the name stuck). Buzz was the first man Joan dated that her oil executive father approved of for her, especially because he knew Buzz's father, a colonel in the Air Force. Unfortunately, there was zero chemistry between the two. Buzz went to Korea, and Joan pursued her acting career in New York.

When Buzz finished his tour in Korea, Joan's mother had been killed, and Joan, who commuted to New York and lived at home, was left alone to console her father while her own heart was breaking. She didn't lodge a complaint when Buzz pinned his Air Force "A" onto her sweater. Her father declared her off-limits to all dates while Buzz was out in Nevada working as an Air Force instructor.

A couple of months later, Joan convinced her father to go on his two-week vacation in Las Vegas, near where Buzz was a flying instructor. The night before Joan was to return to Jersey, Buzz proposed. When the minister stared into her eyes and pronounced her Buzz Aldrin's wife, Joan felt she was playing the greatest role of her life. Joan's first year of marriage was hell. The gregarious city girl was married and in a flash living at the Squadron Officers' School in Montgomery, Alabama, with a hubby who was usually away flying, or locked up inside his own head. "I was always alone," said Joan. "I was naïve; I had been brought up as an only child; probably I was spoiled. Men don't really chatter as women do, and Buzz is not a man who talks a lot. I am a talker, and I am very direct. It was hard for me, not to have him there to talk to."

The other astronauts gave him the moniker Dr. Rendezvous, because when he was earning his doctoral degree at MIT, the subject of his thesis was "Manned Orbital Rendezvous," which he dedicated to the Mercury Seven astronauts. It turned out to be the rendezvous program NASA used to get to the Moon. "Boy, he's really something," his colleagues said. "He could correct a computer." Given his proclivity for spending time with a slide rule, he wasn't exactly a scintillating dinner companion.

Buzz seemed to be able to shut off his emotions as if he were turning a valve. Part of being a good pilot was remaining totally unemotional, being on the ball and ready for anything, with the ability to make split-second decisions that saved lives. Such a man didn't necessarily make for a good husband. Buzz could be heartbreakingly cold. Joan learned that all too starkly with the arrival of PoPo II, her unwanted Christmas present from Buzz that year.

Sue Bean couldn't believe Joan put up with the animal. Just a regular old squirrel monkey, he was significantly bigger than darling PoPo I. As Sue sipped her tea at Joan's, she'd see the beast scampering around. It seemed so uncivilized! Sometimes the little fellow would run up and down on their shared fence, bare his teeth, and make obscene gestures. He was just awful to Joan. Even when she locked him in his cage, the monkey danced around, mocking her.

"Buzz, I've had it," Joan finally said. "It's either the monkey or me. Somebody's leaving."

Buzz turned around very slowly and looked at his wife silently, as if to say, *Well, what are you waiting for?*

"I've done it now," thought Joan. "I'd better just shut up."

At last came the day when she found PoPo II floating face-down in the backyard pool. Joan breathed a sigh of relief; she'd gotten her wish, though she'd never admit it. She felt very guilty about it, too.

10

The Astro-Pageant

Betty Grissom and Barbara Young were thrilled that they and their husbands were being treated to a free trip to New York and prime seats for the hit musical *Hello, Dolly!* Their husbands were going to be flying together on the upcoming Gemini mission, kicking off the new two-man phase of the space program. Since a duo would be going up in all the missions, the program took its name from the twins of the Gemini sign of the zodiac.

Gus's partner, John Young, was an animated speaker, fond of such expressions as "dam-gum-it" and "what the dickens." Nevertheless, to some of his neighbors he was basically an introverted wisp of a fellow, just the opposite of his wife, a big brunette who had a heavy hand with the eyeliner. John was a hard worker with wildly creative ideas. For him, nothing ever seemed to be right, including his Barbara.

Betty liked Barbara well enough, but couldn't help noticing that she acted more like John's mother than his wife—she was always needling him about why he didn't come home as much as the other guys. Everyone in the space burbs knew Gus didn't come home much either, but Betty didn't give him a hard time about it. She knew how hard Gus and his "space twin" had been training over the past few months.

As the commander of Gemini 3, Gus wanted to make damn sure the hatch of his capsule wouldn't blow this time as it had on his Mercury flight. The new and improved Gemini capsule was fitted with individual James Bond–like ejection seats with parachutes that would lift Gus and John away from the new Gemini Titan rocket, should the beast, which had almost double the thrust of an Atlas, explode upon liftoff.

"Gemini's a Corvette," Gus proudly told Betty. "Mercury was a Volkswagen."

His fellow astronauts had named the Gemini capsule the "Gusmobile." Gus had had such a hand in its design that it fit his wiry five-foot-five frame like a glove. The others just barely fit inside it, which might've been Gus's plan all along. The NASA contractor that built the capsule, McDonnell Aircraft, was outside St. Louis, so Gus and John shared a little two-bedroom apartment there in the months leading up to their flight. Betty thought it was a little weird how every time Gus called home, when she asked if John was there with him, he'd say no. The two were alone, living together like bachelors. Wouldn't they at least have dinner together now and then?

Betty tried to push these sorts of questions far from her mind as the couples took in the grand, gaudy spectacle of Broadway. After the play, the Grissoms and Youngs were invited backstage to meet the googly-eyed star, toothy blonde Carol Channing—*Hello, dollies!* Alas, the magic of the New York trip wore off quickly.

It wasn't too long after that a new drama opened for Betty in Timber Cove. One day she found a threatening note in her mailbox. She always opened Gus's mail for him, but her stomach bottomed out as she read the scribbled note:

> HOW CAN A GOOD FELLOW LIKE YOU WITH TWO CHARMING CHILDREN HAVE A NO-GOOD, TWO-TIMING WIFE?

It was obviously written by a woman. After all Betty's sacrifices—slaving away as a telephone switchboard operator to put him through engineering school at Purdue, sticking with him during Korea and through a time when they lived in a trailer and he only made $105 a month (and Gus later said, "She must have felt that flying equaled poverty!")—someone was writing to tell her husband that *she* was no good?

When Betty showed Gus the letter, he said he had no idea who'd sent it, and reassured his wife that he knew she wouldn't cheat on him. He told her not to pay any attention to the crazy woman who'd written the letter.

"Well, maybe I should," retorted Betty, "because if she's after *you—I'm* the one who's going to end up dead."

Gus just smiled and shook his head. "You don't pay any attention to that."

He didn't stick around to calm her fears. Come Monday morning, as always, he was off again to St. Louis. Betty tried not to think about what was really bothering her. Gus was probably screwing around on her. One particularly nasty story that circulated was that after a party in Cocoa Beach, Gus had driven Betty to the airport only to return to the festivities with another girl. Betty was the first to admit that Gus didn't come home as much as the other guys, but she always maintained that it was because he worked harder than any of them.

"I'm not saying that Gus didn't have girlfriends," said Betty, "but whenever I thought of things like that, I just tried not to think about those possibilities."

A few weeks before Gus's launch on Gemini 3, Betty joined him at the Cape. To protect her, he never wanted Betty to be there for a launch, just in case something went wrong, but this was a little treat to squeeze in some alone time before the launch. The Astrowives called it "patting the booster."

One day Gus and his space twin, John Young, took Betty for a ride along the Strip. Sitting next to her in the backseat was a young woman named Susy. Who was she? Betty didn't dare ask John, who'd ushered her into the car. The gal was skinnier than John's Barbara. "Probably younger, too," thought Betty.

They drove in silence past Cocoa Beach's low-rent motels. Then Susy piped up: "Oh, there's our old apartment."

Dry-mouthed and uneasy, Betty stayed mum, refusing to give this Susy, whoever she was, the satisfaction of acknowledging her comment.

"Okay, that's the answer to *that* puzzle," Betty thought to herself. "I guess he's been living with her."

That's why John was never around when Gus called. He'd found himself a Susy in St. Louis. Susy was probably already in the picture during the couples' romantic Broadway trip. John should've gotten a bouquet of roses thrown in his face for his performance as the loving husband.

Alone with Gus, Betty cut to the chase. "Are any of the *other* guys messing around?"

Gus wouldn't answer, so a skeptical Betty later flared her nostrils and muttered under her breath, "I guess they are."

Soon she was back home with the gossiping wives of Togethersville, and this time she had a *real* death threat to worry about. Gus had told her that someone was threatening to kill him.

"Why would anyone want to kill you?" asked Betty.

Gus was evasive about the specifics of the threat. He just told her that NASA had given him the warning. He shrugged it off.

She kept on asking for more details. "Okay, how 'bout John? Are they threatening to kill him?"

"I don't know," was all Gus said. He had been staying at the Holiday Inn and was assigned a Secret Service man.

"Everywhere I go, he's there," Gus told Betty when he called home. "I go into a bar, he's there. I go to eat, he's there. I finally just gave up, and moved out to the astronaut quarters at the Cape."

Betty was glad to hear that.

On March 23, 1965, Betty sat in her living room with the Mercury wives, old pros watching the countdown. Her boys and Sam the Dog, "a sad-eyed basset hound," were watching with them. The Grissom boys munched on fried chicken, ham sandwiches, avocado salad, and chocolate cake, washed down with milk. Betty ate skimpily. Following *Hello, Dolly!* Gus had decided to name his Gemini capsule after another popular musical, *The Unsinkable Molly Brown*. NASA absolutely hated the name, but after Gus threatened to rename it the *Titanic*, the space agency reluctantly agreed.

Over at her home in El Lago, Barbara Young was grateful for all the company she had during the first launch party starring a New Nine astronaut wife; the more the merrier. Her fellow New Nine wives were there to make sure their hostess didn't have to lift a finger. Instead of keeping the press at bay as Betty Grissom did, Barbara brought out pots of coffee and home-baked goodies for the hungry journalists camped out under a lone tree on her property. She even offered to clear her cars out of the garage so they could have shelter.

Back inside, settled in front of her TV, Barbara began to chain-smoke, an occupational hazard of being an Astrowife. She was a former art student, and her old paintings hanging around the family room raised some eyebrows.

"John looks mean this morning," said Barbara, setting down some napkins and lighting yet another cigarette, her big brown eyes glued to the television as her husband prepared to launch into space. Someone kept a flow of coffee on the burner and emptied the ashtray filled by the chain-smoking artiste. The special red emergency phone NASA installed in each astronaut's home before he went up kept ringing and ringing, but every time Barbara picked it up she was met by eerie silence on the other end. Finally, halfway through the morning, the NASA repairman arrived to fix the phone. After it was rewired, Deke Slayton called from the Cape and assured Barbara that all systems were "Go."

The reporter from *Life* magazine who had been assigned to cover Barbara's launch party gave some of the wives the creeps. They thought his questions and comments were just plain weird, and overly focused on the dark side of things—the existential meaning of it all, which Barbara was currently too preoccupied with the possibility of John blowing up to consider.

Spotted red and white with chicken pox, Barbara's six-year-old Johnny ran around screaming manically: "Daddy's got a rocket ship! Daddy's got a rocket ship!" She didn't bother trying to control him. Dashing out the front door and into the crowd of well-caffeinated newsmen, Johnny soon returned to the living room and set loose a frog he'd caught from a tin can.

The house was abuzz. The New Nine wives were taking the launch party to a whole new level, with the kind of panache that made the old pro Betty Grissom say, "One thing that has always kind of bothered me: some of the other wives, as soon as their husband is in orbit, they had their champagne. And I thought: 'What are you celebrating? They're not down yet!' " There were already cases of bubbly on ice at Barbara's. The new minimum was thirty pounds of ice. Now the regular phone was ringing off the hook, so Marilyn Lovell took control of the receiver while keeping an eye on the elaborate spread of launch party fare—shrimp and tuna casseroles, devil's food cake, deviled eggs, always deviled eggs. *Why did her journey with Jim always seem to revolve around food?* Marilyn Lovell wondered. They'd even met in their high school cafeteria! It was fate, probably, just like with her parents, who'd met in a candy factory and later ran their own chocolate shop. Marilyn had grown up in the candy kitchen of her parents' shop, watching her mother hand-dip chocolates while her father made peppermint sticks.

Applause broke out as the black-and-white television reported that the Gusmobile had landed. *Pop!* Marilyn enjoyed the champagne along with the rest of the wives.

The tremendous success meant Gemini 4 was on course to launch in June. This mission would feature the first "space walk" by an American. The Russians had just chalked up another space race victory by beating the United States to this feat. Cosmonaut Alexey Leonov floated in space on the end of a long, snakelike tether attached to his spaceship.

Jim Lovell was one of the backup pilots for Gemini 4, and

even though he wouldn't be flying this time around, Marilyn wanted to make sure she looked her best for the launch. She went on a diet, only this time she couldn't seem to lose a pound. She actually gained. When she went to the doctor, she learned she was pregnant.

What a time to have a child! Jim was not only a backup, but expected he'd be assigned to Gemini 7, an ambitious two-week mission scheduled for December 1965, right when their new baby would be due. Marilyn had a terrible feeling that if NASA learned of her pregnancy they would take the flight away from him. A pregnant wife about to pop would be viewed as a major distraction for the astronaut.

"What am I going to do?" Marilyn cried to her doctor, the same one who had once confused her with Jane Conrad. "They're going to take this flight away from him—I can't tell Jim! Please don't tell anyone I'm pregnant."

"My hand on the Bible, I swear," said Dr. Adels.

As the weeks rolled on, Marilyn's dresses were getting harder to fit into. She was four months pregnant when Jim drove her and the three kids down to the Cape to watch Gemini 4 take off. Marilyn was sick the whole way there. Jim had to keep stopping so she could go to the bathroom.

"Oh, I have a bladder infection," she insisted. She still hadn't told Jim she was pregnant, and miraculously, he hadn't noticed. He was never around long enough to notice, thought Marilyn.

They finally reached the Holiday Inn at Cocoa Beach. The Lovells were offered two one-dollar-a-night rooms for Jim, Marilyn, and the three kids to squeeze into. To stave off her morning sickness, Marilyn hid saltines underneath her pillow and nibbled away at them in the middle of the night.

"What's wrong?" asked Jim, awoken by her mousy noises. "Why are you eating crackers?"

Marilyn sighed. She had to tell him. "You'll never believe this."

"Believe what?"

"Well, I hate to tell you this, but I think...I know...I'm pregnant."

"Oh my God," groaned Jim, "pinch me tomorrow and tell me I had a nightmare."

After a while, Jim calmed down and told Marilyn he hadn't meant what he'd said, but what a shock for both of them! They decided it would be best to keep the news from NASA for as long as they could—at least until Jim had proven himself irreplaceable for Gemini 7.

Back in El Lago, New Nine wife Pat White couldn't sleep, worrying all night about her husband, Ed, who in a few hours would be blasting off on Gemini 4; he was to be the first American to step into space. Many in the neighborhood considered war-decorated Ed to be NASA's "next John Glenn." He'd certainly proven himself El Lago's hero a few months before.

The Armstrongs, the Whites' next-door neighbors, had been awakened in the middle of the night by the smell of smoke, to find their entire living room wall in flames. Ed White, who had almost qualified for the Olympic high hurdles, cleared the six-foot fence dividing their yards, landing in the Armstrongs' backyard. Neil handed his ten-month-old son through a window into the safety of Ed's arms. The story of Ed's heroics spread like wildfire. Strong, athletic, and redheaded to boot, "Red Ed" did indeed seem to be the next John Glenn. He stood out in the neighborhood full of workout-obsessed, overachiever astronauts, up at the crack of dawn, jogging around the suburban streets, decked out in sweat clothes. He made the younger wives in the neighborhood swoon. At one of their gatherings, they crowded around the window to watch him go by.

Delicate-as-porcelain Pat had met Ed at a fall football weekend at West Point. Even after a dozen years of marriage, she was still very much in love with her husband. She loved that Togethersville thought of him as a hero. She'd happily go to the end of the Earth with Ed, to the Moon, maybe even the White House. He had a kind and attentive manner that some of the other spacemen in the neighborhood lacked. Just like John Glenn, Ed always tried to be home with his family on Friday nights.

On June 3, 1965, Pat sat on her bed and watched Ed taking off with his Gemini space twin, Jim McDivitt. This was the first flight to be directed from the new Mission Control at the Manned Spacecraft Center here in Texas. Previously flights had been controlled from the Cape. As would become the tradition, NASA had installed in Pat's house a "squawk box," an amazing space-age device that let her tune in to the transmissions going on between Ed in orbit and Mission Control. The mission would take four days, so along with the box in her living room, NASA had installed one in her bedroom so that she could go to sleep listening to her Ed, coordinating her own sleep schedule in Texas with his in space, and silently wishing him sweet dreams. Of course, there were limits. She'd been told that in case of an emergency, NASA would shut the box off, so Pat knew things were going all right as long as it squawked.

Still, she chewed on a pencil, and when the doorbell rang was presented with a beautiful bouquet of gladioli from Ed. While only the launch could be televised, he knew she'd be listening in the rest of the time, so he had timed the delivery to only a few minutes before he took his first step into space.

In grand Texas style, Lyndon Johnson was trying to do everything at once, pushing through the greatest triumph of his presidency while sowing the seeds of his destruction. With his Great Society program, which included the establishment of Medicare, Medicaid, and the Voting Rights Act of 1965, he hoped to save America's soul. At the same time, he was planning to increase the country's involvement in Vietnam, adding another 50,000 to the 75,000 American soldiers already there.

He welcomed the festivities of June 17, 1965, when he faced Ed White and Jim McDivitt in the Rose Garden and hailed them as "the Christopher Columbuses of the twentieth century." Especially Ed, for performing the first American space walk.

He could not celebrate without thinking about the large numbers of American troops lost just the week before at Dong Xai, when the Vietcong had overrun an American Special Forces camp. The weary president hoped the spacemen would provide some relief and optimism, saying, "Men who have worked together to reach the stars are not likely to descend into the depths of war and desolation."

The space twin families had been invited to stay overnight at the White House. Lady Bird ordered a Walt Disney movie to be "laid on" for the Astrokids while their parents headed to the State Department, where the astronauts would narrate for Lyndon, Lady Bird, and a host of politicians a screening of the footage, in color, that they'd filmed of their trip into space. The lights dimmed and everyone watched spellbound as Ed, bulky in his white marshmallow space suit, pushed himself out of his spacecraft and into the void. The only thing keeping him from drifting off into space was a twenty-three-foot umbilical cord. He squeezed a gun that squirted invisible puffs of gas to change his position, twisting his body above the beautiful blue Earth.

His visor was gold-plated and it covered his face. "This is fun!" faceless Ed had said as he floated.

Some said they heard an infinite longing in his voice. He was rumored to be experiencing the "ecstasy of the deep," a sort of space narcosis or euphoria. When his twenty-minute space walk was over, he wasn't ready to return to the capsule. He was having the time of his life.

"Come on," Jim McDivitt had coaxed from inside the capsule. "Let's get in here before it gets dark."

When Jim's efforts to reel his partner in didn't work, Mission Control worried things were getting dangerous and sent up an ultimatum. Finally Ed relented, but as he climbed back inside the capsule, he'd confessed, "It's the saddest moment of my life."

Lady Bird called it "a thrilling, incredible, heart-in-the-throat moment." She wrote about the evening in her diary, "This was one of those incredible days that would make a book." LBJ was elated. Ed White was his own John Glenn, not a little fellow, but big and tall like Lyndon Johnson, and with a sweet little lady who wouldn't *dare* shut him out of her house. The president had big plans for Ed White, who, when asked how he was feeling during his space walk, said, "Red, white, and blue all over." At the close of the film LBJ unveiled a Texas-size surprise.

"This may not make me too popular with your families," said LBJ, glancing at the Pats—Pat White and Jim's wife, Pat McDivitt. "But I am going to ask you tonight—in the very next few hours—to take the presidential plane and travel outside the country, again."

The astronauts and their wives wouldn't be spending the night at the White House as planned, but instead would leave at four in the morning to attend the American Air Show in Paris. There the astronauts would have a meeting with two Soviet cosmonauts, including the first man in space, Yuri Gagarin. It was sure to be a vodka-fueled meeting.

After preflight drinks at the White House, Lady Bird led the Pats through her office into her private dressing room, with the promise of finding evening dresses, at least one for each. "After all, what does any woman think about when she hears she is going to Paris—clothes!" Lady Bird wrote in her diary.

To her delight, it turned out the Pats were both a size ten. "That's great—so am I," Lady Bird noted approvingly.

Picking up her First Lady's telephone, Lady Bird called her secretary and suggested they put on an impromptu fashion show. The Pats were getting a very rare privilege indeed. "Maybe 'Le Grand Charles' might invite them to a reception," cooed Lady Bird, referring to France's president, Charles de Gaulle.

The Johnsons' two teenage daughters volunteered to babysit for the Astrokids while their parents were in Europe. As the helicopter lifted from the White House to deliver the couples to Air Force One, waiting at nearby Andrews Air Force Base, Pat waved an excited good-bye to her seven-year-old Bonnie and her son, Eddie III, who were standing with Luci and Lynda on the lawn in pajamas and robes.

Jane's husband, Pete, went up next with Trudy's Gordo on Gemini 5. Perhaps influenced by his rootin'-tootin' grandma who'd ridden a covered wagon westward when she was a girl, Gordo picked the image of a wagon for their mission patch, with the slogan "8 Days or Bust."

Afterward, their worldwide tour, which had become a new tradition, took Trudy and Jane to Haile Selassie's Jubilee Palace in the heart of Addis Ababa, Ethiopia. When the plane doors opened, a noble and slightly bored lion greeted them at the top of the metal steps and had to be led down with great ceremony before they could disembark. Two chained leopards greeted them on the palace steps, which smelled of big-cat urine.

In the middle of the night, Jane awoke to find palace servants at the foot of her golden swan bed, which Queen Elizabeth had recently slept in, gathering her clothes to be washed and pressed by morning. Throughout the Middle East and Africa, Pete and Gordo were presented with the traditional props of tribal warrior heroes, Masai spears and jewel-encrusted daggers (and cigarette cases). Haile Selassie presented Jane and Trudy with bracelets of gold and elephant hair. In Kano, Nigeria, the emir, in his royal robes and a striking turban that revealed only his eyes, took Trudy and Gordo aside and asked if they would consider leaving their teenage daughters, sixteen-year-old Cam and fifteen-year-old Jan, to join his harem.

A week before liftoff of Gemini 7 (which was going up eleven days before Gemini 6, with the two craft scheduled to "rendezvous" in space), the NASA electrician was installing Marilyn's squawk boxes and emergency phone when the Lovells' collie, MacDuff, bit the poor man in the crotch of his pants. MacDuff got him bad, and it was a good thing the doctor lived next door. It was general chaos with Marilyn running around in a flap when Susan Borman arrived to take her to a wives' coffee at Marilyn See's house on the lake in Timber Cove. It turned out to be a surprise baby shower! It was a real shocker to Marilyn. Pacifiers and white leather baby shoes were lovingly hung from boy-blue ribbons affixed to the chandelier. Marge Slayton and Jo Schirra were there along with the New Nine gals, who had all chipped in to buy Marilyn a beautiful rocking chair.

"Did his voice change?" asked Marge when Marilyn recounted the harrowing NASA technician dog-bite saga.

Life snapped away, but was very nice about not taking a body shot of Marilyn, who hated the sight of herself full-Moon pregnant. In case the stork came while Jim was in space, he had arranged for a "crew" and "backups" for taking her to the hospital:

1. Call Pete and Jane Conrad, who live a few blocks away.
2. Call Ed and Pat White if the Conrads cannot be reached immediately.

Ever since Jim had found out she was pregnant, he'd been teasing Marilyn that he hadn't been home long enough to get her pregnant. "If the baby has a gap between his teeth, we'll know Pete Conrad is the father," he joked.

"Gaps run in my family, too!" Marilyn laughingly reminded him.

Before Jim left for space, Marilyn told *Life*, he cleaned out the garage, balanced the checkbook, and gave the old bassinet a fresh coat of white paint.

Blown up like a balloon, a very pregnant Marilyn smiled broadly for the magazine's embedded photographer. Jim would be going up on December 4 and spending two weeks in orbit, seeing if humans could survive up there for that long. Jim had always gone with his family to get the Christmas tree, but this year Marilyn decided to pick it out the night before he came back. She'd invited the neighbors to come decorate it with cranberries, popcorn, and gingerbread cookies.

Susan Borman's Frank was commanding Gemini 7, and she and her two boys, Ed and Fred, went down to the Cape to watch the launch. Overcome with the emotion all the astronaut wives felt during liftoff, she couldn't help but show it.

The newspapers printed the most devastating pictures. Susan was so upset that her face practically looked red in the black-and-white photos. In one, she was covering her face with her hands, hiding the tears running down her cheeks. Marilyn felt guilty when she saw those pictures. She was afraid that in comparison to Susan, America might think her uncaring.

Back in El Lago, looking at the pictures of Marilyn smiling for Jim, how could Susan not face the obvious? It didn't look good for an Astrowife to appear so distraught and worried. If Susan wanted to do her part to get Frank picked to go to the Moon, she'd have to steel herself and show she had the right stuff like he did. Frank always maintained the tough-as-nails, brash, rally-the-troops manner he'd adopted when he was a test pilot instructor at Edwards.

"Next to my old boys," said Marge Slayton on behalf of the Mercury wives, "I like him the best."

Susan did her best to keep calm over the next two weeks until her husband finally came back to Earth. She called the scene unfolding at her house the Death Watch. When Gemini 7 finally splashed down, the cases of champagne were brought out and the corks popped.

11

The Lemon

One foggy, snowy February morning in 1966, New Nine astronaut Elliot See was flying his T-38 toward the runway of the St. Louis airport. Down below, directly adjacent to the airport, was McDonnell Aircraft Building 101, where his Gemini 9 capsule was being built. Elliot and Charlie Bassett, who sat behind him, were there to see the finishing touches. Behind them in another T-38 were their Gemini 9 backups, Gene Cernan and Tom Stafford. Elliot zoned in for landing, but miscalculated his approach. He turned a sharp left to compensate and slammed into the roof of Building 101, sending his T-38 spinning like a pinwheel into the parking lot below. It burst into flames and exploded. Both men were killed instantly.

Astronaut John Young knew the new NASA protocol. Because Elliot See's wife lived down the street from the Lovells, he called Marilyn Lovell and told her that there had been an accident. As soon as she was assured it was not Jim, he instructed her to go around the corner to be with Marilyn See.

Marilyn Lovell couldn't believe what she was hearing. "You want me to be the one to tell her that Elliot was killed?"

"No," he said. "I want you to do something much harder—not tell her. She can't be told anything until I can come over and tell her officially. We don't want some overeager newspaperman knocking on her door."

It was shortly after 9 a.m., and having received similar orders, Jane Conrad dashed across the street, curlers flying out of her hair like plastic tumbleweeds as she ran. She tried to take out the rest and hid them in the pocket of her housecoat as she stood on Marilyn See's doorstep. Trying to catch her breath, she rang the bell.

Marilyn looked confused to see her this early in the morning. Jane had to pretend she'd just popped in for a friendly visit. Marilyn invited her in for a cup of coffee and the two went back to the kitchen. Soon the doorbell rang again. Jane knew what was about to happen; she had been dreading getting such a visit for years. But it wasn't John Young at the door. It was Marilyn Lovell, who came into the kitchen, also in curlers (she had just bathed her newborn, Jeffrey, and fortunately the baby nurse was there, so she could leave). She glanced at Jane. They could see they were burdened with the same shattering news. How could they explain both of them visiting this early in the morning?

Marilyn See poured another cup of coffee, but the wait was excruciating. Marilyn Lovell was so nervous, she could barely hold her mug, so she lit another cigarette, forgetting about the one still burning in the ashtray. As she tore off a match, her hands shook as she tried to light it. Staring at her strangely, Marilyn See exclaimed, "Marilyn, you're a chain-smoker!"

Finally the doorbell rang. John Young looked desolate as he delivered the news. Marilyn See began to cry and the three of them didn't know what else to do but huddle around and hug her. Still, no time could be wasted. Marilyn Lovell raced out the back door to pick the See children up from school, praying she'd get there before the press got to them.

After the news of Ted Freeman's death had been so bungled by NASA and the press, Togethersville banded together more than ever, especially protecting its widows and wives from the outside world. Family and neighbors dropped everything and started arriving at Marilyn See's and Jeannie Bassett's, ready to stay all day if they had to.

After hours of phone calls informing relatives of the news, Jane started off toward the door, but three-year-old David See hung on to her, needing to escape his mother's ceaseless crying. Jane took him home with her for the rest of the afternoon and put him into her bed to read him a storybook.

"My daddy's asleep," he said to Jane. "And now I'm going to go to sleep, too."

Over the next few weeks Jane went to Marilyn See's almost every evening around five, the hour when Jane longed for Pete to return. She also visited Jeannie Bassett. It wasn't easy for either of the widows. Jeannie, Charlie's widow, hadn't been told the gory details until she read about it in *Time* magazine. Her husband had been decapitated. Unfortunately for Marilyn, Elliot had been flying the plane when he and Charlie died. An airplane accident was always seen to be the head pilot's fault, an opinion that got passed on to some of the wives, so, in addition to heartbreak, there was also an undercurrent of blame.

Women around the country were finally organizing to stand up for their rights. In the three years since *The Feminine Mystique* had been published, the women's movement had been steadily growing. Its mission, as Betty Friedan had scribbled on a napkin, was "to take action, to bring women into full participation in the mainstream now." In the summer of 1966, the National Organization for Women (NOW) was formed, just around the time of the first official meeting of the Astronaut Wives Club. The intent of the latter was, however, quite different from NOW.

The meeting was held in the ballroom of the Lakewood Yacht Club, overlooking the inner harbor of Clear Lake. With over fifty wives in total, there were simply too many members of this exclusive club not to have official, organized meetings. In addition to the Mercury Seven, the New Nine, and the Fourteen, a group of nineteen more astronauts was added in April 1966. The new boys called themselves, tongue in cheek, the "Original Nineteen." Everybody wore handwritten nametags. Upgraded to sophomore status, one of the Fourteen wives peered down to read the names of the incoming freshmen, like Jan Evans and Gratia Lousma.

"I hope one day we don't need the nametags anymore," she said sweetly.

It was 10:30 a.m. on the first Tuesday of the month, which would be the day for all future meetings. Though the wives would take turns acting as hostess, everybody knew that it was Marge Slayton who was really in charge. The "A.W.C." was Marge's baby, and along with Louise Shepard, she coordinated it. It was only fitting since their husbands, Deke and Alan, were running the Astronaut Office together over at the Manned Spacecraft Center. The younger wives called them Mother Marge and Lady Louise. Marge had chosen Tuesdays because it was usually such a drab day, with husbands gone until Friday. The A.W.C. was something for all of the wives to look forward to, especially the younger ones. After doing some bits of business, welcomes, announcements, updates on the last Gemini flights and the upcoming Apollo program, Marge asked if there were any questions before they settled down for coffee.

The new wives had plenty of questions. Perky Nineteen wife Jan Evans had attended a tea party at Marge's when she'd first arrived in Togethersville, where she'd seen a recent picture of the Mercury wives next to a photo taken of them at the beginning. Marge had arranged them in their frames side by side as a conversation piece. It was amazing how different the two photos looked—from babes in the woods, some a little chubby or a little frumpy, to strong, confident women in full command of their position as astronaut wives—as dramatic a change as the "before" and "after" pictures in a magazine makeover. How did the Mercury wives do it? The new wives were itching to know, but in a group of fifty women, each of whose husbands was jockeying for the upcoming Apollo missions, they were afraid of asking the wrong questions. What if a gal said something that might reflect badly upon her husband? The ballroom fell silent. There were no questions.

On her own time, Rene Carpenter visited newcomers, who were often in awe of how glamorous she was. Rene dropped by one new wife's house wearing a chic pale blue blouse. Waving her hand in a circle, Rene told her, "You only get to go around once." The moral the new wife took from these words was: savor every minute of it because you only get one life to live.

Rene was beginning an exciting new career. Gus Grissom had caught wind in the *Houston Chronicle* that Rene had been offered a syndicated newspaper column. After going to the trouble of having no windows put on the front of his house, Gus didn't want to worry about the press coming in through the back door.

"So, you gonna write about me?" he asked.

"No," Rene assured him. "You're not interesting enough."

Her woman's column would be exploring what it meant to be a wife, a mother—friendships, relationships, that sort of thing. (She first had to come up with twenty sample columns to prove her writing prowess.) Rene also let Gus know that having a job was something she needed to consider, especially now that her and Scott's marriage was beginning to dissolve.

Gus was relieved. Ever since it had been insinuated that he had "screwed the pooch" on his Mercury shot, Gus had come back with a vengeance. He'd piloted the first Gemini mission and now he was going to command the first Apollo mission. "I didn't give a good goddamn about the White House, but my boys did, and Betty did." Gus laughed. "Look at her, she's still mad."

Rene had come up with a name for her new column, A Woman Still, inspired by a verse from an Edna St. Vincent Millay poem: "A flutterer in the wind, a woman still: I tell you I am what I was and more."

In one of her columns, Rene tackled the dynamic of the original group of seven wives. "Now at a call we run across lawns with uncombed hair, drive at unsafe speeds to hug and hold, make coffee, fix a drink and wipe the kitchen counter."

The Mercury wives liked Rene's columns, which Jo cut out religiously and pasted into her scrapbook. Fan letters started pouring into Rene's mailbox. She was writing three columns a week. It was hard, rewarding work. Editors around the country admired her unique voice. Soon thirty-five papers picked up her column. There was a thumbnail-size picture of her next to her byline.

Talk show host David Susskind invited Rene to be on his show. Susskind was known for flicking his cigarette ashes over his shoulder and stopping the evening's show when he was bored or too tired to continue. Guests were ushered onto his acid green and purple felt–lined set, and sat in one of his big chartreuse lounge chairs. He asked Rene about being an astronaut wife, how she'd coped.

Rene slipped into her Primly Stable role, and Susskind loved it. She was such a smash that people wondered if she might host her own show. Certainly her personality could carry one. In December 1966, Neil Simon's *The Star-Spangled Girl* opened on Broadway. The title character had actually been inspired by Rene, whom he'd met at a New Year's Eve party in New York.

"Eclipsing the Astronauts," headlined a *Newsweek* feature. "There may be a rising TV star in the family of astronauts—Rene Carpenter, wife of spaceman Scott Carpenter. She is witty, strikingly blonde and the author of a highly personal column..."

There was a fuss over Rene, but her home was in Houston. Her kids needed her. Still, her days in television were far from over. She would later get to appear twice on *The Tonight Show* as a guest of Johnny Carson, and cohost for one night the top-billed *Mike Douglas Show*. One of her guests was producer/director Mel Brooks. Rene talked about the columns she'd written on high-pressure schools and sex ed, and in the cooking segment, shared her recipe for taco pie.

A year after the T-38 accident, both Charlie Bassett's and Elliot See's widows were still lingering in Togethersville. Military custom dictated that when a man gets killed, his wife leaves right away. Her presence alone is an unwelcome reminder to the troops. But the two widows didn't want to uproot their kids from school. Besides, neither had finished college or had any job experience. At least they had their $100,000 *Life* insurance policies.

Everybody kept on telling Jeannie that she could afford to wait a year before making a decision about whether she should go or stay. Meanwhile, snide remarks bounced around Togethersville like, "They're coddled in this program. If they were Air Force, they'd have thirty days to get out and nobody would ever have heard of them." From tough former Air Force wives, "Bitterness, of course, is a part of grief... but people are supposed to get over it after a while."

The men were even worse. Deke claimed that "Elliot See flew like an old woman," and that's why he crashed the plane and got himself and Charlie killed. Nevertheless, Marilyn See stuck it out through a year of dirty looks and hushed silences. It was Jeannie Bassett who first decided to get the hell out of Togethersville. As she put it, "When you're in the program, you're *in in in*. Then something happens and you're out. I don't want to hang around and be the big happy fifth wheel." She packed up and headed off to San Francisco. Besides, as *Life* quoted Jeannie, "My daughter has two great dreams. One is to meet the Monkees, the other is to have a new father." Actually, ten-year-old Karen wanted her old daddy back. Without knowing it, Jeannie was moving into the teeth of the 1960s, the Summer of Love just around the corner. The wives gave her a coffee before she left—and the gift of a golden whistle with the message: "If you need us, whistle."

* * *

The Apollo program seemed to be beyond any individual's control. The space program was going corporate. Gus didn't get the same sort of input into the design of his capsule that he'd had with the Gusmobile. NASA was still determined to get a man on the Moon before the decade was out. One of the workers at the NASA contractor North American Aviation, which was building the Apollo capsule, told Gus the deadlines were so draconian, they'd ship the spacecraft "ready or not." No one was listening to Gus's complaint—not only was the Apollo ship not a Corvette, it was worse than a Volkswagen.

Coming into the kitchen one morning before he left for the Cape, Gus held up a giant Texas lemon he'd picked from the tree in their front yard.

"What are you going to do with that lemon?" asked Betty.

"I'm going to hang it on that spacecraft," said Gus, kissing her good-bye. Considering the slapdash way he thought North American was assembling his ship, he figured that's what it was.

A lemon.

After he left, Betty considered the situation. Gus was down in the dumps. There was no humor in his voice, which just wasn't like him. He liked to be havin' "a ball," but he made no effort to hide his disapproval of Apollo 1.

There was some good news. His upcoming Apollo 1 mission would only be testing the new lunar spacecraft in orbit, but soon enough, he'd also be going on another Apollo mission, the one that really counted. Gus had told Betty that Deke, who was now in charge of flight assignments, had tapped ole Gus to be the first man to land on the Moon.

On the Cape's Launch Pad 34, the lemon was perched on top of the giant Saturn IB rocket, a 141-foot behemoth that in a month's time, on February 21, 1967, was scheduled to take off with 1.6 million pounds of explosive liquid oxygen thrust. Betty didn't know exactly what about that capsule worried him, since she always told him not to bother her with the technical details, just tell her as much as she needed to know.

The night before a prelaunch test, he called home to check in.

"Can you promise me one thing?" said Betty.

"What's that?"

"Don't do the flight before you are ready."

The following morning, January 27, 1967, Gus climbed into the Apollo 1 capsule with his crew, Roger Chaffee and the "next John Glenn," Ed White. This was a dress rehearsal for the actual flight, so while the booster was not fueled, the Apollo 1 capsule would be sealed and pressurized with pure oxygen as they ran through everything, including a T-minus countdown.

Tensions were high on the launch pad with a string of goof-ups that Gus called his colleagues out on. "How do you expect us to get to the Moon if you people can't even hook us up with a ground station?" he radioed from inside the capsule. "Get with it out there!"

It was a drab Friday evening on Pine Shadows Drive in Timber Cove when Betty heard the doorbell ring. She hoped it was the deliveryman. She had bought herself a late Christmas gift, a modern new sofa, upholstered in a rich cream silk embroidered with cheerful orange blossoms. Gus had promised her one for years and she'd finally gotten the go-ahead. Betty had put up with the same dingy furniture since Enon, Ohio, because Gus preferred putting his cash into fast boats and cars. He'd even started a company with Gordo and Jim Rathmann called Performance Unlimited to design and build a race car for the Indy 500.

Peering through the small peephole in her orange door, she saw her freckled redheaded neighbor Adelin, whose husband, Jerry, was in charge of the Apollo program's landing and recovery unit.

"Hi," Adelin said. "I guess the poker game is off."

Betty gave her a serene, almost devious smile, and she relaxed. It was the norm for husbands to stay late at the Manned Spacecraft Center, though Jerry usually tried to come home early on Fridays so he and Adelin and the Grissoms could play poker with a few other neighborhood couples. It now looked as if Gus wasn't going to be flying home until tomorrow.

"Shucks," said Betty. "Well then, Adelin, let's you and I have a little drink."

Betty made two gin and tonics. Adelin was hilarious, always telling funny stories like the one about the time she had to go to the bathroom in a four-person passenger airplane with no toilet. *"Oh God yes."* She had to go so bad that she went in an upchuck bag and made everybody sing so they wouldn't hear her. They were giggling and happy when Jo Schirra walked in from next door, arriving via the rabbit hole. Her face looked flushed.

"There's been an accident at the Cape," said Jo. "I think Gus was hurt." She explained that she had gotten a call that something bad had happened on the launch pad, adding that "nobody knows how serious." She told it to Betty straight; she wasn't about to try to hide anything from her friend. But Betty knew this was it. "It's over," she thought.

The next minutes were the longest, and worst, of all their lives. The three women just sat there, trying to talk and drink their drinks. When Dr. Berry, the astronauts' physician, arrived with his black bag they even knew the worst had happened. He'd come with the official word. Betty didn't break down. She told Adelin that she'd "already died 100,000 deaths." If you could be trained for this, Betty had been.

Her older son, Scotty, took his mother's stoic lead. Mark, who was thirteen, asked, "Can I still come and get my shots in your office?"

"Sure. Of course, son," the doctor said.

With that, Mark turned his back and walked away. Betty's worst nightmare had come true. Gus, veteran of both Mercury and Gemini, had been killed, along with fellow astronauts Ed White and Roger Chaffee, during a prelaunch test for the Apollo 1 mission, on the ground.

Over in Nassau Bay, twenty-nine-year-old Martha Chaffee was clearing the table after giving her two young kids dinner. Even when she wore her "at home" slacks and went barefoot, she always put on her makeup. Only her short frosted blonde hair, cut in a mod style like the model Twiggy, was not as perfectly groomed as usual. It showed signs of going a little feral, but she had an appointment at the beauty parlor the next day. She and Roger were supposed to be going to the annual Time-Life dinner-dance gala on Saturday night. All of the astronauts and their wives were to attend. Roger was flying home tomorrow in time for it.

The doorbell rang. At the door was Sue Bean. Sue smiled sweetly. "I thought you might like some company."

Then another Fourteen wife, Clare Schweickart, appeared,

and then a neighbor whose husband worked for IBM. They told Martha there had been an accident; that's all they knew.

Martha thought, "It can't be Roger... he isn't flying tonight."

She felt a terrible urge to scrub the kitchen floor and wash the windows. She went into the family room and fluffed up the pillows. Then the gentlest of the astronauts, Mike Collins, came to the door, and Martha *knew*. His wife, Pat, had already arrived.

Mike was struck by how beautiful Martha looked that night. "I have to talk to you," he said as he led her to sit down. Martha had to coax the news out of him because he was having such a difficult time delivering it.

"Mike, I think I know, but I have to hear it," Martha said.

She felt as if she were outside of herself, looking down at what was happening. Martha felt bad for Mike, because he was having such a hard time. All three astronauts testing the Apollo 1 capsule were dead, he told her. A flash fire in the highly pressurized, pure oxygen environment of the sealed cockpit had burned them alive. The hatch had been impossible to open. The NASA technicians and doctors were still trying to figure out how they died, whether from asphyxiation or from burns.

Mike asked if she wanted to tell her children. How to explain the finality of death to an eight-year-old and a five-year-old? Martha didn't think they even knew what the word meant. She brought in her kids and, calling them "sugar," told them that something had happened to their daddy. Martha worried that her youngest, Stephen, wouldn't even remember his father because Roger had been gone so much of his life.

In Timber Cove, the Grissoms' house was filling with astronauts and their wives, as well as some security people who had been sent over under the guise of protecting Betty from the press. Betty wasn't fooled. She knew they were really protecting NASA from what the loosest cannon in Togethersville might shoot off about that lemon.

All of Togethersville was ready to hold up its end of the social contract and take care of ole Betty, at least for one night.

Jobs were delegated, but Betty didn't want to give away any of her responsibility. Dr. Berry volunteered to call Gus's parents in Mitchell. But Betty wouldn't hear of anyone else letting Dennis and Cecile Grissom know. That awful job was hers.

Some of the men said Gus had died within seconds—seconds, and that to Betty's mind meant that he hadn't suffered. "They didn't feel anything," said Betty, as she looked to the TV for more information.

All of a sudden, glancing up, she saw a woman sporting a perfectly coiffed hairdo.

"No reporters!" screamed Betty, only the lady wasn't a newswoman. She was New Nine astronaut wife Pat McDivitt, who'd just gone to the beauty parlor.

Betty's neighbor, Wally, was put in charge of making the arrangements for the funeral. "What do you want?" he asked her.

"The whole nine yards," Betty told him. "The whole thing, whatever they do, do it."

NASA called Betty to inform her that a NASA Gulfstream would fly out of D.C. to pick her up and fly her to Gus's funeral in Arlington. But NASA wasn't going to start pulling anything over on Betty Grissom. Being the most senior of the widows, she insisted she get to fly out on the Gulfstream already parked in Houston. "How about the Houston airplane?" she kept asking until NASA finally rejiggered the plans.

Having heard the terrible news on the airwaves—*the capsule on fire, and everybody burning up*—Betty's hairdresser figured her client could use a touch-up. Betty had a standing Friday appointment for a shampoo and set, and had gone just that morning. She had come a long way from the plainspoken Hoosier who once upon a time had refused to have her makeup done for the Mercury wives' first *Life* cover shoot.

"I can't let you go to Washington looking like that," the hairdresser said.

All the wives sitting with Betty followed her down the hall to her bedroom. Betty closed her eyes and allowed herself to relax in the girl's expert hands. The kind stylist also worked her magic on the other wives. Betty still pretty much followed Gus's orders of "Don't mess with your hair."

Over at the Whites' home in El Lago, Susan Borman sat with Pat White for hours as Pat cried her eyes out. The following night, after seeing the capsule burned like a "fire-blackened charnel house," Frank and Deke held their own version of the Irish wake, smashing glasses and watching a NASA man perform handstands. Frank felt very strongly about Ed White. He thought Ed was marvelous.

Back in his Edwards days when a guy bought the farm, famously tough Frank took a moment to be glad it wasn't him. He never got all "clanked up," but remained stoic and quiet. After the fire, his face was stripped of its fighter pilot unflappability. In the days and weeks to come, Pat White asked Susan her terrifying questions.

"Who am I, Susan? Who am I? I've lost everything. It's all gone."

After the fire, Martha Chaffee woke up in the middle of the night and realized she'd unconsciously switched to Roger's side of the bed to be closer to him. Her two kids, Stephen and Sheryl Lyn, were sleeping right beside her. The doorbell was ringing. It was astronaut Gene Cernan from next door. He'd been out at the Apollo contractor North American in Downey, California, and had flown home to be with her and his wife. Martha cried all over him, because he was a man, and they'd been such good friends ever since Purdue.

The cars lined up to make the trip out to Arlington National Cemetery. "I'm in the first limousine this time," Betty said to the other Mercury wives. "Catch up to me."

The flag-draped wooden coffin was in a caisson drawn by six black horses; three were riderless with their saddles empty. The trees at Arlington were gray and barren; it was the dead of winter. Rifle shots sounded, then a bugler played "Taps" as three jets roared overhead in a "missing man flyby," with one peeling off in memory of the fallen astronaut. It was very moving.

Betty wore navy blue, seeing as how much Gus hated black. She squinted at the wives, watching suspiciously to make sure they acted appropriately.

Gus's six Mercury colleagues were the pallbearers. When Betty saw the old gang together again, she thought, "Gus was a lick above them all." She figured they all knew it, too. Why else had they dismissed him as a naïve Hoosier from the beginning?

Gus had been picked to fly the first missions of both the Gemini and the Apollo programs, and Betty knew if he had lived, he would've been the first man to walk on the Moon. Where were the others now? Scott Carpenter was now working as an "executive assistant to the director" at the Manned Spacecraft Center and as an aquanaut. Chief Astronaut Al and Coordinator of Astronaut Activities Deke, while in charge of the Astronaut Office, were both grounded from flight. John still peacocked around like he owned the place, but he was retired from NASA and working as an executive for RC Cola. Gordo was still with the agency but too cocky about his skills, not giving his all to learn the new technology. Wally was still flying, but today he was just plain irritating Betty, standing too close to her side by the grave. She was pretty sure that Wally had been assigned to babysit her, but Betty didn't think she needed any damn wife-sitter! She could handle herself perfectly well on her own, thank you very much.

As her Gus was lowered into the ground, LBJ bent down to whisper into the widow's ear.

"What did he say?" Wally wanted to know.

Betty hadn't heard what condolences the gloomy vulture LBJ had offered, and she didn't care to ask him to repeat them. She didn't want to play the mourning wife. Gus had always said that if he died, she needed to have a party. She had promised him she would, and besides, Betty would never be able to say good-bye. But all things considered, she thought the funeral was pretty nice.

Next was Ed White's; NASA had been terrible about where he was to be buried. He'd wanted to be laid to rest at his alma mater, West Point. But NASA had insisted he be buried at Arlington beside Gus and Roger.

Pat White was beside herself, but she didn't have the guts to stand up to NASA. Her friend Susan Borman did. Frank phoned the Pentagon and convinced them. Ed would be buried at West Point. That's what Ed's father, a major general in the Air Force, wanted. That's what his widow wanted.

The pilots roared over and the missing-man plane peeled off as "Taps" came to an end. Afterward, Lady Bird comforted Pat behind her black veil, and little Bonnie and Eddie. Pat was the only Apollo 1 fire widow who went to all three services: Gus's first, Roger's next, then two hours later she was on a plane bound for West Point. She functioned. She thought she was doing all right. Later she would remember little of those days.

"Well, I'll get a color TV for the children," Pat told the press, wanting one of the new marvels, "and we'll take a trip."

One of the astronauts had taken over Pat's business affairs, and told her, "Now Pat, you aren't going to be able to do these things for several months."

NASA was still in the ladies' business; they'd been screening their mail since the fire.

Pat shrugged it off. "It's annoying," she said to a friend, "but perhaps it's for the best. Some people send pretty nutty letters. Even obscene ones."

What would Pat do with her time now? Ed had always filled her days, even when he was off working. She had dedicated everything to him. She had cooked gourmet meals. She had handled all his correspondence.

"She just worked at being Ed's wife," said one of the wives, "and she was wonderful at it, and that was all..."

12

Women's Lib

With Deke still grounded, Marge was no longer an astronaut wife like the others, but she was Mother Marge to her girls, as she thought of the Astrowives. Her girls were going through such heartache. She knew that Betty was tough and would be all right, but what about poor pretty Martha Chaffee, and dear Pat White? Marge wanted to bring as much comfort as she could to her girls. The monthly coffees and teas of the Astronaut Wives Club served the same purpose she did: "If you need us, come."

They'd lost Jeannie Bassett to San Francisco, but Marge considered the A.W.C. a lifetime membership. Regardless of how NASA treated the space widows, considering them excess baggage, as far as Marge was concerned, Faith Freeman, Marilyn See, Betty Grissom, Martha Chaffee, Pat White, and Jeannie Bassett would always be astronaut wives.

Marge had imagined the Astronaut Wives Club as a port in a storm: the wives would see each other through trying times, offering homemade casseroles, a stiff drink, or a shoulder to cry on. But somehow, after that first meeting, her baby was failing to thrive. Nobody really opened up; they carefully skirted the big issues, and only talked about safe things.

The meetings had become routine—discussing launch parties, sharing recipes, and planning bake sales to raise money for the POW/MIA wives whose husbands were missing in action in Vietnam. The taboo subjects of depression and alcoholism, T-38 crashes and fatal fires, were strenuously avoided. So was pretty much anything that had to do with their husbands' competition and extramarital activities. And the Cape Cookies, who presented a much-loathed rival group to the astronaut wives.

One morning, with the assistance of Lady Louise, who drove in from Houston for every meeting, Marge drew up a phone tree on a blackboard that she wheeled in. She explained how, in case of another terrible emergency, they should first call the women in their respective groups who lived nearest them. She described how the wives should be dispatched to care for the woman and her children, until an astronaut arrived to officially inform her she was now a widow. God forbid it should happen again.

The women nodded—didn't they *know* this already? But Marge knew they were scared, all of them, especially the younger ones, and she wanted to put it front and center.

"Ever since the accident," said Marilyn Lovell, "I've been telling Jim I want him to be a postman. Can you imagine him delivering mail?" She added, "Nobody chases a postman but dogs." As Barbara Cernan put it, "When I'm reincarnated, I want to marry a nine-to-five man, not an astronaut."

"I think it's a wonder this hasn't happened before," said another. "Do you know how many miles they fly, all the time? And all the other things they do? It's a wonder."

The Apollo deaths haunted not just the astronaut wives, but the entire nation. LBJ was too dragged down by Vietnam to send NASA budgets unquestioned through Congress, where the term "Moondoggle" now echoed down the marble halls. The Apollo program was stalled for eighteen months as the Apollo capsule underwent redesign, and until NASA could come up with some answers to what had happened.

Gene Cernan figured that if he had to sit out on the bench for a year and a half, he might as well put his T-38 skills to good use. He was sick of hearing about the antiwar protest movements raging around the country. It made him angry. He loved his old college pal Roger Chaffee and mourned his loss, but he also was getting leery of hearing about astronaut heroism all the time when his old Navy buddies, good soldiers all, were out there in Nam getting shot at every day, dying and being thrown into POW camps. That "hairy furball of guilt," as he called it, was lodged in his throat, and Geno had a powerful urge to hack it out by roaring over North Vietnam and carpet-bombing the godforsaken place back to the Stone Age. He marched over to Deke Slayton in the Astronaut Office to tell him what was on his mind.

"You can go," said Deke, "but I won't guarantee a job when you come back."

Geno stayed put.

Ten days after the fire, one of the wives was amazed to see Betty at a party, sitting in a chair, sparkling. Betty had loved and lived for Gus, but when he died, she said to herself, "Betty, you're on your own now. You have to start looking out for yourself from this moment forward."

People would call up worried that she was alone now, but Betty had to admit that things weren't all that different. "Well, I'm going to miss the phone calls," she said. "That's mostly what I had of him. The phone calls."

Some of the wives thought now that Gus was gone, Betty felt he truly belonged to her. She didn't have to share him with the program or his hobbies.

Wives would run into her in the grocery store and Betty would stop them just to chat, talking a blue streak. She told everyone that she and the boys could go right on living the way they had. "Gus always said he'd take care of us, and he did." The change was evident in Betty. There was no doubt she was coming out of her shell, turning into an extrovert. She said to one wife, "All my life, ever since I married Gus, I've felt as if I were sitting on top of a volcano."

Now the volcano had erupted, and she was free to live as she wanted. She joined a bowling league in La Porte, Texas, just up the highway, and was having her teeth capped. She had to make weekly visits to the dentist. All those years as a test pilot wife and worrying about Gus had wreaked havoc on her jaw. One day, in the window of a local antique store, she saw the sort of player piano she'd wanted all her life. Its front featured a carving of wizened old men and trees and queer little Oriental dwellings. It was made of mahogany inlaid with iridescent pink-and-green mother-of-pearl. Betty bought it.

Her fellow space widows didn't seem to be faring as well. Unable to sleep through the night, Pat White was consoled a bit by the books of Catherine Marshall, the widow of the chaplain of the U.S. Senate. Mrs. Marshall's books, touching on the afterlife, helped her during her time of need. She insisted that reading *To Live Again* might also help Martha Chaffee.

One thing in the book bugged Martha, how Mrs. Marshall said that after death there is no time. Martha considered the possibility of an afterlife reunion with Roger. "If there's no time then I'll be seventy-six and Roger will still be young—that won't be right!"

A huge framed color photo of eternally young Roger hung over the piano in the Chaffee family room. There weren't many books at Martha's save for the one Pat had lent her. Feeling like a guest in her own home, she'd walk around past the color TV and the big blowup color photo Ed White had sent her months ago of the Apollo 1 crew. She loved that one of Roger smiling, Ed laughing behind him, Gus by his side.

"They were so happy, they loved what they were doing," she thought.

Martha had never been to a funeral before Roger's at Arlington. She never did get to see her husband's charred remains; she didn't even know if he had been buried in his military uniform. During the funeral, she had just followed NASA's orders. Thirty-one-year-old Roger was the rookie, the youngest and least known of the three dead astronauts.

After the funeral, Martha worried about his headstone. Was there one? The burial had been such a blur that she couldn't recall the details.

She went to visit Roger's grave. NASA gave her a driver. There was her love. NASA had taken care of the headstone, which looked just like the rest at Arlington, white and official. She hadn't even realized that Roger and Gus were buried side by side. Seeing that made her feel better. She visited Ted Freeman's grave, Charlie Bassett's and Elliot See's. Then JFK's. There were a lot of people standing before the Eternal Flame. An older woman muttered to Martha that she used to come to Arlington to read because it was so peaceful, but now there were just too many tourists.

Frank Borman, the only astronaut assigned to the Apollo 1 Fire Review Board, visited Martha's home on Barbuda Lane several times, offering to answer any questions she wanted to ask about what had happened. Frank gave Martha the report of the investigation, all three thousand pages of it. It described a scream in the capsule, "Hey, we're burning up!" and implied that it was Roger's.

Her five-year-old Stephen hadn't talked about the accident after it happened, but that summer, a few months later, he had some questions. He obviously was trying to come to terms with his father's death.

"Why weren't the suits fireproof? Did they burn up?"

"Your daddy didn't burn up, he suffocated," Martha said, explaining that the fire had burned up all the oxygen in the capsule, and the men couldn't breathe without oxygen.

The day after, she bought Stephen Mexican jumping beans, but they stopped jumping.

"Are they dead?" he asked.

"Well, if they are," she said, "we'll make them a present for Daddy."

What would she do when school started? Like Roger, Martha hated just sitting around. She needed to be busy. She considered joining the Clear Creek Community Theatre, which Buzz Aldrin's wife, Joan, was heavily involved in. Martha applied for a job in television, but she didn't get it. Then she went to Los Angeles with a friend who had quite a lot of money. They went to lots of "in" parties. L.A. was really a happening place in 1967, its music scene exploding with Buffalo Springfield, the Mamas and the Papas, and the Byrds, who sang, "Hey, Mr. Spaceman." They visited movie sets and met movie stars.

Martha's friend wanted her to move there. "You'll get in a rut in Houston, Martha," she warned.

Back in Nassau Bay, Martha was a night owl. She'd gotten so used to Roger being away from home to begin with, it wasn't hard to pretend he was just away again, training for Apollo. Whenever she couldn't stand being alone in the house at night and had to get out, Martha would call Gene and Barbara Cernan next door and say, "I have to have a drink," then go across the lawn to their house.

Sometimes when she came home, she still couldn't shake her insomnia. It was hell, just hell.

Finally she went to the family medical center at the Manned Spacecraft Center and talked to Dee O'Hara, the astronauts' nurse. Dee cut quite a figure. She drove an electric blue Mustang, which she parked alongside the guys' hot rods. She wore her signature pink-grape lipstick and a white cap with the small red cross over her short black hair. She was friendly with the wives, but would never give away the guys' secrets. She called Martha "hon" and "dear."

"At 3 a.m., I'm still wide awake, like this," Martha emphasized with wild eyes, heavily outlined in mascara. "I'm so lonely, Dee, I'm just so lonely."

There were nights she tossed and turned for hours, holding on to her American flag like a security blanket, the one that had been handed to her at Arlington after being draped over Roger's casket. When she really couldn't sleep, she'd go out and sit on the edge of the diving board over her pool and look up at the stars and feel so close to Roger. He had wanted to go up there so badly. One night, staring at the Moon, she completely lost it.

* * *

Since her husband Elliot's death in the T-38 crash over a year before, Marilyn See had traveled to Acapulco and Mexico City, and now she was about to take off on a grand European tour. She'd been studying to be a court reporter, not just to keep occupied but to make some money to get on with her life. Before he'd joined the Navy as a pilot, Elliot had been at General Electric. That was where they'd met. Marilyn had been his secretary. Now Marilyn was ready to spread her wings and fly a little. The wives organized a bon voyage party to send her off. They gathered around, insisting she open her presents. She held up a lacy corset with a quizzical expression. The wives had sewn a padded behind onto it as a joke.

"It's because those Italian men like to pinch!" squealed Jane Conrad.

Betty was there to see off Marilyn, too. She thought Marilyn had gotten a raw deal with all of Deke's gossiping about Elliot flying like an old woman. Alan Shepard had been even worse. Marilyn had told Betty that when she had gone to the Manned Spacecraft Center to pick up some of Elliot's things from the Astronaut Office, Shepard had tried to bar her from entering. She had to drive home and call a NASA higher-up to help sort things out. Then when she went to Ellington Air Force Base to pick up her dead husband's car, the guards gave her the run-around.

While the two women were having a private chat that evening, Marilyn had a sudden idea: "Why don't you come with me?" she asked Betty.

"Shoot," said Betty. "I don't even have a passport." She

started making her usual excuses but then shifted gears. Well, why not? Her sister Mary Lou could come stay with the boys, Mark and Scott; and besides, Scott, who was seventeen, was practically old enough to stay on his own.

"I think," said Betty, "I might just take you up on that offer."

The party was on Saturday night, and come Monday morning Betty was downtown filling out the forms for her passport. As the youngest space widow, Martha Chaffee seemed to be traveling around in her own circuit, off to Los Angeles and all, but Marilyn asked the newly widowed Pat White to come to Europe, too. Pat was still grieving, and refused the invitation with a simple "I can't plan that far ahead. One day at a time."

Betty thought about Marilyn See as she packed—if Betty hadn't accepted the invitation, Marilyn would've gone to Europe alone. "I wouldn't have done that myself," thought Betty, "but then again, maybe I would."

They started their trip in New York, where they spent a few days taking in the Big Apple. *The Unsinkable Molly Brown* had long sunk on Broadway, as had *The Star-Spangled Girl. Hello, Dolly!* was still going strong, although now it was an all-black cast starring Pearl Bailey as the irrepressible widow, as well as Cab Calloway and a young Morgan Freeman.

Then they took off for Europe. Betty wasn't sure that they would get along. At thirty-five, Marilyn was still one of those "younger ones." Forty-year-old Betty was pleasantly surprised. Marilyn had planned the trip brilliantly, and the two did not have the usual sorts of trivial arguments both were used to having with their husbands on their rare family vacations.

First they went to Greece, then Italy, then Spain. If Betty had mapped out the trip herself, she would've picked the same countries. They shared rooms in charming hotels, enjoyed ordering breakfast for two, and together studied their travel guides and plotted their plans for the day.

"You always get up in the morning in a good mood," Marilyn told Betty.

That made Betty glow. She enjoyed having a companion. Gus had hardly been around enough to know what she was like in the morning.

At the top of the Spanish Steps in Rome, Betty spotted La Mendola, a world-famous boutique. Rita Hayworth and Anita Ekberg wore La Mendola's custom print dresses. They came in sherbet colors, and bore images of Roman emperors. One shift was printed with the folds of a toga, another a fabric of flames. It was of Rome burning.

Betty ignored the daunting price tags and picked out a screaming pink coatdress lined in psychedelic silk with slits high up the sides. She even bought the matching headscarf. Amazingly, who should walk into the boutique while they were shopping but Nancy Dickerson. The TV reporter inspiration for Primly Stable was the only person who recognized Betty during the entire trip.

In Spain, Betty bought a carved wooden Don Quixote statue, which she called "my little man." She didn't give a second thought to how much money she spent. When she returned to Timber Cove she even bought Gus's share of Performance Unlimited and looked forward to going to the Daytona 500 with the Rathmanns. She loved car racing. She could buy anything she wanted now. Gus had left her with that $100,000 *Life* insurance policy, some investments, and around six hundred dollars a month from his military pension. Of course, it wouldn't last forever, but it was enough to kick-start Betty's new life. She was becoming almost a textbook "liberated woman," just as women were taking up the idea across America.

In the evening, driving her twelve-year-old son, Kent, back from his afterschool activities, Marge would see the bright lights of the cold, clinical, male-centric Manned Spacecraft Center. Sometimes Marge felt ready to storm the place. The MSC stood out against the flat horizon, a flush of petrochemical red streaked across the sky with ominous-looking clouds hanging above. The exhaust from nearby oil plants, which often prevented the wives from having a private moment alone with the Moon, created the most stunning sunsets.

If someone had asked Marge (or any of the Astrowives, for that matter) what her relationship to the nascent feminist movement was, she'd probably laugh, thinking she had nothing to do with it. But in her own way, she did. Marge was trying to create a haven for women in a world of men. The Astronaut Wives Club was the closest thing the space burbs had to a NOW chapter.

And besides, there weren't many card-carrying members in NOW who could say they'd had a heart-to-heart with Janis Joplin. Marge had been attracted to the young woman, who was also from Texas, not because she was a famous R & B singer, but because she recognized a floundering soul in need.

At a social gathering in Washington, Marge had found herself seated on a sofa next to Janis, and though she didn't know that Joplin had been the star of that summer's Monterey Pop Festival, she heard the broken heart in her smoky, Southern Comfort–cured voice.

Marge dosed out some peppy, upbeat advice. There were easy

steps that could be accomplished right away. Janis might not have been conventionally beautiful, but Marge could tell she had a wonderful soul. How about pulling her frizzy hair back from her eyes? A little lipstick, maybe even a frost...

Alas, there were so many souls to save. Even Marge herself had a blues song to sing. She may have had the sweetest smile in Togethersville, but it hadn't been easy growing up on the wrong side of the tracks in Los Angeles, on "skid row," with a drunken railroad detective father. Her family was so poor that young Marge would actually peel warm asphalt from the ground and chew it like bubblegum. Finally her mother, Nanabelle, left the drunkard father, taking her two daughters with her.

"We had to go on the dole," said Marge, but Mama would never let Marge and her sister go with her to pick up the food stamps. She was a proud lady and wanted better things for her girls.

Marge had seen a lot of the world, and though she wanted her ashes to be sprinkled over Mount Fuji, it was Friendswood, Texas, that claimed her heart. Marge's home on a heavily wooded bayou in the Quaker community of Friendswood had an open-door policy. She welcomed all the wives to visit at any hour, especially the younger ones. Marge's mother, Nanabelle, lived with the Slaytons to help take care of their son, Kent, who was fast growing up.

One day, Kent asked his mother about the strange name on the Army footlocker in his bedroom, and Marge had to hedge. He wasn't quite old enough to hear about her ex-husband, but Marge laughed about this story with her friends. Apart from the occasional bump, it was smooth sailing in Marge's neck of Friendswood.

"Those beautiful Quakers!" she'd say. "I've lived in a lot of places, but if I'm from anywhere, I'm from Friendswood."

Every morning she went for coffee at the town's drugstore. Sometimes her smoking buddy Jo Schirra would drive over from Timber Cove and they'd share a Danish and cig at the counter.

"It will never be the same again, the friendship of the first Seven," Jo would complain. But Marge was hopeful for the new generation.

Taking advantage of Marge's open-door policy, Nineteen wife Gratia Lousma came to seek counsel and comfort. Things were so different in Togethersville, and the astronaut life was so intimidating, and, to make matters worse, her dog had just died. Marge was more than sympathetic. She always said that her weakness was that bladder behind her eyes. They sat on her couch hugging each other and crying—Gratia for her pup, Marge for her long-gone Acey.

One night, perhaps thinking about the A.W.C., Marge had the strangest dream that she'd had a baby, but, right after she'd given birth, she'd rushed off and left the baby at the hospital. When she finally remembered to pick her baby up, it had already learned to talk.

It was horrible.

Her dream was fresh in her mind when she walked into Togethersville's new gym, the Bayshore Club, on Monday morning. The endless launch parties had added weight gain to the worries shared at A.W.C. meetings, and while some of the wives concluded that the bigger the hair, the slimmer the body would look, others hit the shiny machines and piles of mats.

Jo Schirra, who was a faithful exerciser, was depressed. "They keep telling me muscle weighs more than fat," she said, but they'd been in exercise class for a month now and she wasn't losing girth. Indeed, she had gained three pounds. Marge sympathized. Though she'd lost eight pounds herself, she was still way overweight. She'd gained thirty when they'd moved to Texas five short years ago. *All that barbecue brisket and those trays of deviled eggs.*

After their workout Marge stopped at the club's juice bar, where Bonita, the pregnant bar and massage girl, whipped her up one of the club's signature milk-and-cucumber shakes. On the walls of the health bar were little mimeographed signs for the Bayshore Club Quick Rejuvenation Diet, which would make you look like Venus: AMERICANS ARE BECOMING MORE AND MORE HEALTH CONSCIOUS. WE BELIEVE IT IS PARTICULARLY TRUE IN THE LAND OF THE ASTRONAUTS. "FIRST CLASS PROTEINS" YOU SHOULD EAT: BRAINS 2 MED. PIECES; FOODS PROHIBITED: ANGEL CAKE. (That was before nutritionists figured out that a pound of sautéed beef brains contains more cholesterol than one needs in a year.)

Martha Chaffee joined Marge for a shake. She'd lost twenty pounds, down from a size eight to a four. Exercise was very good for pounding out all the nervous energy Roger's death had left her with. Though looking girlish and lovely as usual, Martha was feeling blue.

The two women were soon talking and crying, their arms around each other.

Martha finally told Mother Marge about the man she was dating. "He's convinced me there's another life for me, in time."

"Why, honey," said Marge, "just as sure as there are stars in the sky and that the sun comes up in the morning, there's another life for you."

It became clear to Marge that her baby, the Astronaut Wives Club, was alive and well here at the Bayshore Club, where the wives grunted and groaned their way to health.

After her workout, Pat White changed into a pretty dress, instead of the slacks or dungarees the other busy mothers wore. It was amazing how Pat always managed to leave the Bayshore looking as clean and lovely as she had coming in. Some of the gals still couldn't figure out what she did all day, not knowing that she was studying Greek literature at the University of Houston–Clear Lake. Pat had majored in psychology at school but had never finished. Now she was learning all about classical mythology, the gods and goddesses and their fate-bending desires.

Pat continued coming to exercise class, but as the months wore on, she became pale and thin. Telltale signs of stress were in the shadows around her faraway eyes. She still wasn't sleeping. It was going around that Susan Borman, who was big on religion, had been working on Pat about being Mrs. Ed White in the next life.

The other wives also noticed that Susan, conspicuously absent from the Bayshore, was often high-strung and raging about something or other when she'd drop over for a cup of coffee. Then she'd beg off and go nap for the rest of the afternoon.

Hopefully she was doing some good for Pat White, but it seemed that Pat needed a little more Beth Williams in her. Beth was the latest space widow along with Nineteen wife Ada Givens, whose husband, Ed, had crashed his VW Bug in what was rumored to be a drunk driving accident. Beth's husband, C.C., had bought the farm in a T-38 crash in October 1967 near Tallahassee, Florida. The astronaut was flying home to pregnant Beth and their one-year-old daughter.

"He died doing what he loved," the NASA administrator said when he came to make a courtesy call on Beth.

The feisty strawberry blonde didn't want his visit any more than she wanted the loaves of banana nut bread—the loaf of choice for a grieving astronaut widow. The southern belle swore like a sailor, telling NASA where they could shove their goddamn sympathy. "He didn't love NASA. He loved me. If he died doing what he loved, he would've been in bed with me."

Beth couldn't stand smothering Togethersville in the first place, and that's why she and C.C. had chosen to live in Dickinson, Texas, ten miles away. Unlike the Corvette boys, C.C. had driven a green Chevrolet pickup, which everybody made fun of when he parked it in the lot of the Manned Spacecraft Center. He had gotten several parking tickets because no cop could believe that an astronaut would drive a pickup truck with SELMA OR BUST painted on the rear. C.C. wasn't like the other astronauts, and Beth wasn't like their wives. She let it be known that if she received one more copy of *The Prophet*, Kahlil Gibran's eternal best seller, she might throw it at the well-wisher.

Even to the funeral, she'd never worn black. She'd gone wearing a sharp new suit and a gaucho hat C.C. liked.

Like Betty, Beth would be just fine. On the other hand, the wives couldn't help but notice that Pat White usually spoke of her Ed in the present tense. Pat said she often dreamed of Ed, and when she awoke in the morning she could hardly believe he was gone. She'd just *seen* him. It worried the wives how Pat clung to Ed's image as an American hero, and hers as the hero's wife. They thought that after almost a year, it was time for her to move on.

And that morbid Karmann Ghia rotting in Pat's garage? The

wives couldn't imagine *that* was helping her outlook and mental health. Ed had wanted to give it to his son, but until young Eddie III was old enough to drive it in three or four years, the sports car sat up on blocks in the garage. Pat liked having the Karmann Ghia there. She found Ed's car somehow comforting.

What about dating, Pat?

The wives urged her to get out—give it a whirl again, like Martha Chaffee, whom the Cernans had been setting up on blind dates. Martha had even let someone buy her a nice fur. But Pat seemed to be drifting ghostlike through life.

One morning Clare Schweickart went over to visit her and Pat offered to fix lunch. After they finished their meal, Pat gathered up the dirty dishes and the glass of milk she'd served Clare, and poured the half-drunk contents of the lipstick-stained glass back into the carton in her fridge. She looked to Clare like a zombie. That's when Clare vowed she would build a life for herself so that if anything happened to her redheaded astronaut husband, Rusty, she would never be like that. Clare thought it one of the most frightening things she'd ever seen.

When Pat failed to show up at exercise class, the other wives knew something was terribly wrong, especially when nobody could reach her on the phone. Someone called a neighbor, who had to break into Pat's house. Pat was found clutching a bottle of pills, which had to be wrestled from her hands.

How many did she take? What was she *thinking*? the wives asked each other. Then they helped Pat cover up what she'd done.

13

Susie

The Mercury Seven wives hosted a farewell lunch for Rene at Jo's house out by the pool. They took lots of pictures. This time, they felt, the group was really breaking up for good. Early one of the following mornings in August 1967, the Carpenters pulled away from their brick ranch house. Annie and John came out in their bathrobes to see their neighbors off. Two of the Carpenter kids, peering out from the back of the station wagon, watched the disappearing Glenns waving good-bye from their driveway. They were off to Bethesda and their new home.

Scott's heart was still undersea. During Sealab II, Scott had spent a record thirty days in deep-sea submergence living, a virtual isolation tank dropped to the ocean floor off the coast of California, hundreds of feet below the surface. Coming up from that mission, Scott had placed a phone call to LBJ from within his decompression chamber, which was filled with helium. He spoke in an Alvin and the Chipmunks voice. Now Scott was ready to go deeper on Sealab III.

In Washington, Rene was still writing her column, and becoming more political with the escalation of the Vietnam War. She was frequently invited to gatherings at Hickory Hill, Bobby

Kennedy's large white brick manse. His wife, Ethel, held a lovely welcome tea for Rene.

Set on a tract of family land in McLean, Virginia, Hickory Hill had been a flurry of activity since Bobby had thrown his hat into the 1968 presidential race. The Democratic nomination was up for grabs now that LBJ's war in Vietnam was having such disastrous domestic consequences. Since the Tet offensive in January, the war news was ever more dire, and many responsible elders were joining the youth of the country in ever larger protests against the war. After peace candidate Eugene McCarthy beat out Lyndon Johnson in the New Hampshire primary, Bobby saw his opportunity and announced his candidacy.

The scene at Hickory Hill was populated by PYGs, the so-called Pink, Yellow, and Green People. Composed of Pucci-loving socialites and Lilly Pulitzer–clad hangers-on, the PYGs lounged about Hickory Hill as if it were their own, blending seamlessly into Bobby's wife Ethel's very expensive but understated color scheme.

A true individual, Rene had her own style. She now wore her platinum hair shoulder length. A profile in the *New York Times* featured the headline "Rene Carpenter Regards Conformity as a Big Bore." Wearing a green copy of a Pierre Cardin dress for the photograph and posing with the family's fluffy white Samoyed, Rene brought political reporter Myra MacPherson into her bedroom closet, which included a vibrant orange-and-gold chiffon dress by Rudi Gernreich, designer of "the futuristic look." She usually found daring designer clothes on sale—"because I like to wear what no one else dares buy," said Rene. "I'm not the understated type. It bores me to tears." Myra even wrote about the white fur and aqua corduroy dress that Rene had worn in high school for a dance back in Boulder in 1945.

Myra included in her article Rene's vitals: just turned forty, size six, and "totally averse to wearing something just because it was 'in,'" adding, "Mrs. Carpenter willingly classifies herself as 'sort of a kook.'"

Rene said that even when she was an astronaut wife, she'd always resisted being "the professionally brave wife." Because she couldn't keep her political views under wraps any longer, she was giving up her newspaper column for a brand-new adventure—being Ethel Kennedy's right-hand companion during her husband's campaign.

Clearly, Rene was someone who was interested in more than just her miniskirt hem lengths—"from mid-thigh to three inches above the knee and she gets a sick look when anyone mentions midis," Myra dutifully reported, along with Rene's latest declaration: "I will never lengthen my skirts."

"I want to discuss issues," said Rene, ready to stump for Bobby, to make speeches to the many women's groups proliferating across the country.

Getting ready for a psychedelic-themed neighborhood party in Togethersville, Fourteen astronaut Donn Eisele (pronounced *eyes-lee*) painted "Love Bug"–style daisies on his wife Harriet's naked knees, using her eyebrow pencil and lipstick. Choosing something as simple as the right shade for the flowers, be it red or purple, could prove too much for Donn. He admitted to Harriet that it sometimes took him an hour to decide which hammer to use from the garage for a repair project. In Donn's Air Force days, Harriet had a standing request from the squadron commander to encourage her husband to get to work on time. Even now when Donn was a big-shot astronaut, Harriet needed to keep him motivated and give him the occasional swift kick in the pants.

The other wives were amazed by four-foot-ten Harriet, who wore her short dark hair in a high tease. "She's a dynamo," they said of the pint-sized, big-hearted mother of four. Harriet was indefatigable, always doing what needed to be done.

Every morning she drove her four-year-old Matt, who had Down syndrome, to a special school half an hour away in Pasadena, Texas. The class was run by the Houston Council for Retarded Children and lasted for two and a half hours. It pretty much shot her day. Harriet also had a newborn and two other children to care for, but she never complained. Matt was very special to her. He loved Snoopy and singing songs and was so good at throwing his toys up on the roof that Harriet was constantly having to climb a ladder to retrieve them. She and Donn joked that he might one day join the Major Leagues.

Harriet had been a nurse back in Ohio. One time, when she was in training, a psychiatrist needed help holding down a squealing patient for electroshock therapy, and little Harriet volunteered.

"Oh, honey, you can't, you're too little," said the doctor.

"But I've got muscles," Harriet told him as she showed him her biceps, and then she did it. After that, the doctor requested her every time and they got to be good friends.

Now that she was living in Texas as an astronaut's wife, Harriet longed to see a DeBakey heart operation. Dr. Michael DeBakey had implanted the first artificial heart in a human in 1963, having created a prosthetic artery on his wife's sewing machine. And he was right there in Houston! Harriet was so interested in what was going on in the world of medicine that the wives suspected she may have regretted having given up her career to marry Donn.

Harriet enjoyed the Love Bug party and the other neighborhood gatherings, be it shrimp boils or luaus. But she didn't like the high-society galas, at least one every weekend, which took her and Donn away from the precious little family time they had as it was. With the guys gone all week, Harriet didn't think that it was fair to their children to abandon them on the weekends. The only wife she knew who liked the galas even less was her best friend, Faye, who lived across the street in El Lago.

A pleasingly plump big-hair blonde and the Astronaut Wives Club's top pastry chef, Faye Stafford had been Football Queen back in Weatherford, Oklahoma, but rolled her eyes at the stuffy society queens at the fancy Houston parties she was expected to attend. The ladies were too far removed from her reality to understand that the astronauts lived on government salaries, no matter what perks they received. With *Life* money going to college funds, the wives really couldn't afford expensive gowns. Now, with fifty men strutting around the neighborhood calling themselves astronauts, that *Life* pie was sliced paper-thin.

"Casts-of-thousands dinners," Faye called those gatherings that were becoming more frequent as NASA got closer to landing a man on the Moon.

At one of the annual Moon Balls, while others were waltzing on the rooftop of the posh Warwick Hotel, Faye snuck out onto the veranda by the pool. She took a good long look at the Moon, thinking it (or she) must be far less hostile than the upper-crust denizens of Houston.

Though she allowed her husband, Tom, to drag her from one party to the next, Faye was a homebody. Her idea of a great evening was staying in doing needlepoint with her Pomeranian pups and her two teenage daughters. She and Louise Shepard had plans to open up a cozy yarn store, the Penelope Shop, in Clear Lake.

Faye did like going to the neighborhood get-togethers, but the nurse in Harriet couldn't help but notice her friend's many phobias. Faye didn't like flying in planes or traveling, although she'd go out to eat or shop with Harriet. In the future, Faye's antisocial tendencies would inch toward full-blown "phobic anxiety disorder," or agoraphobia. She got to the point that she was afraid of leaving her own house.

Harriet had arrived in Togethersville with her own problems. At a get-together at her and Donn's home before they'd moved to Togethersville, Harriet had walked into her bedroom to find Donn kissing another woman. Donn could be very "wishy-washy" and it didn't take much to convince him to do things he didn't necessarily want to do, so Harriet didn't make too big a deal over it, but her trust was a little shaken when she arrived in Houston as a fabulous new astronaut wife. Marge Slayton tried to make light of the situation by saying how all of the wives were in the same boat: "People throw themselves at them—it wouldn't matter if they had two heads!" But soon Harriet had bigger worries.

"No nurse ever makes a diagnosis" was one of the key tenets that Harriet had learned in nursing school, but she'd always been good at diagnosing, and it was clear to her that there was something wrong with her son Matt. Harriet noticed blood blisters on his little body; he was cranky, and just wasn't himself. She was certain the blisters were petechiae, a telltale sign of leukemia, not uncommon in kids with Down syndrome.

"I think I need to bring Matt in, but I'm scared," Harriet told a NASA doctor she saw at a party. Unfortunately, her diagnosis was correct. Matt was taken directly from the family medical center at the Manned Spacecraft Center to Texas Children's Hospital. He was in and out of the hospital for a year and a half. Only once during that time, when Donn was home from training, did Harriet ask him to spend the night with Matt in the hospital. The next morning, Donn told Harriet that he was so upset by Matt crying out in pain that he couldn't bear to stay in the room. He never stayed at the hospital again.

Matt had two remissions and was able to go back to his school for a time, but his second remission was short. In the last weeks of his life when Matt's condition was rapidly deteriorating, the doctors told Harriet, "I think we need to call Donn."

But Harriet knew she couldn't find him at the Cape. She had suspicions he was with another woman and she couldn't deal with that now. During this time, the wives supported Harriet, keeping her freezer stuffed full of Tupperware dishes, with no names so she wouldn't have to write thank-you cards. One wife came over and mowed the lawn without saying a word.

Donn was with Harriet at the hospital the day six-year-old Matt died. Harriet sat holding her little boy and Donn was on the couch. Both were devastated, but Donn rarely talked about his feelings, saying, as many of the astronauts did, "I'm not given to introspection."

Afterward, Donn flew off to the Cape, where he would begin training for Apollo 7, the first manned mission after the Apollo 1 fire, and Harriet was left to deal with the emotional fallout. Donn rarely came home the summer before his flight, and Harriet's sense that there was another woman in the picture continued to grow. Donn would give her the typical excuses, blaming it on his crewmates not doing their jobs, which forced them to work overtime. "Wally and Walt are goofing off—if I don't stay, we're all going to be killed," he'd tell her. He accused Harriet of ruining his concentration, suggesting that her pestering him with her crazy worries could also get the whole crew killed.

Then Donn started leaving clues—Harriet found out he'd been at some movie star's house (which she thought was a big deal and would have enjoyed being taken along, but Donn excused it as a trifle). She also found a matchbox from the Beverly Hills Hilton. It was as if he wanted to be caught, as if he were living a second life and wanted to get rid of his first. He kept on denying it, and when Harriet raised her suspicions, Donn bought her flowers and told her she was acting even crazier than usual. She began to be afraid that she was imagining things. There was that unspoken belief, especially among the guys, that if you got a divorce, you'd be done for. At the height of the intense competition for assignments for the Apollo program, guys aching to be chosen to go to the Moon believed selection went hand in hand with a textbook marriage. The tighter the marriage, the thinking went, the better the flight position. Broken relationships, screaming fits, no matter, as long as all this remained behind closed doors.

With his Apollo 7 flight just around the corner, Donn had

begun appealing to Harriet's friends, saying Harriet was upsetting him. Even her best friend Faye told her it was all in her head.

"You're crazy," Donn kept on repeating to her.

Harriet finally said to Donn, "If I'm really crazy, I should see a psychiatrist."

"You can't go see a psychiatrist," said Donn. "I'll lose my job."

Flying out in March 1968 to join her husband, Bobby, at his first campaign stop in Kansas, Ethel Kennedy worried about how the conservative midwesterners would react to her husband's progressive platform of civil rights and social equality, and his commitment to end the war in Vietnam. The country was bitterly divided. But when her husband touched down in Kansas City and Bobby stepped out onto the metal steps, a throng of young women were waiting at the bottom, screaming, "Bobby!" As it turned out, the girls were TWA flight attendant trainees, recruited to raise Bobby Kennedy's appeal to rock-star status with the youth of America.

In Topeka, Bobby addressed a cheering crowd in the ballroom of the Ramada Inn. "In 1960," he began, "the American people and mankind looked to John Kennedy." The crowd loved him so much that they ripped the buttons off his coat and his shirt.

That night at the governor's mansion, where the campaign staff was staying, Rene sewed the buttons back on while Bobby was in the next room, walking around in his bathrobe drinking a Heineken and eating a roast beef sandwich. The next morning, Rene awoke to a frantic Ethel knocking on her door.

"Can you please help Bobby?" she asked.

Downstairs, Bobby was having his breakfast while the governor watched in awkward silence. Neither was much for small talk, so Rene came in and saved the day.

Since the beginning of his run, journalists had been asking Bobby if he was scared that "they" were going to kill him, but Bobby just shook his head and smiled. A month later, on April 4, 1968, Dr. Martin Luther King Jr. was assassinated in Memphis. Many of America's major cities, including Chicago, Washington, D.C., and Boston, erupted in riots. America seemed to be spiraling out of control.

In June, on the night he won the California primary, Bobby Kennedy was shot in Los Angeles at the Ambassador Hotel, gunned down in the hotel kitchen. The Glenns were traveling with the campaign and staying there. Early that morning, John and Annie led five of Bobby's eleven kids from the hotel and flew them home to Hickory Hill and tucked them into bed. When they woke up, John had the terrible task of telling them that their father was dead.

On October 11, 1968, sitting at the Formica bar in the Schirra family room, Jo and Marge sat tight for the Death Watch, smoking cigarettes and watching the NBC coverage of Apollo 7. Finally back on track after the tragic fire, this first manned mission in the Apollo program was commanded by Wally Schirra with his crew of Donn Eisele and Walt Cunningham. Apollo 7 was to orbit Earth for ten days so that the crew could check all the features of the new and improved Apollo capsule.

"There's Rene!" Marge's face lit up, clicking the volume up on Jo's "Zenith Space Command" wireless remote.

Smiling on the television, wearing a poppy-red shirt and a navy blue vest, Rene sat side by side with TV's top news duo, Huntley and Brinkley.

I'VE DEVELOPED A NEW PHILOSOPHY. I ONLY DREAD ONE DAY AT A TIME. Harriet Eisele had pinned the huge *Peanuts* button onto her sweater on the day of the flight, letting it do the talking for her.

Reporting for *Life*, embedded journalist Dodie Hamblin, who was fond of Harriet, thought she was the biggest wreck she'd ever seen. Like everyone in Togethersville, she knew that the past few months had been horrible for Harriet, who didn't want to be caught in the glare of publicity.

Over the ten days of Apollo 7, Harriet cowered while the squawk box squawked its incomprehensible numbers and vectors. She was deeply disturbed by the change she heard in Donn's voice. Some felt he was clearly imitating his commander, Wally, who was being a real hard-ass to Mission Control. This was Wally's last mission and he wasn't holding anything back. But Donn unwisely followed his lead, making inappropriate remarks. He seemed to be committing professional suicide. Harriet just thought there was something different about Donn—this was not the Donn she knew.

Finally in November, a month after the flight and right before they went to the White House for the post-flight celebrations, Donn told Harriet about "Susie." Harriet actually enjoyed the trip—because for the first time in months, things were out in the open, and she knew she wasn't crazy.

Harriet thought they had achieved a new openness. Then she noticed Donn had started closing bank accounts.

"You've got to file for divorce to protect yourself and the kids," her minister told her, and she did.

The Astronaut Wives Club was called to order at the Lakewood Yacht Club. One word silenced the clanking teacups.

"Susie."

The name was poison. Even though each wife knew too well that some Susie, however she spelled it, could come between her and her husband, the gals pinned all their fears onto one particular Susie, the new wife of Donn Eisele, the rookie astronaut who'd suddenly made big headlines around the world. *Paris Match* showed up at Harriet's door wanting the inside scoop. The shit hit the fan and Harriet was terribly embarrassed. "Astronaut Donn Sued in First 'Space Divorce'—And More Homes May Break Under Strain," ran a headline in the UK's *Daily Express*.

"The astronaut life is a great strain on marriage," Donn told the tabloid. "It is like a circus. To be avoided."

But Susie married him anyway. And now she wanted to join the A.W.C.

Susie didn't yet comprehend what she was in for. She didn't think she'd done anything wrong. She hadn't hunted Donn like some of the other Cape Cookies. She was a respectable single mother who'd worked at the Cape Kennedy Savings and Loan Association. Some of the wives were exceedingly kind—space widow Beth Williams out in Dickinson was a dear—but the rest?

"It was a living inferno," said Susie. "I figured if we minded our own business, it would be okay. But I did not know how radical this group was."

Susie was up to her ears in alligators and figured the wives who were meanest were the ones whose husbands cheated the most. Donn's new wife didn't stand a snowball's chance in hell in Togethersville.

Susie got a new job at a local savings and loan association in Houston, and as Donn was always working, she wondered what on earth she might find to do in her spare time. It occurred to her to join the Clear Creek Community Theatre, where Joan Aldrin and Clare Schweickart were amateur actresses. The theater put on the all-female Clare Boothe Luce play *The Women*, about a bunch of catty, backstabbing women. They also did *The Crucible*, Arthur Miller's Pulitzer Prize–winning play about the Salem witch trials. But Susie was told that an Astrowife had to ask NASA's permission if she wanted to appear in a community play, and Susie didn't want to. Someone urged her to attend an A.W.C. meeting, but before she even got a chance to consider what she might wear, Susie received a phone call informing her that if she dared to show up at the Lakewood Yacht Club, the other wives would walk out. It wasn't long before Donn was fired from NASA.

14

The Dark Side of the Moon

Dodie Hamblin, a big-boned Iowa girl turned New Yorker, was *Life*'s new bureau chief for outer space. She paddled across Clear Lake in a red canoe, her preferred mode of transportation between the three space burbs of Timber Cove, Nassau Bay, and El Lago. Today she was visiting the Bormans. She'd been told that their yard looked like a pit stop with all the hot rods Frank and his two sons worked on. The grease-stained, buzz-cut trio hunted duck in the backwoods. Dodie hoped they didn't hunt reporters.

Dodie had been getting the lay of the land since the winter of 1967, when she'd been dispatched. One of her first pieces was on the space widows. She certainly felt she'd landed in a curious place. Here, plumbers plumbed at cost, and if an astronaut family had a crisis, all the other families instantly appeared.

She'd found her best material at the gym at the Bayshore Club. One day, feeling fat and uninspired, she spied a woman clutching her bosoms as she ran around in a circle, brown ponytail bouncing behind her. Next, she wrapped the vibrator belt around her tummy to give herself a good jiggle. It was not until Dodie was on the belt next to her and struck up a conversation that somehow turned to Japan, of all things, that she realized she was speaking to none other than Marge Slayton.

Marge asked how Dodie was adjusting to Texas, and started chattering about how she used to have curly hair before she came to Houston.

"But then I got off the plane and it went to hell," she said.

Dodie signed up for the Bayshore Club, which set her back a pricey $200 a year. Unlike the Astrowives, she didn't receive a special discount. Dodie could often be seen at the club, clutching a white terry-cloth towel in one hand, her cigarette holder in the other, as she pedaled away on one of the club's stationary bikes. It was hell, but she got terrific material.

The wives seemed to be living pretty large in Togethersville, what with all the freebies and goodies they were offered. Even so, they were competing to win the prizes in the club's membership drive—postiches, and falls to add to their hair to create the currently fashionable cascading curls. The grand prize was a tacky cowboy painting that reminded Dodie of a bad Andrew Wyeth. To that end, Dodie gave her "referral" to Jane Conrad, who in turn gave it to Susan Borman, who was apparently crazy about that painting. The cowboy looked like Frank.

Dodie thought she'd better pay a visit to the Bormans. Frank was about to spend Christmas in a capsule orbiting the Moon. He was the commander of Apollo 8, the first manned voyage to the Moon, scheduled for that December 1968. The Astrowives believed the mission was the nation's best hope to redeem the tumultuous year. After the assassinations of MLK and RFK and the riots in Chicago during the Democratic National Convention, Nixon had won the election, but America was still in turmoil. The wives barely recognized the country they read about in *Life*: kids "getting high," young men burning their draft cards, women setting bras on fire, men looking like long-haired bums.

Living in Togethersville, happily trapped in the fifties, the wives might have been on birth control pills, but they were still buying the clean-cut, all-American image one hundred percent. Barbara and Gene Cernan had actually walked out of the prime seats they'd been given to the free love rock musical *Hair*, which had just opened on Broadway, because it featured nudity and sex. They thought it was un-American. The wives didn't even seem to know that America was in total upheaval—students had taken over Columbia University, the militant Black Panthers had hijacked the civil rights movement, and radical feminists had emerged from the women's liberation movement. In June, Valerie Solanas of SCUM (her Society for Cutting Up Men) had shot Andy Warhol. Though they all had plenty of cans of Campbell's stacked in their cupboards (cream of mushroom soup being a key ingredient in casseroles), most of the wives probably didn't even know who Warhol *was*! And forget radical feminists. What about plain, garden-variety feminists?

Were any of the wives up on the current literature of the burgeoning women's movement, from *The Feminine Mystique* to Gloria Steinem's Playboy Bunny exposé and also the more mass-produced fare? Who couldn't help but admire Helen Gurley Brown's *Cosmopolitan*? As its editor in chief, Brown claimed women could have it all, "love, sex, and money," while also advising them on beauty treatments that were quite a bit more modern than the Edna Wallace Hopper white clay mask. "Spread semen over your face," one of Ms. Brown's pieces advised. "It's probably full of protein as sperm can eventually become babies. Makes a fine mask—and he'll be pleased."

Sometimes Dodie wanted to scream, it felt so outdated and claustrophobic here. "Togethersville can be a warm and loving family," she typed up for *Life*, "or just a great gelatinous blob that closes around and smothers the individual."

Docking her canoe, Dodie found her way to Frank's newly mown lawn. The two teenage Borman boys, fifteen-year-old Ed and seventeen-year-old Fred, were huge. Frank greeted her and Susan offered her a drink.

Knocking back a round and gesturing flamboyantly with her cigarette holder, Dodie was a charming guest, offering them the use of her apartment should they ever visit New York. That was clearly the wrong thing to offer Frank Borman.

The Bormans weren't like their sophisticated best friends, the Collinses. Mike and Pat were connoisseurs of French wine, readers of literature, and lovers of those old and dirty and crappy cities, as Frank deemed Chicago and New York. Frank felt very much at home here in Clear Lake City; he tolerated Houston because it was a new, clean city.

He even communicated in his own home via telephone, which Dodie found surpassingly bizarre. Frank called upstairs to the boys to ask, inexplicably, permission to use their car to drive to a restaurant.

"Could I please borrow it, pal?"

Ed, or perhaps Fred, said okay.

At Eric's Pub on the banks of Clear Lake, they were shown to the best table by Helen, the maître d'. She lived on an old houseboat tied up outside. Princess Grace and Prince Rainier had recently lunched here, which pissed off Frank to no end. He'd been asked to meet them and, as a result, had missed an important meeting at NASA. Over the local specialties, Frank regaled Dodie about the future of NASA. When it became all about science and was no longer about test flying, it wouldn't interest him anymore, he declared. He only liked the flying part.

"When we get to the Moon," swore Frank, "I'm getting *out*."

He also shared his feelings about how the entire country was going to hell. There were no winds of change blowing at the Bormans'. Frank couldn't stand the long hair the boys wore: it made a man look like a girl. Hell, if he got down to it, he couldn't stand long hair on a *female*.

Dodie was relieved to paddle toward home, a new apartment complex in Nassau Bay. From the middle of Clear Lake, she could see the space burbs all around her, so quiet, so isolated from the rest of the world. She paddled home as the Moon rose over Togethersville. Perhaps what was going on here was more important historically than the war in the Congo, or the riots in Paris, or even the throngs of hippies wandering around Haight-Ashbury, sleeping in Golden Gate Park. Dear God. This *was* where the sixties were happening. Or, for that matter, the twentieth century! The *millennium*? Certainly the cavemen who beheld the mysterious Moon never thought about meeting the Beatles. Nor would the computer-enhanced beings who might someday inhabit outer space.

A model of composure at A.W.C. meetings, Susan Borman had to work to keep from chewing on her string of pearls in front of everyone. Susan used to be an object of envy at the Bayshore, too, confidently doing her exercises while others were left huffing and puffing. But ever since the Apollo 1 fire, she wasn't burning out her stress on the exercise machines. Nobody knew it at the time, but Susan had been drinking heavily. Eventually, in Susan's struggle to be "the perfect wife married to the perfect husband who was the perfect astronaut in a perfect American family raising perfect children," she became an alcoholic.

For any Astrowife, it was difficult to keep that tight, raw ball of fear inside from growing before her husband's launch. Left unchecked, she could explode like a pressure cooker. A wife could always try to confide in her husband, but as NASA insisted, an astronaut needed to be kept *away* from stress at home. There was no way on God's green Earth that an Astrowife like Susan would openly share her terrors with her peers at an A.W.C. meeting.

The newest arrivals to the ever-expanding confederation were the "scientist-astronaut" wives, who seemed too busy calibrating their husbands' slide rules to understand the code of behavior. But the rest of the wives, the ones who counted, knew just as well as Susan did that an astronaut's wife did not disclose her fears to anyone. They all knew fear was contagious. Even though most of the ladies harbored the exact same dark thoughts, they couldn't risk sharing them.

All the astronauts would give an arm and a leg to be where Frank Borman was, flying to the Moon. It was ironic. Susan had always longed for something like the A.W.C. so that she and the other women wouldn't always be stuck at home alone. She still showed up to meetings, but she kept her mouth shut about the things that really mattered to her, quietly waiting for the day when Frank would leave the program, as he always said he would "after the Moon."

She worried a lot about Pat White and visited her often. She couldn't help but imagine that what had happened to Pat was going to happen to her. Pat's questions echoed in her mind, "Who am I? What do I do now?" "My God, this could be me," thought Susan.

Frank had gotten to know a hell of a lot about the fire when he was on the Apollo 1 Review Board. It turned out that all the Gemini astronauts had flown under the same combustible pure oxygen conditions. The big joke was how he and Jim Lovell had actually carried paperbacks on their two-week Gemini 7 flight, which could have acted as *kindling*! for Chrissakes.

"You just worry about the custard, and I'll worry about the flying," Frank reassured his anxious wife. It was the Bormans' version of the Glenns' "chewing gum" routine.

Susan dreaded the Apollo 8 mission. Along with his crewmates Jim Lovell and Bill Anders, her Frank would be the first human to orbit the Moon, ten times around, a death-defying feat if there ever was one. Susan was convinced that Frank was going to die on his six-day mission. If he didn't explode in a ball of fire at liftoff, he'd circle the Moon for eternity. Susan wasn't sure she'd be able to go to the Cape for the countdown. To her new pal Dodie Hamblin of *Life*, whom the wives had discovered could knock down a stiff martini with the best of them, Susan confessed, "Some of us aren't at our best before a launch, so it's important to know us as we really are."

Her apprehension about Apollo 8 was compounded when flight director Chris Kraft paid her a visit. Kraft was the head honcho of Mission Control. There was no question that it was *he* who decided who was going to get to go up into space. "I am Flight and Flight is God" went Kraft's credo. It was Kraft who had clipped Scott Carpenter's wings. He'd sworn that Scott would never fly again after overshooting his landing on *Aurora 7*, and sure enough, Scott was now scuttling across the bottom of the ocean.

What if Kraft caught a whiff of fear in an astronaut's home, especially the home of the one who was about to take two of his boys on a trip around the Moon? Susan surely didn't want to think about what that could mean for her Frank. "They didn't want an oddball," Susan said later. "We kept it like *Leave It to Beaver*."

Chris Kraft had come out of his cave at the Manned Spacecraft Center on a rare visit to see a *wife* personally. He was here at the Bormans' to discuss the risks of Frank's flight, NASA's most dangerous mission to date.

Susan knew the code of the military wife. Her whole life revolved around supporting Frank's career.

"Hey, Chris, I'd really appreciate if you would level with me. I really, really, want to know what you think their chances are of getting home."

"Okay, how's fifty-fifty?"

Susan wasn't sure if that made her more or less worried.

Marilyn Lovell had been planning for Jim to take the family on a long overdue vacation to Acapulco for Christmas. Having spent more time in space than any man alive (first on his two-week Gemini 7 mission and then on Gemini 12, which had closed out the program), he hadn't been around much to enjoy the comforts of Lovells' Levels. Marilyn was looking forward to bouncing along the high cliffs in one of those adorable pink jeeps at the Las Brisas Resort, where Frank "Brandy" Brandstetter offered free R & R for astronauts. Until Jim mentioned that he wasn't sure he'd make it.

"Well, just where do you think you are going to be?" asked Marilyn.

Susan Borman (right) and Valerie Anders hear their husbands coming around the far side of the Moon during Apollo 8, Christmas 1968.

Marilyn Lovell toasts her husband, Jim, during Apollo 8.

Apollo 11 families "on" the Moon. From left: the Aldrins, the Collinses; at right, the Armstrongs.

Pat and Mike Collins eat breakfast, Nassau Bay, March 1969.

Joan Aldrin cries in relief as she watches on TV as the lunar module lands on the Moon during Apollo 11, July 20, 1969, 3:18 p.m. central daylight Earth time.

Togethersville, July 1969: Pat Collins (in red with beehive), celebrating splashdown at the end of Apollo 11 with friends and champagne. (The bunny is the family's pet, Snowball.)

At home in Nassau Bay, Joan Aldrin applauds as she watches TV coverage of the splash-down of Apollo 11.

The wives (in Hawaiian leis) greet Neil Armstrong, Buzz Aldrin, and Michael Collins in the Mobile Quarantine Facility.

Marilyn Lovell, wife of Apollo 13's Jim Lovell, listens to the squawk box and watches TV coverage of the ill-fated mission at the Lovell home in Timber Cove, April 1970.

Neil Armstrong's family watches from a boat on the Banana River as Apollo 11 lifts off.

Astrowives Sue Bean, Barbara Gordon, and Jane Conrad hold up the club's motto during Apollo 12, November 1969.

"Oh, I don't know," said Jim, proceeding cautiously. "Maybe the Moon?"

Obviously, Marilyn couldn't argue with that. It was such an immense triumph for his career, let alone for all of humanity. Her husband's flight on Apollo 8 was going to beat the Russians. It would be American astronauts who would be the first to orbit the Moon.

Just before Christmas, Marilyn and her four children stayed in a beach cottage near the Cape to spend some time with Jim before he blasted off.

Two nights before his launch, Jim drove Marilyn to a lookout on the beach so she could behold, off in the distance, the floodlit Saturn V rocket. The 363-foot whopper was bigger than any rocket ever launched, fueled with fifteen hundred tons of liquid oxygen, enough thrust to shoot Jim up to the Moon.

"Don't get frightened when it takes off, because the rocket is going to lean to one side," Jim warned her. "And the ground will shake for miles!"

Jim began laughing, but Marilyn had no idea what private joke he was enjoying.

Suddenly he took out a large black-and-white photo of the Moon, taken by a satellite, which he'd used in training. He showed her a pert little triangle-shaped mountain near *Mare Tranquillitatis*, the Sea of Tranquility, where the first lunar landing was supposed to take place with Apollo 11. Tapping his finger on it, he said, "I'm going to name that mountain for you." For all eternity, it would be known as Mount Marilyn.

Jim had always maintained there was a certain amount of romance in his job, and now he was including Marilyn in it.

What could be more romantic than a Moon mountain named after you?

In El Lago, Susan Borman remained curled up on her bed, watching the hours tick away on the clock. She could do nothing but be the vigilant wife waiting till dawn. With each hour that passed, she just knew that Frank was going to die.

Finally it was time to get up, dress, and greet the wives who'd been invited for her Death Watch. Most of them were from the New Nine cohort, and they arrived not only with deviled eggs but also bottles of champagne. "Standard operating procedure," Susan called it. All she had to do on launch day was sit back, surrounded by women who knew what she was going through, and watch her husband ride a Saturn V rocket into the unknown on national television.

On the outside, Susan was a model astronaut wife. As always, she was beautifully dressed, literally for the pages of *Life* magazine: pearls on, buttery blonde bob flipped up. After the successful liftoff, Susan finally stepped out onto her lawn. "I've always been known as a person who had something to say," she said to the waiting reporters. "Today I am speechless."

After that she returned to her kitchen and lit another cigarette. Her sons, Ed and Fred, had been begging her to quit, and Susan had promised she would right after their father landed safely home.

The day after liftoff was a Sunday and Susan sat for services at St. Christopher's Episcopal Church, her hands composed in her lap, and her strapping boys by her side. Only a few hours earlier, she'd gotten a call from the NASA doctors. "Does Frank often have trouble sleeping?" they wanted to know.

It turned out that Frank had radioed in to Mission Control asking permission to take a Seconal sleeping pill. Frank had always been adamant about never taking pills. But at one in the morning on his first night in space, Frank had found it impossible to sleep, and he knew it was important to get some shut-eye on such a mission as this. He radioed down to Mission Control, who gave him the A-OK, and Frank swallowed the pill with a squirt of liquid from a water gun. He tried to get to sleep in the lower level of the spacecraft, but soon he started to vomit, and green particles floated into other parts of the spaceship. A big gelatinous sphere sailed by his crewmate Bill Anders, the rookie. It splashed onto Jim, "like a fried egg." Unfortunately it wasn't only vomit floating by, but diarrhea as well.

Susan came home from church to find plenty of food brought by the wives. She wasn't hungry, but her boys insisted she eat. The squawk box transmitted Frank's voice from space. Susan snuck into her bedroom, curled up in bed, and listened to her private squawk box.

Marilyn flew back from the Cape to Timber Cove that morning. She and her son Jay watched Jim's first television appearance from space. "This is known as preparing lunch and doing P23 at the same time," said Jim on the small screen.

Posing before the state-of-the-art black-and-white video camera, built specifically for NASA by RCA, Jim showed how to make chocolate pudding by squirting a shot of water into a bag of brown powder. The crew had been offered new and improved food, but commander Frank had declined, wanting to keep things as meat and potatoes as possible. So they were stuck eating mostly space kibble. Focusing the camera on a floating toothbrush, Frank told the world that he knew the rookie on board, Bill, had been "brushing regularly." In a subsequent broadcast, the camera captured Earth through the spacecraft's window. Jim described the bright blue marble as being "about as big as the end of my thumb." It was terrifying how small home was, but its beauty enthralled him.

"What I keep on imagining is, if I were a traveler from another planet," mused Jim, "what would I think about the Earth at this altitude—would I think it was inhabited?"

Using two hand controls, Frank put the ship in "barbecue" mode with the spacecraft slowly spinning like a rotisserie once an hour, distributing the heat of the sun.

On Monday, Marilyn drove over to Mission Control. With its bleacher seating behind soundproof glass, walls lined in felt to absorb all sound, the VIP section was set up like a crying room in an old-time movie theater, overlooking the high-octane operations. The spacecraft was at the tipping point between the Earth's and Moon's gravities. Then Apollo 8 slipped away from Earth's gravity and was pulled in by the Moon.

"Have you seen Susan yet?" astronaut John Young asked. He'd been assigned to Marilyn to explain everything that was going on during the flight.

"No," said Marilyn. "Would you like to go over there?"

"Well, why don't we both go."

When they arrived at Susan's house in El Lago, they found a few people in the living room, milling around the tinsel-draped Christmas tree, having drinks, sipping coffee, munching on holiday candy and peanuts. The boys had snuck off to go duck hunting earlier that day. Susan was holed up in her bedroom. Marilyn decided she would wait for Susan to come out and greet her, but it became apparent that Susan wasn't coming out and

Marilyn wasn't being invited in. After waiting an hour to see her, Marilyn asked John to take her home.

When Marilyn returned to Lovells' Levels, she fixed herself a scotch on the rocks. She sat at the brick bar in the family room and cried her eyes out, the tears literally streaming down her face into her scotch. It was humiliating. Their husbands were on their way to the Moon together, and Susan couldn't come out and say hello? Marilyn felt like they, too, were on a mission together.

Jim was going into lunar orbit very early the next morning, Christmas Eve, which meant the space capsule would disappear around the far side of the Moon (Jim and the astronauts were sticklers about calling it the far side instead of the dark side because it was permanently turned away from the Earth; it wasn't always in shadow). On the far side, all radio contact with Earth would be cut off. *Would he make it back?*

Marilyn couldn't allow herself to go there, couldn't bear to consider the question. Of course he'd come back. He had to. She always told her friends she couldn't live without Jim.

Soon she had some company with teenage Betsy Benware from next door coming over to give her and the kids a home-cooked meal. Betsy's father was the head of a company that supported Mission Control, and her mother was Marilyn's best friend. Marilyn could tell Betty Benware things that she wouldn't dare say to another Astrowife, even Jane Conrad.

Betsy handed over the tray that her mother had prepared, but Marilyn wasn't very hungry. The girl quickly realized how upset she was.

"Are you all right, Mrs. Lovell?"

"Oh, yes," Marilyn replied, but Betsy didn't believe her.

Betsy headed home, and within minutes, her mother took over as Marilyn's Mission Control. Soon other close friends began arriving, called over to Lovells' Levels because Betty Benware had decided they were going to come over to support Marilyn and cheer her up. Now that she was relaxed after some food and a few cigarettes and laughs, Betty told her she better get some sleep before Jim went around the far side of the Moon. She laid a gentle hand on Marilyn's shoulder and led her back to her bedroom.

"Lie down. I am not leaving this room until you lie down."

At first Marilyn resisted, but soon she let her body settle onto the bed. She awoke a few hours later around 2 a.m. on Christmas Eve.

Padding down the hall to the family room, where the TV was on, Marilyn found one friend sleeping in a big chair, another on the sofa, and a couple on the carpeted floor. It really touched her how they'd all made themselves beds just so that they could be there for her.

Over in El Lago, Frank squawked through Susan's box. "As a matter of interest, we have as yet to see the Moon." The astronauts were about to arrive at the Moon. NASA gave Apollo 8 a "Go" for lunar orbit, and just before the Apollo 8 crew went over to the far side, Susan asked Mission Control to pass along a message to her husband: "Frank. The custard is in the oven at 350."

"No comprendo," Frank replied. He'd forgotten the reference that was so important to his wife—"You just worry about the custard, and I'll worry about the flying." After that, her squawk box went silent.

Why Frank hadn't responded to their private joke? Susan

only prayed that the engine would work and slow the spacecraft down so that it came into lunar orbit at the proper angle. She couldn't bear the awful silence on the squawk box. Would they ricochet off the Moon's gravity field and be lost forever in space, or crash into the Moon?

Finally, the squawk box came to life.

"Apollo 8, Houston. Over."

"Go ahead, Houston," crackled Frank. "This is Apollo 8. Burn complete."

"Apollo 8, this is Houston. Roger... good to hear your voice."

Susan closed her eyes in relief. For the next twenty hours, Frank would be orbiting ten times around the Moon, from late Christmas Eve into early Christmas morning. On Christmas they'd head home, but first they'd have to perform the most critical part of the mission, the one Susan dreaded the most—trans-Earth injection.

Dear God, she didn't know if she could survive it. She kept vigil in her kitchen, ears alert to the squawk box, eyes glued to the television. The sun still hadn't fully come over Houston Christmas Eve morning at 6:30 a.m. when the TV in the den broadcast the first lunar telecast, the video from Frank's camera surveying the bleak, pockmarked lunar terrain.

Susan had greater things on her mind than to be fascinated with this glimpse of another world. The only thing that mattered was that Frank came home.

As the navigator, Jim Lovell identified landmarks from the Moon maps—the Sea of Tranquility, Dry Gulch, Apollo Ridge, Twin Peaks. Nearby was a lunar mountain range.

"I can see the initial point right now, Mount Marilyn," Jim

radioed to Mission Control. Astronaut Mike Collins, serving as Capcom, was puzzled. "Roger."

That afternoon, Marilyn Lovell phoned her priest, Father Raish. It was between services. "I'd like to come over to the church," she told him.

When Marilyn arrived, the church was empty save for Father Raish and the organist, who was playing the music for midnight mass. The church was lavishly decorated with poinsettias and holiday garlands, but she didn't expect to see it alive with hundreds of candles like tiny dancing stars.

"You did all this for me?"

Father Raish knew she wouldn't be able to attend regular midnight mass, since her husband would be performing some critical maneuvers then, but there was something godly about going around the Moon. He wanted Marilyn to have a special Christmas. She and Father Raish knelt down at the altar. As they prayed, tears welled in Marilyn's eyes.

Driving home from church, her whole heart was up there with the Apollo 8 crew. As she was pulling into Timber Cove, she looked up at the sky, just as she and Jim had when they were teenagers back in Milwaukee and he'd point out the constellations to her and they'd neck. It had been cloudy all week, but suddenly the clouds parted. There was the Moon, the bright, beautiful half Moon.

"My God, my husband is going around the Moon at this moment," Marilyn thought. "I'm blessed, I'm truly blessed."

Susan sat down at her kitchen table. She took out a piece of paper and a pen and began writing Frank's eulogy. *If they don't get the Apollo 8 crew back safely, the press will really have a field day. Three dead astronauts circling the Moon,* she thought. *They'll stage a big funeral in absentia, but I'll be damned if they are going to tell me how to run it.* She didn't know where to start, but then she had an epiphany: *What a magnificent place to die.* She wrote down her feelings that the world should feel uplifted. After all, Frank was watching over them, orbiting the Moon for eternity. Susan thought that was what Frank would want. No brown mud-earth grave for him at Arlington or West Point, but the smooth silver orb that lovers had stared at for centuries. Susan could look up whenever she needed a connection.

"Mom, what are you writing?" Fifteen-year-old Ed had come into the kitchen.

"Your father's memorial service. He might not come back."

"Just remember, Mom," said Ed. "Dad gets to choose the way he goes—you and I don't have that privilege."

Ed took the pen out of her hand and Susan slid the paper with the eulogy from sight. Later she would hide it in a drawer.

That night at 9:30 p.m., it was time for the crew to make their special Christmas Eve television transmission. "We are now approaching lunar sunset," said Frank, "and for all the people back on Earth, the crew of Apollo 8 has a message that we would like to share with you."

"In the beginning, God created the heaven and the earth. And the earth was without form, and void; and darkness was upon the face of the deep," said Bill, reading from the book of Genesis for a live television audience around the world, "And the spirit of God moved upon the face of the water. And God said, 'Let there be light.' And there was light. And God saw the light, that it was good. And God divided the light from the darkness."

Jim picked up next. "And God called the light Day, and the darkness he called Night. And the evening and the morning were the first day..."

"They must be in God's hands," Marilyn said to herself, as Moon shadows flickered on her TV.

"And God called the dry land Earth; and the gathering together of the water called the seas; and God saw that it was good," Frank continued. "And from the crew of Apollo 8, we close with a good night, good luck, a Merry Christmas, and God bless all of you—all of you on the good Earth."

Susan cried as her husband concluded the broadcast. Marilyn took her kids for a walk around the neighborhood, past the pool shaped like the Mercury capsule and their friends' homes lit up with reindeer and lights. Jim and the Apollo 8 crew were about to go over to the far side one last time.

Trans-Earth injection, or "TEI," was next. Susan was still dreading it, and soon the rookie Bill's wife, Valerie, would be arriving to sweat it out with her. Earlier in the week, the two women had decided they'd sit together for the midnight event.

Bill had actually named a lunar valley for his wife. He wanted the name, Valerie's Valley, to stick. But it didn't quite have the ring of Mount Marilyn.

For the *Life* photographer, Susan wore a gray-lilac sheath and her signature strand of pearls, which she intermittently chewed on. Somebody had stuck a red pin on her that said SANTA LIVES!, but Susan didn't look as if she believed it. Valerie wore eggshell blue trimmed in squiggly white rickrack. Both women had sweaters around their shoulders, for comfort as much as anything else. Two white squawk boxes, one for each, were dead silent.

Over on the far side, Frank was supposed to be kicking off TEI. Susan closed her eyes and her jaw, and the muscles around her neck tightened. It was a 12:34 a.m. on Christmas morning. Time for her to hear something.

"Apollo 8, Houston," crackled the Capcom. "Apollo 8, Houston, Apollo 8, Houston, Apollo 8, Houston."

Ten seconds of silence. Twenty. Thirty. Forty. Fifty. Fifty-one. Fifty-two...

"Houston, Apollo 8," crackled Jim. "Please be informed. There is a Santa Claus."

"That's affirmative. You are the best ones to know."

At Mission Control, the men clapped their colleagues on the back and lit up cigars. The boys were finally on their way home.

The sun rose over Timber Cove and the Lovell kids ripped into their presents, delivered the night before by a jolly neighbor dressed up as Santa. Marilyn couldn't wait for her gift—Jim's return home in two days. The waiting was the hardest part, but Marilyn was certainly used to it.

The doorbell rang. It was a deliveryman from Neiman-Marcus. He'd pulled up in a Rolls-Royce and wore a chauffeur's cap. He had a big box wrapped in blue-and-silver foil. Perched on top was a mobile of the Moon and Earth, two Styrofoam balls studded with sequins. A minuscule white spacecraft was going around the silver-sequined moon on a wire. Marilyn looked at the card.

TO MARILYN

FROM THE MAN IN THE MOON

She tore into her gift. Silver stars sparkled in the light blue tissue paper inside.

"A mink jacket!" she exclaimed. Jim knew she had always wanted a mink—didn't every woman?—but it was a total surprise. Marilyn thought maybe he figured that in case he didn't make it back, she would at least have that fur.

Marilyn danced around the family room in her mink, loving the feel of the fur against her skin. A little exhausted from all the excitement and stress, she let herself fall in a heap on the sofa. Wasn't it crazy? Here she was, lying on the sofa, wrapped in her mink, and Jim was a quarter of a million miles away.

15

The Giant Leap

Joan Aldrin couldn't begin to wrap her mind around the enormous significance of the Moon landing scheduled for July 20, 1969. It would be years, decades, centuries, perhaps, before mankind comprehended the impact of the step her Buzz was about to take. She was sure that Apollo 11 would be the capper of Buzz's accomplishments, which were many. Most wives in the A.W.C. wished their husbands were postmen, but Joan had a better idea.

"If Buzz were a trash man and collected trash," she told the *Life* reporter, "he would be the best trash collector in the United States."

Once as they watched the garbagemen make their rounds early in the morning in Nassau Bay, Buzz commented that he thought they didn't take enough pride in their work, listlessly slinging the bags up into the truck instead of giving it their all. Joan knew that Buzz gave everything his all. He would undertake his Apollo 11 flight with vim, vigor, and gusto, and though he'd be a hero to the rest of the world, she knew he'd return to Earth the same thoughtful, brilliant man he'd always been. "A curious mixture of magnificent confidence, bordering on conceit, and humility," she'd told *Life*. He was not one to become puffed up and peacocky. She took great comfort in that.

A year before, immediately after Martin Luther King Jr.'s death, there had been a peace march in Houston organized by some of the churches for Palm Sunday 1968. Buzz told Joan that he felt obligated to participate. That made Joan very pleased, especially since she was not used to seeing such strong passions stirred in Buzz. That Sunday afternoon, he marched to city hall, and the next day his picture appeared on the front page of the *Houston Chronicle*. Joan was a little worried because she didn't know how NASA would respond when they read the caption about an astronaut marching. Luckily the caption didn't say *who* that astronaut was. She was amazed at the number of people who didn't recognize the photo as being of Buzz.

On Monday morning at the astronauts' weekly meeting, one of the guys mentioned, not exactly encouragingly, how he had heard some astronaut marched in "that peace parade yesterday."

Buzz hadn't said a word. His peers weren't exactly civil rights activists. And for that matter, they hadn't liked him very much to begin with. With his PhD from MIT, they thought Dr. Rendezvous was an overly intellectual square. *Let them think what they want*, Joan said to herself. Let Buzz be a square, so long as he'd still be square when he returned from the Moon.

Now, in the summer of 1969, Joan had a much more sanguine outlook on Buzz's spaceflight than she had three years before, when Buzz manned Gemini 12. She'd assumed that after his space walk, he'd be much less cold than he usually was, that he'd share his feelings about what he'd experienced. She'd expected him to have a profound spiritual transformation in space, like Ed White's ecstasy of the deep, so that back on Earth he'd become closer to her, more emotionally engaged. She told Dodie Hamblin of *Life* that she'd envisioned their sometimes tenuous and distant relationship becoming "so much more magical and meaningful and magnificent because he had done this wonderful thing."

Unfortunately, after Buzz's Gemini flight, their marriage was unchanged. Buzz was still gone most of the time; his moods were still heavy and impenetrable. He was as withdrawn as ever. "Maybe six months later I realized that our marriage was exactly what it had been before, that if we had an argument, we argued still over the same things, but we still shared the same ideals and principles," said Joan.

In January 1969, while they were standing in a local Laundromat waiting to pick up their clothing, Buzz had told Joan that he'd been assigned to the first crew to land on the Moon. Joan tried to be thrilled but felt curiously numb. She wrote in her diary, "It was a day, the first of many, I'll bet, of walking on eggs, of normalcy tinged with hysteria. I wish B were a carpenter, a truck driver, a scientist, anything but what he is. Now I understand how Susan Borman felt—wanting to run and hide. I want him to do what he wants but I don't want him to."

A few days later she wrote, "Had a long talk with Buzz, but still don't understand what he was driving at. Who makes the first exit from the LM on lunar surface is still very much of an issue. And B was upset because he heard, via that terrible institution, the grapevine, that Deke's opinion was that Neil should be the first for historic reasons if nothing else."

Apollo 11's commander, Neil Armstrong, was a civilian, and both NASA and President Nixon felt it was important for Apollo 11 not to be seen as a form of military action, of lunar conquest, especially with the Vietnam War still raging. When the crew—Neil, Buzz, and Mike Collins—designed their mission patch, they picked an eagle to represent the "LM," the lunar module *Eagle*, and placed an olive branch in its sharp talons.

Joan prepared for the eight-day mission by focusing on all the housekeeping chores she'd been avoiding. "Wash the windows, paint the walls, anything to keep sane," she told Dodie. She even ordered a new salmon-colored velveteen armchair from a local furniture company to reward herself for all the cleaning and redecorating she planned to do. It looked like a big mushroom.

In the weeks leading up to launch day, Joan broke out in pink blotches, but luckily she knew from her acting days how to apply a thick layer of pancake makeup so she'd be presentable for the press on her lawn. Dodie told Joan that she looked like Shirley MacLaine, which made Joan very happy. The actress in Joan viewed Apollo 11 as her big moment. She'd have a worldwide television audience!

Her plans for cleaning the house during the flight were never realized. She couldn't even bear to sit on her new armchair. Instead, she sat cross-legged on the floor, curling into a ball, and gleefully kicked her legs before her television set after a risky maneuver had been accomplished.

It took the crew three days to fly to the Moon, which meant a lot of time to endure for the wives. To avoid the press, they had to lie down in the backseats of neighbors' cars under blankets while being driven to the grocery store or the mall to go shopping. When one of them braved the beauty parlor undisguised, a female reporter was on her tail. With thick green shag carpet, gilt mirrors, and chandeliers, Parisienne Coiffures at the local shopping center was owned by a very "au courant" bearded French hairdresser who wore colorful suits without lapels. He had chosen Houston because he wanted to be where the action and glamour were. So had the two mod English girls who worked for him. The Astrowife sat under a hair dryer listening to a handheld radio account of the flight as the reporter watched her every movement from a nearby chair with her notepad on her lap. "Comb me out slowly," the reporter told her hairdresser.

Annie Glenn had sent the Apollo 11 wives each a yellow orchid, potted in a champagne glass with a note: *May God watch over you and your family. Fondly...* For the next few days, the living rooms of Togethersville were as tense as NASA's control room. One day, Joan sat in a blue polka-dot swimsuit chain-smoking in front of the television, while out in her backyard the Apollo 11 wives hosted a pool party. "It's like a dramatic television show, but it seems unreal. There are just no words. Don't you agree?" Joan said to one of her visitors. It was still very much uncertain whether Neil and Buzz would be able to land successfully on the Moon. They wouldn't know for sure until they touched down, and then they wouldn't know if they'd be stranded there until they lifted back off into lunar orbit.

On Sunday, July 20, the lunar landing module *Eagle*, a silver spider with aluminum pads for feet, detached from the main spacecraft, *Columbia*, which was being flown by Mike Collins. He would orbit the Moon alone while Neil and Buzz descended through the frozen silence of space. *Eagle* floated slowly over Mount Marilyn and across the Sea of Tranquility, kicking up a cloud of dust.

"Okay, engine stop," Buzz called out over the squawk box.

It was 3:18 p.m. when Neil Armstrong said, "Houston, Tranquility Base here. The *Eagle* has landed."

Joan experienced an ocean of feelings surge inside her. Her very own Buzz had just landed on the Moon! The entire world would remember just where they were at this very moment for the rest of their lives. Beside her sat Dee O'Hara, the astronauts' personal nurse, who knew "the boys," as *Life* said, "better than any woman except their wives."

"It was probably the only time I've experienced a surreal moment," said Nurse Dee, awestruck. "I don't know how quite to describe it, but it was truly unreal. I saw the TV flickering and the LM was there, and we were told it was the Moon, and the LM was on the surface of the Moon. Of course, we were so relieved that they had landed. But it just simply wasn't real. Intellectually you know it is, and, of course, Joan, as was everyone, was terribly relieved that they had landed. I remember sitting there. I kept shaking my head. I thought, this can't be real, it just can't be. Here we are, on another planet. It was goose bumps all around."

Joan's movements were tentative as she rose from the sofa and then fell to the floor. Of course the *Life* photographer caught the odd moment—Joan in baby blue polyester pants and a white-and-red polka-dot blouse lying still on the tile floor.

They got a much more emotionally readable photo when Joan, who had stood up and leaned against her wood-paneled wall, dramatically fell into the arms of Buzz's eccentric uncle, the serendipitously named Bob Moon. As everyone laughed and cried and clapped, Joan, who was surrounded by friends, pushed herself out of Uncle Bob's arms and disappeared into Buzz's midnight-blue study. Her mind simply couldn't absorb it. Joan was so overwhelmed with pure relief that they had landed that she swooned and actually blacked out for a few moments.

When she came to, she was lying on the floor and saw a

matchbook beside her, and the reality that Buzz was on the Moon hit her again. She had to pick up that matchbook, to grab on to something tangible, but she couldn't get her brain to coordinate with her limbs.

It took her a while to compose herself, but compose herself she did. "See, all smiles," Joan would say in a cheerful voice. "No more tears."

The Conrads' was definitely the most "happening" house in Togethersville, which to Norman Mailer was textbook Squaresville. The macho writer thought that Jane was "sensationally attractive." He'd been commissioned by *Life* to write about the Moon landing, and Jane and Pete kindly invited him over for a backyard barbecue. Jane's friends were excited to see "the monster," as Jane jokingly called him, in person, wondering what kind of man would stab his wife with a penknife, as Norman notoriously had done in a drunken rage. Leading Norman under the crepe myrtles, two of Jane's braver, hipper friends danced around him and shook the tree, decorating the writer in bright pink blossoms, soothing the savage beast and showing him a really good time. He'd completely forgotten about his girlfriend from New York City, decked out in black high heels and fishnet stockings, very exotic for the space burbs. The astronauts tried to toss her into the pool, but Pete rescued her.

Norman made a sport of reporting on the Apollo 11 wives, and for the duration of his assignment he referred to himself as "Aquarius." As if imagining himself on a jungle safari, he spotted, through the suburban vegetation of El Lago, something totally unexpected: a Zen manor, spacious, modern, and Japanese-inspired, featuring a heavy green statue of the Buddha in the living room, as well as a pool table. This was the home of Neil Armstrong. Neil had meticulously placed his rocks in the ivy-covered garden, creating the feel of a true Zen garden.

The neighbors thought Neil a bit taciturn, a bit mysterious. Daresay, cosmic? Neil was not a big breakfast eater—or a big exercise man. As he once told a friend, "I believe that every human has a finite number of heartbeats. I don't intend to waste any of mine running around doing exercises." The *Life* photographer Ralph Morse had once snapped the elusive fellow in a chef's hat. It was said he liked to make pizza and light the occasional cigar in celebration. The NASA public relations man was positioning the hot pink pedestal he'd have to haul from lawn to lawn for each of the Apollo 11 wives' press conferences. Aquarius would follow. The reporters fired their questions.

"Will you let the children stay up and watch the moonwalk tonight?" one of the journalists asked.

"Is this the greatest moment of your life?" asked another.

Mailer groaned. He found these questions canned.

"Are you pleased with the Sea of Tranquility as a place to land? What are you having for dinner tonight? Space food?"

Mailer moved over to Nassau Bay to meet Pat Collins, who posed outside her house in a white dress. She'd just gotten her hair done and wore it in a high black beehive. Pat was an Irish Catholic girl from Boston. She had met her Mike in France when they were both stationed at an Air Force base in Chambley after World War II. As the recreational director, Pat had hosted events for the enlisted men during their off-duty tours: Ping-Pong and bridge tournaments, theater acting, historical tours of the local area and surrounding countries, the favorite Bingo Night. Because of her background as a social worker, she also did a fair amount of counseling. She was what the French called *gamine*, Virginia Slims skinny. Aquarius found her "conversationally glittery."

"Mrs. Collins," asked a reporter, "do you mind that your husband is *not* landing with the others?"

Mike was remaining in the mother ship *Columbia* while the other boys were on the Moon. Like her husband, Pat insisted that she *didn't* care. But Aquarius didn't believe her. How could she and Mike not care that he had traveled all the way to the Moon and couldn't even go down and take a stroll on its beachy surface? Mailer waited for Pat to crack, but it was not to be.

So he was off to Joan Aldrin's, whose glistening pool surrounded by a fence seemed to be an oasis of tranquility. *What darker things lurked beneath the placid surface?* Aquarius wondered. It started to rain, a summer thunderstorm beating down on the roofs of Nassau Bay, and the reporters had to put on their red and yellow ponchos.

"Mrs. Aldrin," one of them asked, "what were you doing when they landed?"

"I was holding on to the wall," said Joan, emotionally exhausted. "I was praying."

Aquarius could almost smell that something was amiss here at the Aldrins'. A strange bird, this Joan, but what kind of beast was her Buzz? Mailer sensed, even from this brief glimpse, that Joan was trapped in a marriage full of raw agony. (With four marriages already under his belt, three to aspiring actresses, Aquarius knew of what he spoke.)

"Listen," Joan asked. "Aren't you all *excited*? They did it! They did it!"

But the crowd of wet reporters seemed bored and ready to go home. They'd grown jaded after a decade of covering the wives. After Joan returned inside, with no more wives to cover that day and the Moon landing that the country had been anticipating for a decade now behind him, Aquarius suddenly regretted that he hadn't paid Joan, whose husband had just landed on the *Moon*, the attention she deserved.

At just before 10 p.m., on that same day, July 20, 1969, six and a half hours after they'd landed on the Moon, Neil Armstrong stepped off of *Eagle*'s footpad onto the Moon.

"That's one small step for man," declared Neil, "one giant leap for mankind."

Only after Neil had planted his foot on the Moon, which reminded him of the American high desert, was Buzz allowed to join him. "It's like making an entrance onstage," said Joan. The second man on the Moon described his view as "magnificent desolation."

Joan threw kisses toward the TV screen, laughing, her whole body shuddering on the verge of tears as Buzz bounced across the lunar surface, doing what the wives named the Kangaroo Hop.

"How can you be serious about what you're doing when you're doing *that*?" asked Joan. "He's gotten more TV time in the last two days than I ever did in a year of trying!" Still, she couldn't shake how devastated her husband was that he had to be second. The glory would forever be Neil's, who would always be first.

After the astronauts completed a two-and-a-half-hour moonwalk and spending twenty-one hours on the Moon, the *Eagle* prepared to lift off to rendezvous with Mike in orbit. As Buzz got closer and closer to Earth, Joan felt sweeter than ever toward her big cosmic baby, coming home to Mama. "Bless him. Bless the baby! They're on their way back to Mother. That's a good boy. Just think, tonight we'll have that beautiful big burn and then—look out, world, here we come! I don't have any more tears. I think I've just cried for the past two weeks."

"I called three of, in my view," said President Nixon, "three of the greatest ladies and most courageous ladies in the whole world today—your wives."

The man who had once schooled Khrushchev on the virtues of America's greatest cold warriors—the true-blue housewives of the U.S. of A.—was now speaking in person to the Apollo 11 astronauts upon their safe return to Earth, and brought a message from their wives.

"I bring their love and their congratulations. And also, I've got to let you in on a little secret. I made a date with them."

The astronauts couldn't do much about that one, seeing as they were speaking to the president from behind glass, quarantined in the MQF, the Mobile Quarantine Facility, a tricked-out silver Airstream parked aboard the USS *Hornet*. Scientists thought there was a possibility, no matter how remote, that the astronauts might have picked up some alien Moon germs that could produce a lethal global epidemic. Flying off shelves in bookstores, Michael Crichton's bestselling novel *The Andromeda Strain* dramatized such a consequence of an extraterrestrial plague.

"I invited them to dinner on the thirteenth of August," continued Nixon, "right *after* you come out of quarantine. It will be a state dinner held in Los Angeles. The governors of all the fifty states will be there, the ambassadors, others from around the world and in America. And all I want to know—will you come? We want to honor you then."

Neil Armstrong smiled. "We'll do anything you say, Mr. President."

"This is the greatest week in the history of the world since the Creation, because as a result of what happened, in this week, the world is bigger, infinitely, and also, as I'm going to find on this trip around the world... as a result of what you've done, the world's never been closer together before," said the beaming president. "Incidentally, the speeches that you have to make at this dinner can be very short. And if you want to say *fantastic* or *beautiful*, that's all right with us. Don't try to think of any new adjectives. They've all been said."

The headlines were thrilling:

MEN WALK ON MOON. ASTRONAUTS LAND ON PLAIN.
COLLECT ROCKS, PLANT FLAG
A POWDERY SURFACE IS CLOSELY EXPLORED
ANCIENT DREAM FULFILLED

Twenty-one days later, the biomedically swabbed astronauts were deemed free of any Moon plague by the time they waltzed into the Apollo 11 Moon Ball, a grand, extravagant, star-studded affair. The guest list was a veritable who's who of the entire country, including practically every American official in the chain of succession as well as the justices of the U.S. Supreme Court and every member of the cabinet. And of course, there was NASA's own German rocket scientist Wernher von Braun;

Charles Lindbergh; World War I flying ace Eddie Rickenbacker; Mrs. Robert Goddard, the widow of the rocket pioneer; Howard Hughes; and Jackie and Aristotle Onassis. There was also "a delegation from the entertainment world": Fred Astaire, singing cowboy Gene Autry, and Joan Crawford. LBJ and Lady Bird had sent their regrets.

The astronaut couples were put up at the new nineteen-story, crescent-shaped Century Plaza Hotel in Los Angeles on the corner of the Avenue of the Stars and Constellation Boulevard, the perfect setting with its space-age design and spectacular Celestial Fountain. Flown in by helicopter, the Nixons were staying in the Presidential Suite, which boasted a view all the way to the Pacific Ocean. Everything was Moon-themed. The band played "Fly Me to the Moon" and "Moon over Miami." The menu featured the finest foods from around the world, including kiwi fruits from New Zealand and Dungeness crab fingers from Seattle. Two new desserts had been created for the occasion: "Moon Rock" petit fours, and Claire de Lune, a delicately textured marzipan, meringue, and blackberry confection. Everything, like the Moon, was topped with an American flag.

All the astronauts were at the ball, from the Nineteen to the Fourteen to the New Nine to the original Mercury Seven. Eight astronauts had been lost along the way—Ted Freeman, Elliot See, Charlie Bassett, Gus Grissom, Ed White, Roger Chaffee, Ed Givens, and C. C. Williams—but with six months to spare, America had landed on the Moon, fulfilling Kennedy's goal to reach it before the end of the sixties. It was perhaps the greatest adventure America had ever undertaken, a Manhattan Project for peace.

Outside the hotel, three thousand demonstrators had a different view. After a decade of sit-ins and be-ins, the counterculture thought the occasion perfectly demonstrated the skewed values of the country. With all of the problems ravaging America, the poverty and the inequality rampant across the land, the soldiers dying by the thousands in Vietnam, we had to waste so much brainpower and money going to the *Moon*? And then celebrate it with a decadent "ball" sponsored by the military-industrialist complex? Raising their fists at the arriving limos and smoking pot in the open air, the protesters had somehow managed to drape a huge banner from the upper floors of an office building across the street from the hotel, summing up their point with two words: "Fuck Mars."

Next up was the "Giant Step" world tour, which would extend over forty-five days and feature visits to multiple heads of state in twenty-three countries. Rechristened goodwill ambassadors, the crewmen and wives of Apollo 11 were briefed by the State Department on the customs of the different countries they'd be visiting: when they should bow or curtsy, whom to address as "Your Majesty" or "Your Royal Highness." Joan learned that one should never turn her back on a king or a queen. She'd need to remember that.

"Three kings in two days! Do you believe it?" Joan asked her fellow travelers, reviewing their mimeographed itinerary.

Loaded onto Air Force One was her mountain of luggage, ten suitcases bearing tags identifying the specific climate for which each had been packed. Joan also brought along a special travel journal, plastic-protected in green-and-black houndstooth. "Beginning the grand tour," she wrote on September 29, "arrived Mexico City eleven a.m. local time. Wild motorcade through city. Lunch with President Díaz Ordaz. Didn't finish till five p.m. Press conference for wives at hotel. Awkward! Reception at Ambassador McBride's. Saw Brandy. Supper with party here—Gina Lollobrigida. Tired."

"I thought Gina was interesting," said Buzz when they returned to their hotel room, a little spice finally peppering his flat manner. Since he'd returned from the Moon, Joan thought that his blue eyes were *different*, a little bluer and a little more animated. Nurse Dee observed that all of the boys came back from space slightly changed: "They have something, a sort of wild look, I would say, as if they had fallen in love with a mystery up there, sort of as if they haven't gotten their feet back on the ground, as if they regret having come back to us... a rage at having to come back to Earth." Though Joan had been hoping Buzz would share more of his deep feelings about the experience of walking on the Moon with her, he kept telling her he was sick and tired of talking about the Moon. He'd already said what he had to say at the many press conferences that had followed their twenty-one-day quarantine. "It was a unique, almost mystical environment up there," he'd said, and it had smelled to Buzz like gunpowder or spent cap pistol caps.

"Gina is giving us a party in Rome," Buzz told Joan. "I accepted."

Joan didn't even try to cover up her irritation. "You did? Well, tell her I don't want to hear the gory details of her car accident again. And I don't want to see her *scars* in the ladies' room again."

"You got to see her what?"

"Her s-c-a-r-s."

On just the second day of the grand tour, the White House called Buzz *back* to the States from Bogotá to attend an AFL-

CIO convention in Atlantic City. Buzz was not a happy camper. Dr. Bill Carpentier, the Apollo 11 flight surgeon, who was along on the tour, asked him to step aside for a private chat to see if he was feeling okay.

"I don't think so, Bill. I think I'm overwhelmed."

"I think you all are."

The doctor prescribed some pills to help with the anxiety. Buzz unhappily went off for a few days in Atlantic City while Joan continued on to Buenos Aires. She retired to her hotel early one night and wrote in her diary, "Planned to go to a show, but pooped out and had a bowl of soup in my room. Rain and fog."

The next morning, she found herself in Rio de Janeiro at the Copacabana Palace Hotel accepting three awards for Buzz. The NASA public affairs man congratulated her on her fine performance. At the hotel, alone again, Joan hummed a popular song, "Whaddaya do on a rainy night in Rio"—adding her own lyrics—"without a husband?"

Buzz was to rejoin the troops in four days in the Canary Islands. When Joan arrived at the Maspalomas Hotel after a long nighttime drive, she found Buzz sound asleep in their room. He woke up long enough to eat a sandwich with her, then went back to sleep. She felt as alone with him as she had without him.

In Paris, just before leaving for Amsterdam and Brussels, Joan awoke to find an official telex from the American embassy in the Netherlands in her room—"Queen Juliana insists, repeat, insists it is imperative for women to wear black for audience." Over breakfast, Joan muttered about Queen Juliana, that "mean old biddy." Queen Fabiola of Belgium hadn't made such a request! Joan didn't want to go to all the trouble of figuring out how to get the one black dress she'd stuck at the back of one of her garment bags, which were stowed on the plane. As it turned out, Queen Juliana was sweet and without airs, and actually favored pastels, leading Joan, conspicuously in pink, to conclude that Pat Collins had played a practical joke by making up and sending that telex.

In Amsterdam, cheers and showers of rose petals and open displays of affection met them. A woman put a bouquet of roses under Buzz's nose and asked the Moon man how he liked her city. Of course, a microphone was hidden in the bouquet, but at least the gal showed real initiative.

As Air Force One flew to Oslo a couple of days later, Joan was presented with "the Pat Nixon Medal—for displaying the qualities of quiet and determined restraint most evident in our First Lady in not upstaging her husband when the public obviously wanted to see *her*, not Buzz."

Buzz was really excited to go to Norway. He was proud of his Scandinavian descent. If any country might add him to the pantheon of the gods of Valhalla, it was Norway. The flat behavior of the Norwegians watching the motorcade put Buzz into a blue funk.

When a helicopter took all the Moon couples to the Norwegian defense minister's lodge high in the mountains, Buzz decided he'd had enough of these "fresh-air fiends" with their cool demeanor. Joan would have to tell their hosts that he was not going to be joining them for dinner. When she came back to their room later that night, Buzz was sitting in an armchair, still in a funk. What was his *problem*? Buzz hadn't even liked Paris!

She reached for the bottle of scotch, fixed them each a generous nightcap, and settled down to talk. Expression heavy as a boulder, Buzz became angrier and angrier as Joan tried to convince him that their lives would "eventually return to normal."

"Joan, I've been to the Moon, and I'm never going to be allowed to live the way I once lived. Neither are you and neither are our kids. Your belief isn't right, it's only a hope and it won't work. Let's try to make it as worthwhile as we can."

He told her that all three of the astronauts and their wives were "fakes and fools for allowing ourselves to be convinced by some strange concept of duty to be sent through all of these countries for the sake of propaganda, nothing more, nothing less." It was an interplanetary dog and pony show.

He called Joan a fake, too. They got drunker and drunker until they eventually fell asleep.

Two days later in London, the astronauts presented a genuine Moon rock to Queen Elizabeth. Rome was next. At the Vatican, the wives wore black lace mantillas for a private audience with the pope. The couples sat on thrones under a Renaissance ceiling painted with angels and clouds. After receiving his blessings, Buzz wanted to head immediately back to the hotel. That night was the big party at Gina Lollobrigida's.

Before they left, much to her chagrin, Joan got hit with a bad case of stomach flu. She spent her time in the bathroom while Buzz went to Gina's. Buzz didn't waltz in until dawn. He had spent the night as part of the international jet set. He may have felt he'd been in a scene right out of Fellini's *La Dolce Vita*. But it was clear that he was now in the doghouse.

16

Everywoman

Practically everyone Jane Conrad had ever known was at the Houston socialite's party at the Eau Gallie Yacht Club near Cape Kennedy on the eve of Pete's Apollo 12 Moon launch. It was an elegant evening, but Jane couldn't shake the feeling that it was all a dream. Familiar faces from all the way back to St. Mary's Hall, the boarding school she'd attended in San Antonio before Bryn Mawr, mixed with those she'd previously seen only in movies and on television: Jimmy Stewart and African American country singer Charley Pride, whose music Pete was taking with him to listen to on the way to the Moon. Pete's old space twin, Gordo Cooper, was chatting up some French starlet, Yvette Mimieux, and the Astronaut Office's giant stuffed ape mascot wore a tux for photo ops. It all seemed surreal to Jane.

Jane's hair was cut into a short geometric Vidal Sassoon bob, and she wore a candy-colored jersey minidress with kaleidoscopic swirls of deep purple, green, and bright sky blue that had been specially designed for her by Emilio Pucci. It had been a surprise personal gift from "The Marquis," with one stipulation. She had to wear it during the Apollo 12 launch festivities for good luck (and free advertising).

At one point Jane was called to the phone. She clacked across the dance floor in strappy black heels. "Dearie," as she called Pete, was quarantined over in the astronaut quarters at the Cape. "I love you," said Jane. Pete found it difficult even to say "I love you" back. All he ever said when Jane told him how much she loved him was a swift "Love you more." Whispering her good-byes, without ever saying the actual word "good-bye," as per the Astrowife tradition, Jane handed the receiver to her four ash-blond boys. They took turns talking to their dad.

In the weeks prior to his flight, Pete had practically disappeared from Jane's life, floating farther and farther away from her as if he were already in space. He'd done the same before Gemini 7, but then he'd snapped back upon his return to Earth. She wasn't quite as delicate with him this time around. One weekend when he was home, he sat in the living room on the sofa, upholstered in bird print, flipping through his latest issue of *Aviation Week*.

"When you come back next time," interrupted Jane, "why don't you take a room at the Kings Inn, so I won't be tempted to bother you? I bet you don't even know you are home, do you?"

She knew he was busy training, but the old Astrowife routine of getting up at five in the morning to cook him steak and eggs seemed so *dated*. Jane felt a change coming over her, too, as Pete was getting closer to going into space. Her own "personal countdown" was how she phrased it to friends.

After liftoff on November 19, 1969, Jane returned to Houston to ride out the ten-day mission. As one reporter noted, there were "no tears, no handwringing, no high drama" for Apollo 12 wives Jane, Sue Bean, and Fourteen wife Barbara Gordon. Barbara was affectionately known in the neighborhood as "the zookeeper" for wrangling her six rambunctious kids as well as a menagerie of pets, including a baby boa constrictor. If a neighbor was about to raise their shovel and murder a big ole poisonous viper, they'd better think twice because it might be "one of the Gordons' children's pets."

Apollo 11 had gotten all the festive rejoicing because it was the first Moon landing. Since Apollo 12 was a repeat, with the exception of landing on the so-called "Snowman" crater in the Ocean of Storms rather than the Sea of Tranquility, everyone expected a calmer reception. What had been accomplished once could be accomplished again. The press dubbed playboy Pete, Alan "Beano," and Dick Gordon (known among the astronauts as "the Animal") "the go-go crew," because unlike taciturn Neil, Buzz, and Mike, this crew was intent on having a ball. The three had gotten matching gold Corvettes from Jim Rathmann, and drove them around the Cape wearing gold aviators and their powder-blue NASA flight suits.

For the duration of Apollo 12, Togethersville turned into a giant community slumber party. At Sue Bean's home, guests were wrapped in blankets on the floor in front of the TV, munching on cookies and swilling Cokes at all hours. Sue's daughter Amy and Barbara Cernan's daughter Teresa Dawn ("Tracy," or "Punk," to her dad) sat with their mothers, two generations of best friends. Gene had come over with Barbara, but the lone man was soon sent home to sleep solo for a few nights.

After landing on the Moon, Pete cried out "Whoopee! Man, that may have been a small one for Neil, but it's a long one for me." He and Beano went through their checklist flipbooks attached to the wrists of their white space suits. Their backups had included a surprise in their books: *Playboy* centerfolds. Miss

September spread across Pete's lunar checklist with the caption "Seen any interesting hills & valleys?" The line above Miss December's voluptuous body was "Don't forget—describe the protuberances."

Setting their special Westinghouse Lunar Color Television Camera on its tripod (another technological improvement made since the primitive black-and-white camera used on Apollo 11 only months ago), Beano accidentally pointed it directly into the sun, burning out the lens. The TV networks were beside themselves—they had counted on covering the entire moonwalk—until someone had the bright idea of building a mock-up of the Moon in the studio. Actor stand-ins walked around in moon suits, synched to the live transmission of the real astronauts' voices.

"Dum de dum-dum-dum," hummed Pete.

Jane hummed along with her Moon man. Her superstitious live-in maid refused to believe that Pete was on the Moon. "Oh no, Mrs. Conrad, you pullin' my leg."

It was the wee hours of the morning when Jane's Moon landing party finally petered out. Wandering out to the backyard and staring up at the sky, she remembered how she used to look for the Man in the Moon when she was a girl.

"Now there is a man *on* the Moon, and it's my husband!" thought Jane. It was amazing. There was a numinous reality in it that far transcended life in Togethersville, and for a moment, she felt part of it. She wondered if this was what it was like to be on LSD.

For their press conference, Jane Conrad, Sue Bean, and Barbara Gordon wore matching white knit pantsuits and tied patriotic Ed White Memorial Fund silk scarves, autographed by all of the astronauts, around their waists as belts. They emerged from Jane's house wearing their best Astrowife smiles, perfected now over many years, and raised high above their heads cardboard signs they'd decorated with their kids' red and blue magic markers. Jane held up HAPPY, Sue held up PROUD, and the third wife, Barbara Gordon, was THRILLED.

The Moon mission was on a roll. Jim Lovell was set to land on the Moon next on Apollo 13. This time, Marilyn got her trip in beforehand. They went to Florence, Siena, and Pisa.

On April 11, 1970, as Jim lifted off on Apollo 13, Marilyn stood in the VIP bleachers at Cape Kennedy, overlooking the eager crowd. She watched until the Saturn rocket carrying Jim, Jack Swigert—"a swinging bachelor with a girl in every airport," *Life* reported—and Fred Haise rose out of sight. Down on Earth, Fred's wife, Mary, was seven months pregnant.

Two days later, an oxygen tank exploded on the spacecraft. The lunar landing was aborted, but that was the least of NASA's concerns. With the damage caused by the explosion, Mission Control was unsure if Apollo 13 would make it home. Jane Conrad arrived at Lovells' Levels on the back of Pete's new red Honda motorcycle and was there with Marilyn when she heard the news that Jim was stranded a quarter of a million miles from Earth in a crippled spacecraft. The three crewmembers were running out of usable oxygen and had to squeeze into the two-man lunar lander, which had now become a lifeboat.

Marilyn's house was filled with people for days. Moon mementos of Apollo 8, which hung on the family room walls, created an ominous stage set. Father Raish was expected to come over to offer communion to Marilyn and her friends, including Jane and Jo Schirra.

Marilyn's twelve-year-old, Susan, became hysterical when she saw the priest at the door. Marilyn found her lying facedown upstairs in her bedroom. She told her daughter that just because the priest was there, they weren't preparing for the end. Susan didn't seem persuaded, so Marilyn took her downstairs and tiptoed out the back door. She led her down their sloping backyard to the canal on Taylor Lake, where they sat in the shade of a favorite tree.

"Now, tell me exactly what you're worried about," said Marilyn.

"What do you mean?" Susan asked, sniffling. "I'm worried Dad's not going to come home."

"That?" She smiled at Susan. "*That's* what's bothering you?" Marilyn shook her head. "Don't you know your father's too *mean* to die?"

Susan looked astonished. "Dad's not mean."

"No, of course Dad's not. But Dad's stubborn, right? And he's the best astronaut I know."

Susan nodded.

"Now, do you really think the best astronaut either one of us knows is going to forget something as simple as how to turn his spaceship around and fly it home?"

She was right. Jim and his crewmates made it home. Two weeks later, when Jim flew out for routine NASA business, Marilyn, who had held it together through the entire space debacle, completely fell apart. She just knew that she would never see him again. Jim came home in one piece, of course, but now whenever he headed off in his car to do some mundane errand,

Marilyn was gripped by fear that she'd never see him again. Finally, she decided she had to see a psychiatrist, no matter the taboo. Her fears were unbearable.

Apollo 14 took off on January 31, 1971, commanded by Alan Shepard. Louise Shepard remained as composed as ever. The day before, Alan had told her not to expect his 5 p.m. call. "I'm going to be leaving town," he said. Louise, the wives' own "Jackie O," had been telling the papers, "I'm constantly aware of the Moon these days. It takes on a whole new look when you know your husband is going up there for a visit."

But everyone wondered what was going on in her new white-columned mansion in River Oaks, referred to as a "swankienda" in Maxine Mesinger's Big City Beat gossip column about Houston's elite in the *Chronicle*.

Alan had made some shrewd business maneuvers, including becoming the co-owner of a local bank. He was still keeping up his reputation as a skirt chaser; like the wives, the Shepards' rich new Houston friends wondered if he and Louise had some sort of "arrangement."

Alan finally had surgery for his Ménière's syndrome, defying Louise's Christian Science beliefs. Just like that, he recovered his balance, and after almost a decade on the bench running the Astronaut Office, he was eligible to fly again.

"It's been a long way, but we're here," forty-seven-year-old Alan, the oldest American astronaut, said as he took his first step on the Moon. Surveying the Fra Mauro Highlands landing site, he cried at the view of Earth. "Before I went to the Moon, I was a rotten S.O.B.," he would say afterward. "Now I'm just an S.O.B."

He'd stowed away the head of a Wilson six-iron on his craft and attached it to a lunar sample-scoop shovel. Holding the makeshift golf club in his thick spacesuit gloves, he swung before the live television camera. The ball didn't go far, but Alan was no quitter. He whacked a second one, which soared, as he put it, for "miles and miles and miles."

"Astronaut Does ESP Experiment on Moon Flight" read the headline after Apollo 14 landed. A reporter had caught wind that on the way back from the Moon, Alan's rookie crewmate, Ed Mitchell, had tried to telepathically transmit his thoughts to his friends back on Earth. Ed's tomfoolery enraged Alan and NASA, not to mention Ed's wife, Louise, who'd been waiting in vain for her husband to come down to earth since long before he left it. She knew Ed wasn't doing himself any good with his ESP talk. He'd tell her how he wanted to explore the field of parapsychology. Ed had been getting into hypnosis, also Eastern religions, as had lots of young men, including the Beatles with their very own "giggling guru," Maharishi Mahesh Yogi.

Now Ed was telling her that he'd had a "Savikalpa samadhi" experience on his way home. His ego momentarily dissolved and he *grokked* the immense fire spirit governing the universe. It was enough to make Louise throw up her hands. Ed later accused her of wanting to be married to a shoe salesman. Louise and Ed divorced shortly thereafter.

Now that it was the seventies, the spirit of the sixties was finally seeping through the cracks of Togethersville. The ladies began smoking their Virginia Slims out in the open, even in front of reporters. The Bormans were long gone, packed up and moved out of town after Frank went to the Moon on Apollo 8.

And since NASA had gotten "soft," there was no one left in

Togethersville to grab the "token hippie" in the Astronaut Office, as Pete Conrad called Rusty Schweickart, throw him into the basement, and cut off his long red hair and scruffy beard. In fact, it wasn't *that* long; it kind of curled cutely around his ears, but it was long compared to a crew cut. His wife, Clare, stumped door-to-door for liberal causes. The neighborhood kids loved her and gathered at her house, where she would entertain by playing her ukulele and singing folk songs. It was her version of *Hootenanny*.

Clare was a free spirit. She had five kids, including twin boys, Rusty Jr. and Randy (whom she used to get confused before she started dressing Rusty in red), and was taking graduate school courses at the University of Houston–Clear Lake on the African independence movements. She and Rusty participated in a couples' book club in the neighborhood, which discussed the latest consciousness-raising literature, like a book titled *Sexual Suicide*, but she didn't particularly love Rusty's scruffy look either—his long sideburns were awful-looking, and what's more, he knew how she hated them. She knew that he wasn't growing out his hair for her and it upset her to think that he might be growing it out for *somebody else*. Clare tried to keep an open mind as Rusty encouraged her to. He was partial to picking up any New Age craze and once told her, "Jealousy is an outmoded emotion." In fact, Clare was inclined to give him a taste of his own medicine. But was she really going to find a partner at her usual spots? The Rendezvous, a family restaurant near NASA, or Weingarten's, the Nassau Bay supermarket? As Mother Marge once said, deploring the dearth of available men for her widowed girls, "There just aren't any good bachelors here or in Houston."

The signs didn't show a very bright future for Rusty at NASA, ever since his space sickness on Apollo 9 when Mission Control almost had to cancel his space walk (because if he threw up into his helmet he could've choked out there and died). Now that his career was basically shot because of his weak stomach, Rusty seemed to be doing everything in his power to expand his horizons.

Like the Beatles, he'd gotten into Transcendental Meditation, and felt greatly honored when Maharishi Mahesh Yogi came to visit the Manned Spacecraft Center. Walking barefoot across the Schweickarts' lawn and into their Nassau Bay home, the long-haired Indian guru in flowing robes sat cross-legged in their living room on a soft little deerskin one of his followers laid down before him. Smelling of flowers and incense, Maharishi gave Clare the gift of her own secret mantra.

Apollo 17 would be the sixth and final flight to the Moon. In total, the American space program had taken the work of two and a half million people and had cost nearly $25 billion. During the landing of Apollo 11, President Richard Nixon had made what he called "the most historic telephone call ever made," from the White House to the Moon. He told Neil and Buzz, "Because of what you have done, the heavens have become a part of man's world. As you talk to us from the Sea of Tranquility, it inspires us to redouble our efforts to bring peace and tranquility to Earth. For one priceless moment, in the whole history of man, all the people on this Earth are truly one." But in December 1972, Nixon canceled the Apollo Program.

Saddled with a major budget crunch caused by the Vietnam War, Congress just didn't want to fund unlimited spaceflight. Critics asked what exactly was America getting out of the Moon except a few rocks? Most Americans could only point to Tang,

Teflon, and Velcro. They could not imagine how profoundly the advances made by NASA would affect their daily lives. The satellite communications networks of the 2000s, a direct result of the space program, were still the stuff of science fiction. Though Saturn V rockets for Apollos 18, 19, and 20 had already been built and were ready to go, President Nixon shut down the remaining flights.

In 1972, during the final Apollo flight to the Moon, the wives went through a particularly traumatic experience. The Black September terrorist group, which had attacked during the Munich Olympic games, announced that it might be planning something more bizarre: going after the crew's families. Security details were attached to every family whose man was going to the Moon, with plainclothesmen following the wives and their children at all times. Miraculously, the press was kept in the dark.

The first night launch, Apollo 17 took off at 12:15 a.m. on December 7, 1972. Mission wives Barbara Cernan and Jan Evans and their families and friends watched the Saturn V lift into the sky on a brilliant burst of flame. The rocket's tremendous vibration of the Earth woke up the fish in the Banana River, causing them to thrash and jump out of the water.

"*Aaaha!* There she goes!" astronaut Ron Evans exclaimed in his ship *America*.

Back when Ron was in Vietnam, flying combat missions from the carrier *Ticonderoga*, his wife, Jan Evans, had called up Deke Slayton and volunteered him for the astronaut program. Now a nice fellow in a semi with open side doors lay down paper towels before lifting petite Jan up to have a chance to sit for a while. Also on the scene was a forty-one-year-old journalist in a white suit, Tom Wolfe, covering the launch for *Rolling Stone*. He was inspired to go back to the beginning and write a book about the Mercury Seven, *The Right Stuff*.

After the launch, both wives returned home. Barbara Cernan was grateful this was the last mission, describing Apollo 17 like the final chapter in a good book. She was ready for it to be over. "I'm going to take the phone off the hook, take a bath, and go to bed," she told reporters.

As her nine-year-old daughter, Tracy, slept—she'd told the host of the *Today* show how her daddy promised to bring back "Moonbeams" for her—Barbara sat in the dark by the squawk box. On his previous Apollo 10 mission, a "dry run" for Apollo 11, Geno had radioed back to Houston that riding around the Moon was a piece of cake.

"It was definitely not a piece of cake for me," said Barbara. "If you think going to the Moon is hard, try staying at home."

She knew "a million things could go wrong" on Gene's final flight. One night when her house was filled with people, she had to escape—but to where? Taking a hot shower, Barbara felt her façade begin to melt away. The pressure was pounding in her ears, and she let out a terrifying scream (which she hoped no one heard). The red, white, and blue excitement that had been following the astronauts since the Mercury days had ballooned to intolerable proportions. It was simply getting to be too much to handle, like the Secret Service men Barbara had to be accompanied by because of the Black September threat.

No one in Togethersville knew what would come next. On the surface, things looked the same. The astronauts still pitched each other into swimming pools at neighborhood parties and still got the perks. All their cigars were courtesy of the American Cigar Institute. Along with Mrs. Nixon, some lucky Apollo wives wore Lunar Module rubies gifted by Van Cleef & Arpels. And if NASA would just provide a few Moon rocks for polishing to Corrigan's, a high-end Houston jewelry store, the gals were promised free one-carat "Moon Rings."

Some of the wives had already put their names on the waiting list for Pan Am's first commercial flight to the Moon, but now that wasn't going to happen. There would be no "orbital newspapers, updated every hour" per Arthur C. Clarke's dream; no Lunar Hilton, which Barron Hilton had proposed; no Lunar Disney; and no chain of A&W Root Beer stands that Pete Conrad and Jim Lovell had planned, half jokingly, to open on the Moon after we colonized.

A space station called Skylab was soon to go up, as well as a "space taxi," a kind of VW bus for astronauts, to be known as the space shuttle. But with Nixon's budget cuts to NASA, the boys definitely weren't going to Mars, as they'd hoped to by the eighties or nineties. The Space Task Group had drawn up a man-to-Mars program that was making the rounds in Washington, courtesy of Vice President Spiro Agnew, but at $78 billion, it wasn't likely to happen. The wives weren't too upset about that one. It would take a husband two years to go to the red planet and back.

The meetings of the A.W.C. diminished in size, the monthly get-together no longer a haven for its members. The faces at the card tables overlooking the boat slips of the Lakewood Yacht Club's marina on Clear Lake were worn out and pinched. Louise Shepard still drove in for every meeting from Houston, but she could see the fatigue in Marge Slayton. Her girls were now scattered here and there like apples—some still crisp, some overripe, some positively rotten.

It had been a patriotic duty to keep one's marriage together in Togethersville, but Harriet's "First Space Divorce" had opened the floodgates. Until then, the men had thought they needed their wives if they wanted to leave the planet. The Susies had been a cancer to the A.W.C. First Donn's Susie. Then John Young, whom Betty Grissom had always kept a wary eye on, left Barbara for *his* Susy. Even Gordo married a Susie after he and Trudy split up for good. There were other names, too, which the gals would just as soon forget.

One day, a friend of Nineteen wife Gratia Lousma called to commiserate with her. She'd heard that Gratia and Jack, who was soon to go up in 1973 to the orbiting Skylab space station, were getting divorced. Gratia was stunned. Unless Jack knew something that she didn't, she assured her friend, their marriage was rock solid.

Gratia was shaken to the core. Deciding she had to do something, she went to the Manned Spacecraft Center to talk to Chris Kraft. She wondered if the formidable Kraft could engineer the saving of some marriages, or do anything to stop the domino effect of Astro-divorces. A visit to the Manned Spacecraft Center was intimidating, but just as Gratia was steeling herself to knock on Kraft's office door, suddenly someone called her name. It was Dr. Terry McGuire. In spite of NASA's prejudices against psychiatrists, the agency had hired him as its psychologist for manned spaceflight. Terry was involved in the interviewing process of picking new astronauts for Skylab and the upcoming space shuttle program.

Gratia told him that she was coming to see Chris Kraft. It

seemed everyone she knew was getting a divorce; she'd just about had it and decided she needed to talk to someone.

Dr. McGuire invited her to step into his office. He was all too willing to help the Astrowives sort out their problems. After all, he was trained for this sort of thing. Maybe a group therapy session?

Gratia thanked him very much for his time. She walked right out of the Manned Spacecraft Center, having gotten cold feet about knocking on Kraft's door. She and Harriet Eisele did end up forming the Survival Group with Terry, which tried to address the wives' marital woes in a responsible manner. It was not officially sanctioned by NASA and met clandestinely in the wives' homes. So the soap-opera, roller-coaster life of being an astronaut wife continued.

"I was looking at the book *Astronauts and Their Families* just the other day," said Wally Schirra, who'd left the program after his Apollo 7 flight, "and I was really shocked how few of those guys were married to those women anymore." Out of the Mercury Seven, the New Nine, and the Fourteen space families, only seven couples would stay together.

"Our marriage has only lasted so long because you were away half of the time," ribbed Jo.

Wally and Jo had traded their Timber Cove home for the fresh Rocky Mountain air of Colorado. They stuck together; so did Louise and Alan, and Annie and John. The Mercury wives had been through a lot together. Some were just now finding themselves. In 1971, Trudy Cooper finally became a Powder Puffer, flying in the Powder Puff Derby, sponsored by Virginia Slims. The cigarette's slogan, "You've Come a Long Way, Baby," was the theme of the year's race.

Two days before the fourth anniversary of Gus's death in the fire, January 27, 1971, Betty Grissom filed a lawsuit suing NASA's largest contractor, North American Rockwell, for $10 million for negligence in the building of Gus's Apollo 1 spacecraft, breaking the code of silence among the space widows. Producers from the *Today* show invited Betty to come to New York and appear on the show to talk about the lawsuit. Betty pleaded her case to America, and hoped that the other two Apollo 1 fire widows, Pat White and Martha Chaffee, might join her in her cause—but in the press they "declined" to jump aboard her lawsuit. Nevertheless, when Betty accepted an out-of-court settlement of $350,000, shared with her sons, Pat and Martha were given comparable settlements.

Hate mail flooded Betty's mailbox. "You said on the *Today* show that you have received no negative comments in regard to your lawsuit, well, you now have mine," wrote one crank from Chicago. Another suggested, "Go to Russia and stay!!" The wife of a North American employee wrote, "You are nothing more than a money-hungry, stupid, selfish female and I'm very glad I don't know you."

Luckily, Betty received other letters praising her efforts as a liberated woman taking on the establishment. Betty would never forget what Gus had once told her: "You know, you're really the astronaut in this family."

In the summer of 1969, Rene Carpenter, who had always been forthcoming with the press, told the Houston column Big City Beat that she had "no plans whatsoever for a divorce." She added, "It's obvious that Scott and I are separated."

After Sealab III, Scott resigned from being an aquanaut and

treaded the waters of private enterprise with his manned underwater consulting firm, which had its offices on the West Coast. He met the twenty-something daughter of a famous Hollywood film producer, Hal Roach, who ran the "Lot of Fun" where they used to shoot Laurel and Hardy films.

In 1972, Rene was given her own television show. She was no longer married to Scott. She'd spent a decade in the limelight in the role of an astronaut wife, but over the years had found her own voice and convictions. Now she was unshakable. She paused a moment as she put on the huge rose-tinted glasses Gloria Steinem had made popular, then entered the TV studio of *Everywoman*, her feminist television talk show. Its mission was "to record the current revolution, to present women who are changing their lifestyles."

Along with hosting guests such as the Continental Airlines flight attendants who confessed how the slogan "We really move our tail for you" made them feel like prostitutes, Rene attacked Barbie and unblushingly displayed a collection of birth control devices to her audience, including a diaphragm. The camera zoomed in tight.

"This is the greatest moment on television," thought Rene.

She was devoted to women's empowerment, and remained unfazed when one of her influential Washington pals said, "That's the most disgusting thing I ever saw."

Epilogue

The Reunion

I think we look like Stepford Wives, don't you?" said Jane Dreyfus, formerly Jane Conrad, looking at an old photo. "Because we all tried to be so calm and so cool and everything, but we were a far cry from Stepford Wives."

"We lived through this amazing time. It's like people who've been shipwrecked together," said Clare Whitfield, the ex-wife of Rusty, the "hippie" astronaut. "They were like rock stars. It was sickening." All the same, it was absolutely thrilling.

"It was hard for them to come home," admitted Faye Stafford. "Who could ever compete with the Moon? I was lucky if I could come in second."

"I was in big-time denial," said another Astrowife. "Somebody else might be screwing around, but of course my husband wasn't."

"There were people there all the time, from sunup to sundown. I was always so grateful for that," said Susan Borman. She had finally gone through rehab for her alcoholism.

In 1991 the first reunion of the Astronaut Wives Club, now rechristened the Original Wives Club (and affectionately nicknamed the K-I-Ts for Keepers-In-Touch), met in Deer Valley, Utah. Two decades had passed since the last mission to the

Moon, enough time that the women were now ready to share many of the feelings and fears they couldn't during the missions. Many were now divorced, trying to make their own way in the world and support their kids. Some were suffering from financial hardship, others from broken hearts.

The wives had talked about a reunion for a long time, but actually pulling it off was not easy. In the mid-eighties, a reunion had been planned for the New Nine wives. A few months before, Pat White, Marilyn Lovell, and Susan Borman met for a girls' weekend down in Florida, where one of their husbands was on a business trip.

It had been many years since the three could simply walk across a lawn to share a cigarette, a cup of coffee, tears, and talk. They were up late into the night listening to Pat's heartbreaking confession. Ed's death in the Apollo 1 fire still haunted her after all these years. She'd remarried a Houston business tycoon, but she was depressed and had attempted suicide on more than one occasion. Marilyn and Susan did everything they could to comfort her, and made her promise she would reach out to them if she had even an inkling of those awful thoughts again. She was about to become a grandmother, and they imagined that would bring some new joy into her life. And there was the reunion of the New Nine wives to look forward to in only a few months' time.

The weekend before the reunion, Pat committed suicide. The news was devastating. They all believed her to be the final victim of the Apollo 1 fire.

Finally, in the fall of 1991, the astronaut wives, from all the different groups, met for the first big reunion since the end of the

Apollo program. Their get-together in Deer Valley resembled a launch party from the "good old days"—an expression that was truer than not, though it still caused some eyes to roll. Back then, each wife was essentially in her own orbit, alone without a tether. None felt she could share her deepest feelings. As Marge Slayton once reflected, "You didn't talk about your personal life—everyone was happily married, everything was lovely."

"Those were the golden years. All the wives were thrilled, proud, and happy," said Joan Aldrin. On the Apollo 11 heroes' "Giant Step" world tour, traveling alongside the other Moon couples, Joan had watched as Buzz went deeper and deeper into a depression. Returning to Earth, her husband, who later inspired Disney's Buzz Lightyear of *Toy Story* (and MTV's original logo), felt that he no longer had structure in his life, with no one telling him what to do and no one sending him on a mission. He eventually crash-landed, having, in his words, "a good old American nervous breakdown." (Pat and Mike Collins's marriage is the only one of the Apollo 11 Moon landing crew that survived.)

For the reunion, Susan Borman and Jan Evans arrived with chili (made in Jan's kitchen and flown in for the occasion) and groceries a day ahead of everyone else, and helped prepare for the arrivals. Drinks were served in Gemini and Apollo glasses, the kind once procured at gas stations or knickknack shops at Cape Kennedy. They raised their glasses to being together, and to those no longer with them.

Annie Glenn, now a senator's wife, had not been able to make it. Still, all the wives were extremely proud of her. Annie had overcome her stutter. In 1973 an episode of the *Today* show had featured a clinic that offered a new approach. Annie saw it and signed herself in.

It was an intensive treatment, for many hours a day. At the end, when she phoned John, he could hardly believe it was his Annie. "John," she said, "today we went to a shopping center and went shopping. And I could ask for things. Imagine that."

"That's wonderful," he said in disbelief. Soon after she arrived home, Annie looked around the bedroom and said, "John, I've wanted to tell you this for years: Pick up your socks."

Louise Shepard was at the reunion, but Mother Marge had died in 1989. Her husband Deke's heart murmur, which had kept him grounded for so long, finally got an override in 1975, clearing him to fly on the first joint U.S.-Soviet space mission, the Apollo-Soyuz Test Project.

"I enjoyed that nice cozy feeling that for the next nine days I would know exactly where my husband was," Marge had said at the time. During the flight, her friends surprised her by showing up at her favorite local hangout, the drugstore in Friendswood, Texas, where they celebrated "Marge Slayton Day," unfurling a banner with a picture of a steaming cup with a smiley face. It said, MARGE, WE LOVE YA! YOUR COFFEE BUDDIES.

Afterward, she went along with Deke on his hero's tour to Russia. At a dinner of astronauts and cosmonauts and cosmonauts' wives, Marge was asked to raise her glass and say a word. She said two: "To love!" The crowd cheered. Not long afterward, she and Deke divorced.

Like many of the wives, Marge just couldn't take it anymore—the lying, the cheating, and the feeling that her husband had abandoned their home for that "harlot of a town," the Cape. Chief Astronaut Al and Coordinator of Astronaut Activities Deke had basically given the boys the A-OK to keep a cookie on the side, as long it was understood that the Cape and Togethersville were separate bubble worlds and never the two would meet. As Gene Cernan put it, "The wives stayed in Texas, and Florida was an off-limits playground filled with Cape Cookies."

After her divorce, Marge's friends didn't call so often, especially Louise, her partner in the A.W.C. They'd been so close, but Marge realized that Louise was still trying to maintain her own tenuous marriage. If she discussed Marge's divorce, she'd just as soon admit that Alan had been running around like Deke. Despite Louise's iciness on the subject, Marge was happy to share her feelings with other wives who might learn from her experience.

At the reunion, some of these matters were discussed in private rooms. Around the living room, it was obvious who was having a tough time of it. Harriet Eisele was way past tears. She'd cried rivers over the years, coping with issues of child support and making it as a single hardworking mom, although she sometimes still felt ashamed about having the first divorce in the community. The other women convinced her that not only was she a survivor, but she had given others the courage to do what they knew needed to be done.

After her divorce, Harriet rebooted her nursing career, first working at a hospital and then as a beloved school nurse for eighteen years. As she grew more confident at her job, seeing as many as 120 kids a day, she'd ask, "Is something bothering you besides your tummy?" More often than not an upset stomach signaled stress at home. So Harriet went back to school and studied psychology at the University of Houston–Clear Lake, earning a bachelor's degree in behavioral science and a master's in marriage and family therapy. When a professor in her women's studies course asked the class to come up with possible research topics about people under stress, Harriet had a brilliant suggestion: astronauts' wives. She would've liked to add in the astronaut kids, who she thought had also suffered. It was hard having a part-time dad who was considered a hero but who was hardly ever at home.

The astronauts' wives pointed out that while their day-to-day lives were similar to the lives of other army wives, although more extreme, their problems weren't all that different from women who are married to celebrities, sports stars, and politicians. While the wives faced the tough task of coping with a volume of stress nearly equal to that of their celebrated spouses, some of their famous husbands just couldn't manage to keep their pants zipped.

Some blamed NASA for failing to take the wives into consideration, accusing them of "using" the wives and ignoring their needs; others were still very supportive of the agency. After his wife's rehabilitation, Frank Borman publicly criticized NASA for not offering counseling and support for the wives. He especially resented any Dr. Feelgood whose remedy for the occasional Astrowife jitters and housewife headache was handing out tranquilizers like Life Savers. He was thankful that Susan had never gotten involved in any of that.

Jane Conrad was "grateful that NASA provided security and opportunity for the family to go to Mission Control, to have squawk boxes in our houses, give us trips and rides in the NASA Gulfstream. I didn't have any beef with how we were treated." She added, "Yes, some of us did ask our doctors for a tranquilizer for a limited time, just to handle all the barrage of reporters and the neighbors' predictions that there would be accidents. It was nerve-wracking and I don't mind admitting we needed a little help now and then. The phrase 'pill popping' today has a more sinister connotation and makes us sound like the *Valley of the Dolls*!"

At the reunion, the wives opened up for the first time and really started sharing together as a group. They realized how much in denial they once were. As Clare Whitfield put it, "We really felt this enormous loyalty to the guys. You just don't see what you don't want to see." The press didn't help matters. "They tried to make them look like perfect American boys. Well, in most respects they were, but they were human, too, just like the rest of us," said Betty. She added, "Sometimes a wife is the last one to know." Clare also observed, "Astronauts get along so well because they don't talk." Women, of course, have to talk. Not surprisingly, the wives have remained closer than the men.

At the reunion, a huge amount of pain was expressed and exorcised, and the friendship shared by the wives during their space program days in Houston was rekindled with a deeper intimacy and honesty, and continues today. That night, the women all gathered around in robes and pajamas and slippers, and talked until dawn. Pretty soon they got the giggles and started telling stories and laughing—about the men. Laughter had always buoyed them through the hardest parts of their missions. And it would continue to lift them in the years to come.

Even today, the wives continue to meet regularly for cruises and getaways, space anniversaries and events, and fervently hope that men and women will continue to explore space. They are fiercely patriotic and very protective of one another, and some have now been friends for more than fifty years. Although they once tried to outdo each other in perfection, if one of their own was ever threatened, as when Donn cast aside his wife to marry a Cape Cookie, they shut the hatch on the outside world. Some wear a golden whistle charm around their wrists as a symbol to keep in touch and call and come when needed. Their flower is the yellow rose of Texas and they wear "space bling," diamond-encrusted gold jewelry featuring their mission numbers and emblems. But the most important things they carry with them are their memories.

During her interview for the book, Marilyn Lovell, with tears in her eyes, spoke for many of the wives when she said, "Those were the best years of my life."

Beth Williams, the water-skier turned young space widow, pointed out, "These were women who were in the public eye and yet pushed to the background all the time. I just think they never got the credit they deserved. The whole thing ran smoothly because of them."

Jan Evans, who wears her golden whistle on her charm bracelet, now maintains the astronaut wives' roster, which she started in 1989 after the death of "our dear Marge Slayton." Since the wives don't have officers, don't pay dues, and don't hold meetings, they no longer consider themselves a club in the formal sense. The monthly coffees and teas at the Lakewood Yacht Club broke up long ago, soon after the first space divorce, which shook the entire community to its core. Still, the club had been important to the women, and they treasured their memories.

After Marge Slayton read in *The Right Stuff* Tom Wolfe's take on the Astronaut Wives Club, she threw the book across the room. She'd read: "Marge organized a couple of coffees for all the wives, the First Seven and the New Nine, so they could all get to know each other. By the second time they met, they all realized without a word—no one had to say it—what this was. This was...the Officers Wives Club, such as existed at every base in the land."

"It wasn't that way at all," explained Marge. "We were all finding our way through an experience that was a *first*—that of being astronaut wives and with the husbands away, we felt the need to support each other. So we began monthly coffees. The message was, 'If you need us, come.' I needed them so it was natural for me to be there. A few of the wives who arrived later were horrified at the loose structure of the group after coming from military lives. But we were now wives of civilians or military men on duty with NASA and not bound by our husbands' service rules." About the widows and divorced wives, she said, "We hugged them to us as tightly and as long as they permitted. We were a lifetime membership."

At one recent reunion not far from Houston, still "Space City, U.S.A.," Clare Whitfield played her ukulele and sang a song she'd written for the astronaut wives about their past adventures being married to spacemen, and how they've moved on, together.

I won't be here to interrupt ya,
I won't be here to contradict ya,
I won't be here to steal your thunder,
You can be Macho Man on your own!

The others joined in on the chorus:

Oh, you can be right about the universe,
You can be right on your own!

Acknowledgments

I still find it amazing that there is more computing power in my iPhone than in the technology that took the astronauts to the Moon. More than that, I am astounded that this incredible group of women has never been written about before. When I asked Jo Schirra how that could be possible with authors like Tom Wolfe and Norman Mailer coming through their homes and interviewing their husbands, she said, "We'd go hide!"

When I called Rene about the book, she advised, "There will be many times when it will just seem impossible."

Betty asked, "You want to talk about naughty astronauts?" To this day, she remains unresolved about Gus's death and is in a tug-of-war with NASA over the ownership of his silver space suit. "One way or another," she said, contemplating the Moon, "I still think ole Gus was up there first."

The remarkable Annie Glenn turned ninety in 2010 after fifty years in the spotlight. She chose not to be interviewed for the book, but her friends shared their memories of her. Jo said, "Annie is really a dream girl. If *she* had run for president, like he did, she would have won." After serving twenty-four years in the Senate, and running for president in 1984, seventy-seven-year-old John lifted off for his second spaceflight, on space shuttle *Discovery*'s mission in 1998. He became the oldest person to go into space to study the effects of spaceflight on golden-agers. Annie didn't want to let him "go up" again ("Over my dead body" were her words), but she relented and did their old "chewing gum" routine.

The book came into being thanks to all of the wives for telling their stories. Thanks to Jo Schirra, Betty Grissom, Rene Carpenter, and Jan Evans. Much heartfelt thanks to Marilyn Lovell and Jane Dreyfus for their warmth, kindness, and girls' retreat in Texas. Jane wrote a memoir, which she sent to Jackie O when she was a book editor, and got "the most beautiful rejection letter." The Most Dramatic Storytelling Award goes to Joan Aldrin; Jeannie Robinson for her laughter; Sue Bean for her sweetness and that great fur she wore to our first group dinner in Houston, arriving on the arm of her best friend, Barbara Cernan, to whom I owe a special thanks. She once said, "My name is not going to be in the history books but I know what I did." Thanks to Martha Chaffee, who is flying free on the Wild Winds Ranch; Pat Collins (who imagined if they ever would "send a woman to the Moon—she would jump up and down and yell and weep"); superhero Harriet Eisele, Clare Whitfield, Beth Williams, and Gratia Lousma. Also Barbara Gordon, Loella Walker, Lurton Ahroon, Dotty Duke, Bernice McCandless, Kathleen Lind, Joan Glancy, Helen Garriott (a scientist-Astrowife and gifted sculptor who back in the day cooked up thousands of Moon Pots), and all of the other wives who were so generous with their time.

Thanks to the astronauts—who thought a book on the wives was a terrific idea, but who may have a hard time being upstaged. Thanks in particular to Jim "Houston, we have a problem" Lovell (who likes to remind people that Apollo 8 is the only crew with marriages that stuck together), Tom Stafford, Alan Bean (who paints with Moon dust), the last man on the Moon Gene Cernan (who thinks "all of these incredible wives should be in the history books"), and Buzz Aldrin for his general flair (and making *Dancing with the Stars* the wives' favorite show).

Unfortunately, some of the old gang are no longer alive. Louise Shepard died in 1998, five weeks after Alan, up in the air on a commercial airline flight en route back to her home in Carmel, California, after visiting her daughter Laura in Colorado. She died at 5 p.m., the hour Alan used to call her to say, "Hello, I love you, I miss you." Her and Alan's ashes were strewn off the seventeenth green, Alan's favorite, on Pebble Beach's famous Cypress Point golf course. As the ashes and rose petals fell to the waves below, two seals came up on a rock and kissed. Louise's girls, to this day, see their parents' story as a love story.

Mother Marge is also gone, but, like others, was remembered through loving memories and notes she kept about her life and the A.W.C. Today you can sit on a bench the wives dedicated to her in Friendswood. She always wanted to make it to Mount Fuji, and perhaps one day she will, but her beloved son Kent sprinkled some of Marge into the Cape's Banana River while watching the last shuttle flight, *Atlantis*, take off in 2011.

Thank you to the Astrokids, including the Shepard girls, Laura, Julie, and Alice; and Kent Slayton, with whom I floated with down the Banana River watching *Atlantis* soar. Thank you to the Lovell kids, Barbara, as well as Susan and Jay (who run the fabulous "Lovell's of Lake Forest" restaurant, where you can sip a Godiva chocolate Mount Marilyn Martini), Kathleen Collins (Pat Collins's daughter, who grew up to be an actress on *All My Children*), Ann Collins, Rosemary Roosa (whose Steel Magnolia Astro-mama went to the same school as Elvis), Suzy Schirra, Mark Grissom, Teresa Dawn Cernan, and others. Thank you to *Life* den mother Fifi Booth and Nurse Dee O'Hara. Thank you to Pat Kleinknecht and Grace Wiesmann, who accepted astronaut wings for her husband, X-15 rocket pilot Joe Walker.

Thanks to all the writers and journalists, past and present, who chronicled space; and the historians, including Jennifer Ross-Nazzal at the Johnson Space Center in Houston, social and cultural dimensions curator Margaret Weitekamp at the Smithsonian National Air and Space Museum, and senior curator Roger Lanius; and also to John and Kathy Charles. Some of the space books that have been especially helpful in the writing of my book are *The Right Stuff* by Tom Wolfe; *Of a Fire on the Moon* by Norman Mailer; *Carrying the Fire* by astronaut Michael Collins; and one of the only other books about the space program written by a woman, *If the Sun Dies*, by the controversial Italian journalist Oriana Fallaci. (In it, astronauts spout Julius Caesar poolside and dream about opening a chain of A&W stands on the Moon.) *In the Shadow of the Moon* by Francis French and Colin Burgess was one of the sources used in the writing of the section on Harriet Eisele. Thank you to the extraordinary Ann Patty; also Kaly Soto, Mark Seliger, Michael Angelo, and Lisa Perry for suiting me up in one of her mod sixties-inspired dresses, and Sarah Self. Thank you to my out-of-this-world agent, Larry Weissman, and his wife, Sascha Alper, for her keen eye.

Thank you to Mission Control at Grand Central Publishing. My wonderful editor Helen Atsma, Jamie Raab, Deb Futter, Emi Battaglia, Matthew Ballast, Julie Paulauski, Allyson Rudolph, Jane Lee, Brad Parsons, Kirsten Reach, Karen Torres, Martha Otis, Andy LeCount, Chris Murphy, David Young, my editor at Headline in the UK, Sarah Emsley, and Mari Roberts. Thank you to all my friends and family, Brooke, Mara, Bob, Niko, Carolyn, Fred, Laura, and most deeply to my husband, Tom. And our two spacey rescue dogs, Ozzy and Lucky.

Reading Group Guide

Questions for Discussion

1. Who is your favorite character? What made you relate to that particular wife?

2. Would you let your significant other be blasted into space? Why do you think these women let their husbands go on these incredible, but also very risky, journeys?

3. Does the sudden celebrity around the astronauts and their families depicted in this book remind you of today's celebrity culture in any way? How does it strike you as different? In what ways are the astronaut wives similar to today's reality show families? In what ways are they different?

4. *The Astronaut Wives Club* depicts the female friendship and female bonding that result from an unusual circumstance. Do the friendships and bonds in this book remind you of friendships you've experienced? What tensions did you see between the different groups of wives? Did you expect more solidarity? Less? Were you surprised at how the friendships evolved over time, so that the wives now meet for reunions and are able to be more open with one another than they ever were back then?

5. In many ways, *The Astronaut Wives Club* is about what it meant to be a "good" wife in the 1950s and 1960s, and how that role changed over the course of the space program. What do you think it means to be a good wife? A good husband? How do you think those roles have changed since the time of this book?

6. The wives in *The Astronaut Wives Club* were often under a high level of stress and intense scrutiny, without the benefit of preparation for or training in dealing with the media. Do you think NASA should have prepared them better to deal with the pressures of public attention?

7. The early astronauts and their families had deals with *Life* magazine to let photographers and reporters into their homes. In many instances, the media seems to have idealized their lives. How do you think those stories affected their day-to-day experiences? How might the published articles have affected the day-to-day lives of housewives who read the pieces?

8. Were you surprised at what happened to the widows of the Apollo 1 fire, such as Pat White? Do you think being in the space program was harder on the astronauts, or their wives?

9. As a contemporary reader, were you surprised to read about the extramarital affairs between a few of the astronauts and the Cape Cookies at Cape Canaveral, Florida? What did you think of the two worlds: the playground of the Cape and the wives' suburban world back home in Houston? Putting yourself in the wives' shoes, do you think you would have challenged the status quo?

10. One of the wives, Rene Carpenter, always seemed to challenge the existing state of affairs of being the perfect archetypal astronaut wife and went on to write an opinionated women's column and host her own feminist television talk show. How do you think she was able to do this?

11. Were you surprised by any of the wives' reactions to their husbands' decisions to go into space? How about the wives' decisions post–space program? What did you think about how going to the Moon changed the men and the marriages (often expanding the men's horizons and leading to divorce)?

12. Do you think Betty Grissom had good grounds for her lack of confidence in NASA, going so far as to sue its largest contractor, North American Rockwell?

13. The wives themselves set up the Astronaut Wives Club, but in many ways the official, all-inclusive organization failed to be the space for open sharing that the founders intended it to be. How did the on-record Astronaut Wives Club differ from the smaller friend groups that formed among the wives? What purpose do you think the official club ended up serving, and why do you think it might not have become what the founders had hoped? Do you think it finally comes together with the reunion group of wives that meets today?

14. The astronaut wives shared intimacies on a daily basis over coffee, cocktails, and cigarettes. What have we gained today that the wives didn't have, and what have we lost?

A Conversation with Lily Koppel

Q: Why did you decide to write about the astronaut wives? What attracted you to this topic?

A: I saw an incredible *Life* magazine photo of the wives in their skyrocketing beehives, outfitted in their swirling candy-colored Pucci minidresses. I've always loved *The Right Stuff* and *Apollo 13* and *Mad Men*, but I never knew how much I wanted to know more about these women until I saw that picture. I now know that what drew me to those movies and the books was an interest in the women. When I learned that they actually have a club—and that they raised their families in the Houston "space burbs" near NASA's operations, in a community known as "Togethersville"—the whole thing was just amazing! I knew I had to write the book and tell their story: the emotional side of the space race.

Q: There seems to be a cultural fascination right now with the 1950s and '60s. Do you think that nostalgia has anything to teach us, today, about our contemporary world?

A: Well, there is definitely a different way of living from the 1950s and 1960s to the 2000s. As the wives told me, they were stay-at-home moms first and foremost. They had tea with Jackie Kennedy and appeared on the cover of *Life* magazine, but they did womanly, wifely things. Revisiting those times was very comforting to me. Just how they would pick up a pink or white rotary phone and call a friend to come over for a cup of coffee and a cigarette, or a cocktail, if they were feeling alone or needed to talk. They walked (and ran) to friends' homes across lawns. One astronaut kid told me nostalgically how his mother used to lock him and his siblings out of the house and tell them to go play with their friends and be home in time for supper. It was a more innocent time. It was a time when people got to live in the moment without yoga, Twitter, Facebook, and all the rest. It was also a magical time when human ingenuity meant everything and America accomplished amazing things. I think today is wonderful, but we need to incorporate some of yesterday's examples into how we live (of course, I am a sucker for '60s fashion, too, not to mention the music).

Q: The scope of this book is wide—you report on many wives and devote attention to a broad range of women, while also focusing on a few notables like Rene Carpenter, Annie Glenn, and Betty Grissom. Given the breadth of the space program, how did you decide what stories to include?

A: I focused on the wives who had the most interesting, dramatic, and, at times, difficult experiences. I let their stories, missions, and personalities guide me in an organic way, focusing on the moments that jumped out at me, like when the Mercury wives were introduced to America like the country's first reality stars, and how this very different group of women bonded and came together. Also, my favorite mission turned out to be Apollo 8, the first flight to the Moon on Christmas 1968, given a fifty-fifty shot (Genesis was read during it), because it showed how two women dealt, in very different ways, with the pressures of having their men go to the Moon. Mission wife Susan Borman truly believed her husband would die orbiting the Moon; while Marilyn, married to Jim ("Houston, we have a problem") Lovell, who later became famous for commanding Apollo 13, kept the faith. Although it is serious history, I always wanted it to read like a page-turner. I hope readers will get into the spirit (with me) of what it meant in a very real, womanly way, to send your husband a quarter of a million miles away—to the Moon (and back)!

Q: This book documents some remarkably intrusive behavior by reporters—one journalist surreptitiously tails a wife to the hair salon hoping for a scoop. As a reporter yourself, where do you draw the line when it comes to pursuing a subject? What obligations do reporters have to their subjects—and what obligations do they have to their readers?
A: I started writing the book by visiting the wives across the country, unlocking the secrets of this very exclusive club of women behind the astronauts with the "right stuff." I was very conscious that the press had often hunted down and harassed the wives (and their children), and so it was important for me to get to know them as women and friends. I interviewed them extensively and spent heaps of time with them. I was lucky that the women were so forthcoming with me. Now in their seventies, they finally felt it was time to let loose a little and come clean. Reporting is always a relationship of trust, working both ways. For example, Joan Aldrin, Buzz's wife, gave me her diary to explore, which she kept on the Apollo 11 "Giant Step" world tour as her husband's life was spiraling out of control.

Q: What other books on the space program do you recommend?

A: *The Right Stuff* by Tom Wolfe; *Of a Fire on the Moon* by Norman Mailer; *Carrying the Fire* by astronaut Michael Collins; and one of the only other books about the space program written by a woman, *If the Sun Dies* by the controversial Italian journalist Oriana Fallaci. (In it, astronauts spout Julius Caesar poolside and dream about opening a chain of A&W stands on the Moon.)

Lily Koppel on Writing *The Astronaut Wives Club*

As the snowflakes swirled outside, I sat inside the home of Marilyn Lovell, wife of Jim Lovell, played by Tom Hanks in *Apollo 13*. Near a roaring fire in her living room decorated with family photos and the pastel Impressionist paintings she collects, I shook out my handbag, arranging my tape recorder, notebook, pen, and other journalistic trappings on her coffee table. As we pored over a photo of Mount Marilyn and the card from "The Man in the Moon" that came on top of Jim's very romantic Christmas present to her in 1968, she started telling me her story of being an astronaut wife.

Marilyn had saved headlines about the Astrowives, such as "HUSBANDS IN HEAVENS, ANGELS AT HOME," and dire Apollo 13 clippings in her scrapbooks all these years. She laughed as she told me how absolutely normal it was for the Lovell kids to make the sign for their father that read "WELCOME BACK TO EARTH, DAD." Because they lived in a neighborhood of rocket scientists, they figured everybody's daddy was an astronaut and a hero.

At one point, reminiscing about the old neighborhood, she started to cry. "Just talking about all these friends— We all had such a good time in those days..." she said as she reached for a tissue. "It was a time in my life that I would never give up. It was the best time in my life." Then she excused herself for a moment, to dry her tears and check on our lunch: "Let me turn on this oven. I hope you like quiche."

After lunch, served with iced tea and warm rolls, she set out coffee and perfectly baked chocolate chip cookies. A few hours and a lot of talk later, Jim came home. When he walked in, I finally got that whole astronaut rock star thing. Even though Jim is in his eighties now, the whole room lit up. In Jim's glowing presence Marilyn can slip into being "the hero's wife." In fact, I noticed this transformation all around the country as I visited with the ladies. When I sat down with some of the wives, I would sometimes have to shoo away an astronaut who was used to being in the spotlight.

"So, whaddya want to know?" asked Captain Lovell, plopping himself down in a cushy armchair by the fireplace.

"Jim," said Marilyn, all eyes (they were high school sweethearts and recently celebrated their sixty-first wedding anniversary).

"Jim," I kidded him, "I came here to interview your wife."

My interviews with the wives were never typical. They nearly always began with the *bing-bong* of a suburban doorbell. I would be introduced to a beloved dog or cat, and we'd go into the living room. Back in the day, to be an astronaut's wife was an immense opportunity that meant you were not just your typical Betty Draper–type stay-at-home mom. The whole country was caught up in the space race, and these women were at the forefront of President Kennedy's New Frontier. They knew in their hearts that they were playing an important role, and they'd attracted the media attention to prove it. But they had now been out of the public eye for forty years.

Harriet Eisele, the four-foot-ten, pint-sized woman who filed for the "first space divorce" following the heartbreaking death of her young son Matt from leukemia, still lives in the same El Lago ranch house that *Life* magazine once shot, where there was a tree house out back and she dedicated her life to raising her four children during the race to the Moon. Harriet offered me coffee in a space mug, the kind all of the wives have from the reunions they now throw every couple years. She made a delicious salad for lunch with her special vinaigrette, and for dessert there was homemade lemon custard and more strong, good coffee. (Harriet herself, who does the lawn and odd fix-up jobs around the house, runs on about five cups a day.) At other homes across the country, I was met with offers of coffee and tea, spreads of cookies and cakes. But the best time was just before five, when one of the wives asked me, "Is it cocktail time yet?"

If some of the wives were a bit skeptical of me at first, they were always kind, open, and welcoming. As one woman wrote to me before we sat down, "The whole expectation of women in those days was far different than now, and I wonder if your research can really reveal the extent of the social changes that occurred before you were born. Hopefully, those issues will be covered in your interviews, and that world we lived in will become more clear to you." As I told them, perhaps I was the perfect person to explore these questions, being the same age they were when they learned their husbands would be sent into space.

After seeing the Technicolor *Life* magazine photo of the Astrowives that sparked the idea for the book and feeling a sense of kinship with those young women, I began the writing process the old-fashioned way—by picking up the phone and calling Jan

Evans, who now keeps the wives' roster. Soon I was off to Arizona to meet her. Jan drove to pick me up at my hotel, greeting me with a hug. Jan told me that she and her friends had talked about wanting to set down their story, but in such a diverse group with different alliances and friendships—not to mention everyone so busy with grandkids (and great grandkids)—they hadn't ever gotten around to it. But she knew, as they all did, that they were all getting older, and time was passing. It was a regular Astrowife domino effect once I spoke to Jan, and the interviews fell into place.

I interviewed over thirty wives and spent a great deal of time in Texas, where many still live. One big thing for me was avoiding the trap the press often fell into by assuming that the men were heroes and the wives their spotless heroines. The wives were feeling brave, and were very encouraging of one another and felt this was the time to tell their story. Marilyn Lovell said to me, "You are so easy to talk to." Interviewing is a two-way street, and I deeply appreciated their willingness to open up their lives and homes to me, sharing their stories, memories, photo albums, scrapbooks (the Pinterest of the '60s), and, in the case of Betty Grissom, her vintage designer wardrobe mostly purchased from Neiman Marcus, including a scandalous pair of fur hot pants!

In some cases, it was harder than I expected to initially get into those living rooms. Afraid to talk, some put up barriers at first. Betty, Gus's wife, was someone many of the other wives thought would be the toughest nut to crack when I first embarked on the project. "Is Betty going to talk to you?" they'd ask, then murmur to each other, "Oh, I doubt it..."

Betty is amazing. After sending me an initial letter inviting me to come to visit her at her home in Houston, she turned out to be a real sweetheart (but don't tell anyone or you will ruin her reputation). She's in her eighties now and uses a walker, but as someone pointed out, "she still looks like Betty." When I interviewed her, I asked about how the wives dressed. She looked at me in all seriousness and said, "Not many people know, but Betty was the wildest one." She likes to refer to herself in the third person as Ole Betty, and to Ole Gus. Then she showed me her fur hot pants circa 1969.

Wild clothing aside, she has devoted her life to ferociously protecting Gus's legacy and has even battled for years with NASA over this, and most recently about a silver spacesuit she claims rightfully belongs to her family. She holds a memorial ceremony every year at the Cape to commemorate Gus and his two fellow astronauts who died in the Apollo 1 blaze, which people come from around the world to attend (one gentleman flies in every year from Japan). Betty wears a denim jacket sewn with an Apollo 1 mission patch. It is incredibly moving.

As tragic as Gus's death was, in a way it sheltered Betty from the troubles many of the wives experienced. As my book documents, "the space program didn't do much for the marriages," Jane Conrad told me. Jane and I have spent loads of time together, just as she once did with another writer fascinated by the male space stuff: Tom Wolfe. He and Jane used to exchange stories over bottles of red wine. Jane has shared with me her memories and her innermost thoughts and worries, and also her writing and painting—she's very talented at both. The first wife of notorious hotshot astronaut Charles "Pete" Conrad, she and Pete divorced in 1990, after he retired from NASA and around the same time one of their sons, Christopher, then in his twenties, died of lymphoma. Pete was killed in a motorcycle crash a couple years later. Theirs was representative of many of the space marriages that ultimately couldn't survive the pressure cooker of the space race and the temptations of the groupie-like Cape Cookies.

Jane also talked to me about the "tackiness," as she tactfully puts going through a "space divorce," and dealing with a second wife, who at one point wanted to make plastic He-Man-type action figures of the astronauts, including Pete. Moreover, she has shared with me her incredibly creative side, along with her sense of humor. Despite the heartbreak inherent in so many of the wives' stories, she has a rare ability to see the bright side of the incredibly exciting period they played leading roles in. (It might help that her story ended happily: She is totally over the Moon about her second husband, Seymour, of twenty-some years.) I couldn't help but smile when she recently e-mailed me a short story in which she imagines what it would be like if *she* were the astronaut and what it would feel like to do *it*, up *there*. It left me knowing what I already suspected: Jane, like the other wives, has the Right Stuff.

One of the more memorable, funny, and touching moments from my interviews with the wives was spending a girls' weekend in Texas with Jane and her best friend, Marilyn Lovell, at the Lovells' home there. It was a girls' slumber party and I felt privileged to be made honorary Astrowife for the weekend. Jim Lovell took us for a ride in his Cessna. At night, we kicked back over glasses of wine and I took notes as the gals sat around talking late into the night in PJs and robes.

Many wives experienced heartache and tension. After the men came back from the Moon, many of the marriages fell apart as a result of a decade of living under severe strain. They didn't know how much their husbands' trips into space would change their lives on Earth. Like the rest of the astronauts' womenfolk, Sue Bean, the former wife of Alan Bean, waited at home in the space burbs. "After the lunar flight, I think sometimes the guys saw things a little bit differently. That type of experience can't help but change your outlook on the world, and we drifted apart," Sue confessed.

She and Barbara Cernan, two big-haired Texas blondes who have been best friends since their their husbands went to the Moon, have one of the most enduring friendships of the group. The wives' relationships have also evolved and today they are much closer than ever before, a symbol of the changing times they've lived through and the fact that without all the competition of the space race they can finally be honest with one another. Surprise, surprise—the wives remain closer than the astronauts. The relationships between them have been evolving and complex. Marilyn Lovell characterized the wives' enduring female friendships as proving ultimately more powerful than many of the marriages.

I reconnected with many of the wives and their children following the publication of *The Astronaut Wives Club*. Many readers have asked me what the space race was like for those kids. I interviewed many of them about their experiences and what it was like growing up as Astrokids. They told me over and over that in many ways, growing up in the close-knit community of astronaut families back when the space program was ramping up in the '60s, was growing up in the cradle of the American Dream! Their mothers often had to pry their kids away from *Star Trek* to watch their dad's launch into space. It was also hard on the kids having a hero dad who was often an absentee father figure, as the Astrowives took on the role of "superhero mom" while the astronauts were away training for most of the week down at the Cape.

After the book came out, I sent all of the wives a patriotic candle—I thought it was a perfectly appropriate souvenir for the keepers of the flame. There were several book launch events (pun intended), but the party we had in Houston was particularly special because many of the wives still live there and attended, as did astronauts, socialites, and Joanne Herring (played by Julia Roberts in *Charlie Wilson's War*). The jazz band played "Fly Me to the Moon." It was like throwing the Moon Ball again. As one of the wives said at the very beginning of the project, "It will be every bit as exciting as watching a Saturn liftoff and over too quickly!"

On the dance floor was Gene Cernan, known as the last man to walk on the Moon. He's the bookend to Neil Armstrong. I gave a speech and thanked all the wives, who were scattered around the room wearing yellow rose of Texas corsages, the A.W.C.'s signature flower. After I was done, Cernan asked for the mike. He first joked and said he was disappointed there was no "former husbands club" for him and his fellow astronaut buddies to join, but his voice faltered as he told the crowd, "If it weren't for the wives who committed their lives to what we were doing, I don't think we would have ever gotten to the Moon."

The wives laughed. They knew how Gene, "Mr. Last Man on the Moon," likes to hold center stage. But more important, they all knew what he said was true. They all knew what they had done. Their tear-rimmed eyes said it all: "Happy, proud, and thrilled!"

Tips from Lily Koppel on Planning an *Astronaut Wives Club* Book Club Night

See more recipes, discussion topics, and tips, including "The Wives Playlist," at www.AstronautWivesClub.com.

For decorations, think patriotic, and for costumes, dress up Astronaut Wives style! Don't hold back, ladies—get your girlfriends together for a night and rock 1960s style with beehive hairstyles. Take a photo and share on your favorite social media platform with the hashtag #AstroWives. Toast the Moon!

Recipes

Moon Eggs (Blue Cheese Deviled Eggs)

The art of the spread seems so 1950s, and if you had asked me about a year before meeting these incredible women, I would have pooh-poohed homemaking as being a prefeminist throwback, going against all I was taught growing up to be a strong, self-reliant woman. (Before researching *The Astronaut Wives Club* I could barely get myself to wear an apron without cracking an ironic smile; I preferred to see my husband in one.) But these women were pros at setting a homey, welcoming atmosphere with a steaming cup and a plate of delectables: the gateway to sharing. These blue-cheese deviled eggs would have been right at home on an Astrowives platter, because they always said the Moon was made of green cheese.

12 hard-cooked eggs
4 tablespoons mayonnaise
2 tablespoons sour cream
1 teaspoon cider vinegar
1 teaspoon Dijon mustard
¼ teaspoon sugar
½ teaspoon salt, or more to taste
¼ teaspoon freshly ground black pepper
½ teaspoon hot sauce, such as Tabasco
½ cup crumbled blue cheese, such as Roquefort or Danish blue
2 tablespoons finely minced parsley, plus extra to garnish

Halve eggs lengthwise. Set whites aside and transfer yolks to a fine-mesh strainer set over a medium bowl. Using a spoon or rubber spatula, press the yolks through the strainer into the bowl. Add the remaining ingredients and stir until smooth. Arrange egg whites on a serving platter. Spoon or squeeze the yolk mixture into the whites and garnish with a sprinkling of minced parsley.

Note: Deviled eggs can be assembled, covered with plastic wrap, and refrigerated for up to 2 hours before serving. (Recipe courtesy of Gail Monaghan)

Perfect Mini Astrowife Chocolate Cookies (or Cape Cookies)

Annie Glenn's famous chocolate chip cookie recipe once graced the pages of newspapers across the nation. Think of these as her cookie's modern update. They also remind me of those Marilyn Lovell served me. When I came back from the road, I tried them out on a friend. They made my New York City apartment smell delicious. "Can I offer you tea, coffee?" I took pleasure in watching my friend's smile grow. "Fresh-baked cookies? A friend gave me the recipe." We sat around the living room, feet up on the coffee table, sipping and snacking and gabbing away as women do. These modern minis are highly snackable and have only 10 or 15 calories each.

2¼ cups flour
1 teaspoon baking soda
1¼ teaspoons salt
2 sticks unsalted butter, softened
½ cup sugar
1 packed cup dark brown sugar
1 teaspoon vanilla extract
2 large eggs at room temperature
8 cups (four 12-ounce packages) chocolate chips

Preheat oven to 375°F.
Sift flour, soda, and salt together.
Combine the butter, both sugars, and vanilla. Add eggs and continue to mix until light and fluffy.
Stir in and evenly distribute the chips.
Using a fork or two knives, form tiny cookies containing just 2

to 4 chips each. Place about ¾ inch apart on parchment-lined cookie sheets and bake until golden, about 8 minutes. Cool on racks, then store in airtight containers for up to a month and frozen for much longer.

(Recipe courtesy of Gail Monaghan)

Mount Marilyn Martini

Marilyn and Jim Lovell treated me to dinner at the restaurant their family owns, Lovell's of Lake Forest Restaurant, which is filled with Captain Jim Lovell's space memorabilia and is a veritable Apollo 13 museum (including a little "Welcome Back to Earth" note from Princess Grace of Monaco and a mural of the steeds of Apollo that once decorated the St. Regis hotel before Tom Hanks purchased it for the couple as a gift at a space auction). If you make it to Lovell's of Lake Forest, be sure to order the Mount Marilyn Martini. They serve this celestial confection there, named after a certain special first lady of space. (Marilyn was raised in a candy shop that her parents owned in Milwaukee, so she's a self-proclaimed chocoholic.)

1 ounce Absolut vanilla vodka
1 ounce Godiva chocolate liqueur (or ½ ounce Godiva chocolate liqueur and ½ ounce Godiva white chocolate liqueur)
½ ounce Baileys Irish Cream
½ ounce Kahlúa

Pour over ice, shake well, and serve in a fudge-rimmed martini glass (put some Hershey's chocolate syrup on a plate and swirl the rim in it). Voila: the Moon in a glass!

(Recipe courtesy of Lovell's of Lake Forest Restaurant)

Out-of-This-World Photographs of the Astronauts and Their Wives

Here's Rene! Platinum blonde Rene Carpenter (pronounced to rhyme with *keen*), wife of astronaut Scott Carpenter, second American to orbit the Earth, poses with her family, May 1962. Rene's trajectory explains how the wives' collective story reflected a new era for women. By the early 1970s, Rene was hosting her own feminist talk show. *(Courtesy: NASA)*

Aviatrix Powder Puffer. Pilot Trudy Cooper, wife of "Gordo" Cooper, and her teenage daughters Cam and Jan watch Gordo lift off during Gemini 5, August 1965. Trudy and her husband had been separated when he was going through the astronaut selection process, and they got back together for the sake of the space race. *(Courtesy: NASA)*

Dream Girl. Annie Glenn, wife of Mercury astronaut John Glenn, smiles, posing for a photo after John is tapped to be the first American to orbit the Earth, 1962. America had been in love with the Ultimate Astrowife Annie Glenn ever since she had caught attention in a *Life* cover story, "Astronauts' Wives: Their Inner Thoughts, Worries." Annie delivered what NASA demanded of each astronaut family—a squeaky-clean image. *(Courtesy: NASA)*

"Betz." Betty Grissom, who worked as a late-night telephone operator to put her astronaut husband, Gus, through college, was destined, against all odds, to become the torchbearer of the space wives. After Gus died in a disastrous 1967 capsule blaze during a routine training, Betty sued NASA's largest contractor, North American Rockwell, and settled for $350,000. Here, Betty and Gus Grissom with their two sons, Scotty and Mark, after Gus's Gemini 3 flight, March 1965. *(Courtesy: NASA)*

The Wife Stuff. Mercury astronaut Wally Schirra's wife, Josephine "Jo" Schirra, was the perfect Navy wife and knew the proper codes of behavior, taught to her by her Navy-wife mother. Here, Jo sits for a portrait in her new home in Timber Cove (a suburb of Houston), September 1962. Jo had furnished the house with a modern Oriental flair. *(Courtesy: NASA)*

Lady Louise (the wives' own "Jackie O"). The first American in space, Alan Shepard received the NASA Distinguished Service Award at the White House from President John F. Kennedy after his *Freedom 7* flight, May 1961. In this photo, Alan's wife and mother are on the left, and the other Mercury astronauts appear in the background. All the other wives were envious that Louise got to be the first to meet Jackie. *(Courtesy: NASA)*

Meet the Lovell Family. From a Florida beach, the family of Jim Lovell (of "Houston, we have a problem" fame) watching the Apollo 8 liftoff on December 21, 1968. From left: James, Jeffery, Susan, Marilyn, and Barbara. Apollo 8 was the first mission to orbit the Moon, and Jim and his crewmates were given a 50-50 chance of survival by NASA. The Lovells are representative of many of the astronauts and their wives: they were high school sweethearts and got married after Jim graduated from Annapolis. Marilyn was with him throughout his test-pilot career. You had to be almost a superwoman to be married to one of these guys, because the job was so dangerous, and the men were so macho. *(Courtesy: NASA)*

Queen Jane. Jane Conrad (now Jane Dreyfus), the wife of astronaut "Princeton Pete" Conrad, in a Pucci dress specially designed for her to wear while her hubby was Moonbound. During Pete's Apollo 12 mission in November 1969, Jane's sanity hinged on having her family and the other Astrowives with her for support (she was also able to hear Pete via the "squawk box," a fabulous space-age device that allowed the wives to hear the transmissions between the astronauts and mission control). Jane compared the anxiety of listening to the squawk box to being pregnant, and "wanting the baby to kick so you know it's OK." *(Courtesy of Jane Dreyfus)*

The Pats. Astrowives Pat White (right) and Pat McDivitt (left) and the Whites' children, Bonnie and Eddie III, visit mission control and sit with flight director Chris Kraft during Gemini 4 (the mission on which Ed White performed the first U.S. spacewalk), June 1965. After Ed White died in the Apollo 1 fire two years later, his wife, Pat, fell into a depression. Tragically, the weekend before the astronaut wives reunion in the mid-1980s, Pat White committed suicide. *(Courtesy: NASA)*

Mr. and Mrs. Last Man on the Moon. Astronaut Gene Cernan, the last man to walk on the Moon as the commander of the final Apollo mission, poses for a family portrait with his wife, Barbara, and their daughter, Teresa Dawn, age nine, at their home in Nassau Bay, near the Johnson Space Center, Houston, Texas, October 1972. In this photograph, Barbara is wearing some "space bling" around her neck. After the missions, the husbands would present to their wives gold jewelry they'd taken into space. And if they were landing on the Moon, the pieces would actually touch down on the lunar surface in a PPK—a personal preference kit—and be flown back. *(Courtesy: NASA)*

Photo Credits

Note: Photo credits are numbered to follow the order in which their corresponding photos appear in the insert.

1. Ralph Morse/Time & Life Pictures/Getty Images
2. Leonard McCombe/Life Magazine/Time & Life Pictures/Getty Images
3. Photo by Ralph Morse/Time & Life Pictures/Getty Images
4. Ralph Morse/Time & Life Pictures/Getty Images
5. Ralph Morse/Time & Life Pictures/Getty Images
6. Robert W. Kelley/Time & Life Pictures/Getty Images
7. Ed Clark/Time & Life Pictures/Getty Images
8. Ralph Morse/Time & Life Pictures/Getty Images
9. Ralph Morse/Time & Life Pictures/Getty Images
10. Michael Rougier/Time & Life Pictures/Getty Images
11. Yale Joel/Time & Life Pictures/Getty Images
12. Lynn Pelham/Time & Life Pictures/Getty Images
13. Lynn Pelham/Time & Life Pictures/Getty Images
14. Ralph Morse/Time & Life Pictures/Getty Images
15. Ralph Morse/Time & Life Pictures/Getty Images
16. Lee Balterman/Time & Life Pictures/Getty Images
17. Bob Peterson/Time & Life Pictures/Getty Images
18. Vernon Merritt III/Time & Life Pictures/Getty Images
19. SSPL/Getty Images
20. Bill Eppridge/Time & Life Pictures/Getty Images
21. Vernon Merritt III/Time & Life Pictures/Getty Images
22. Lee Balterman/Time & Life Pictures/Getty Images

About the Author

Lily Koppel is the bestselling author of *The Red Leather Diary: Reclaiming a Life Through the Pages of a Lost Journal* (Harper, 2008). She has written for the *New York Times,* the *New York Times Magazine*, the *New York Times Book Review*, the *Huffington Post*, and *Glamour*.